White Latino Privilege

Caribbean Latino Perspectives in the Second Decade of the 21st Century

Written by

Dorothy Bell Ferrer, William García,
Ryan Hamilton, Nicholle LaMartina,
Jennifer Loubriel, Julie Ramírez, Raquel Solla
Cesar Vargas, and Gabriel Haslip-Viera

Edited by
Gabriel Haslip-Viera

Cover Art (A commentary on Sammy Sosa) and Cover Design by
Gabriel Haslip-Viera

Latino Studies Press
New York, New York
<haslipviera@gmail.com>
<https://www.facebook.com/Latino-Studies-Press-Gabriel-Haslip-Viera-677991425622664/>
Second Printing

ISBN 978-0-692-99475-7 (Latino Studies Press)
ISBN-10: 0692994750
LCCN: 2018930354

CONTENTS

	Introductory Preface.	1
1	White Privilege, and the Ideology of White Supremacy in the Spanish-speaking Caribbean, its Diaspora and Latin America, 1492-present, by Gabriel Haslip-Viera	9
2	White Privilege and the Effacement of Blackness: Puerto Rico and its Diaspora in the Early 21st Century, by William García	73
3	The Privilege of the White Hispanic: Leaving Out the Rest with Facts, Stats, and Cognitive Dissonance, by Cesar Vargas	89
4	How "*Mestizaje*" in Puerto Rico Makes Room for Racism to Flourish, by Dorothy Bell Ferrer	101
5	Indicators of White Privilege in Latinx Communities by Jennifer Loubriel	111
6	Anti-Blackness in Latinx Communities by Raquel Solla	129
7	Mexican and Argentinian American Perspectives on White Latino Privilege. by Nicholle LaMartina and Julie Ramírez	133
8	White Latino Racism on the Rise: It's Time for a Serious Conversation on Euro-Diasporic Whiteness, by William García	141
9	What Privilege? *Mestilegio*, Blackness and the Contours of Solidarity, by Ryan Hamilton	147
10	Internet Responses to Original Postings by William García and Cesar Vargas and List of Contributors.	157

ACKNOWLEDGMENTS

The editor wishes to thank the many colleagues and friends who have been supportive of my approach to the controversial issues that prevail with regard to identity and race among Latinos—specifically Caribbean Latinos—over the years. I want to thank in particular, the peer reviewers and others who have read earlier drafts of this manuscript. Their thoughtful and constructive comments have been most helpful. It also needs to be said that although the comments and support that contributors received from peer reviewers and others were most helpful, it is the contributors who are solely responsible for all the articulated statements, assertions, errors of fact, and judgments that are made in this book.

Editor's Note: Readers should know that the contributors to this book were free to use the terms "Latino," "Latina," "Latino/a," "Latin@," and "Latinx" when referring to Latinos or Hispanics. They were also free to use "black" or "Black" and "indigenous" or "Indigenous" when making reference to African Americans Afro-West Indians, and Native Americans, or just "Africans" and "Sub-Saharan Africans" when referring to people from the African continent. In addition, internet addresses and links cited in this book may not be accessible in future years.

Additionally, the web addresses in the print or electronic version of this volume may have to be retyped as single lines in address toolbars to ensure that there are no gaps, etc. The editor also has printed transcripts in his possession of the debates from internet web-sites included in Chapter 10.

INTRODUCTORY PREFACE:
"WHO AND WHAT THE HELL IS A WHITE HISPANIC?"

In September of 2014, Christina Saenz-Alcántara posted an item in *Latino Rebels*, an online journal for bloggers and other writers, asking the provocative question—"Who and What the Hell is a White Hispanic?" She argued that a "ridiculous" article in the *New York Times* had just reported that significantly more Latinos had identified as "white" in the final official findings of the 2010 census than had been the case in the 2000 census and that this had generated a considerable amount of discussion, especially in social media, by self-identified non-white and white Latinos, non-Hispanic whites, and African Americans among others. Saenz-Alcántara also claimed that the debate was more about the following than about anything else:

> "It is more about how Latinos are making sense of the confusing label of the 'white Hispanic.' What does it mean to be labeled or take on the label of a 'white Hispanic?' Some in our own social media community have attempted to make sense of the term 'white Hispanic' as a role within and on behalf of our community. Others have seen it as a product of confusion, while even others have dismissed the identity altogether."

Saenz-Alcántara also made reference to internet postings by Geoffery Mullings [no longer accessible] and by City University of New York professor, Hector Cordero Guzman, in *Latino Rebels*. According to Mullings:

> "'white Hispanics' are socially positioned somewhere between being a beneficiary of white privilege and victim of cultural racism. To use their term, 'white Hispanics' are buffers—liaisons between the white elite and the darker non-elite. While 'white Hispanics' may have some upward mobility, they will never be fully accepted into the white elite and hence will never be in a position of power or control."

According to Saenz-Alcántara, Cordero Guzmán also argued that the white-Hispanic:

> "is a result of the social confusion of Latinos having to inhabit the border of two different cultures" that the "percentage of Puerto Ricans in New York City choosing the 'White' category [in 2012] was 44.7 %," that "In Puerto Rico, the percentage was 82.3%;" and that on the island "you are considered white if you have even one white ancestor in the previous four generations—this according to the *Reglas de Sacar*, which were rules used by the more affluent in Cuba and Puerto Rico during the Spanish colonial period to have their race officially re-defined as white for a fee."

Saenz Alcántara also makes reference to Cesar Vargas who is a contributor to this book and whose writings are supported by Geoffrey Mullings and others [see Chapter 3 below]. However, the contributors to this book, who focus primarily on the Spanish-speaking Caribbean and its Diaspora, argue that some of the confusion and misunderstanding may be more concentrated among the younger Cubans, Dominicans and Puerto Ricans born or raised on the U.S. mainland. They also make it clear that there is less confusion on the islands where there is a better understanding of white identity and whiteness as an idea, and where this identity is clearly seen as desirable under the concept of "*mejorar la raza*" [the desire to "improve" one's race].

Loveman (2007), Loveman and Muñíz (2007) and this writer (2009) demonstrated that the whitening process in Puerto Rico actually accelerated after the U.S. takeover of Puerto Rico when local enumerators hired by the Census Bureau decided to re-define certain previously categorized non-white Puerto Ricans [usually referred to as *pardos* and *mulatos*—with light and medium brown complexion] as white because of their desire to demonstrate to U.S. politicians, media, and the U.S. government in general that Puerto Rico was racially white with a white European culture. In various chapters, this book also focuses on how this whitening process, white identity, and the ideology of white supremacy has evolved on the islands in different ways and has been transferred to the U.S. mainland and is still very much alive among Cuban, Dominican and Puerto Rican immigrants, migrants, and many of their descendants who understand and feel that a white self-identification and other mostly class and educational factors may very well give them an edge when it comes to upward mobility in contrast to non-white Latinos and especially Afro-Latinos.

Of course, the focus on the Spanish-speaking Caribbean and its Diaspora results in the failure to deal with some of the different complexities that arise with regard to whiteness and privilege in the other countries of Spanish America [Brazil could also be included]. Here, the issue can be the important Native American component in the Mexican population and the racism and discrimination that still prevails against defined Indigenous peoples in that country [especially in Chiapas] despite the official long-term adoption of *mestizaje* [race mixture] and the propagandistic idealization of the pre-Columbian Indigenous past as seen in the Museum of Anthropology in Mexico City and just about everywhere else in that country. The Afro-Mexican population, concentrated on the Gulf coast around Vera Cruz and the Pacific coast south of Acapulco, was also largely ignored until recently when this population was suddenly granted official recognition by the Mexican government [See Chapter 7 for a Mexican and also an Argentinian-American perspective on this and related issues]. Also, see:

https://www.huffingtonpost.com/entry/mexico-finally-recognized-its-black-citizens-but-thats-just-the-beginning_us_568d2d9ce4b0c8beacf50f6b

All of this has become part of the debate with regard to identity, whiteness and white privilege among Mexican Americans in the

United States since the U.S. takeover of Texas, California and the southwest in the 1840s and continues up to the present—especially when it comes to the Indigenous component. Comparisons can also be made with other countries that have substantial populations of defined Indigenous peoples, such as Guatemala and Bolivia, but these countries have not even adopted the ideals of *mestizaje* as in Mexico which is considered by many, including most scholars, as being more enlightened. Colombia, South America, is another example of the complexities that arise. Most Afro-Colombian are concentrated in the northern *Costanera* region on the Caribbean coast of the country. This population is largely ignored, and there also is prejudice and discrimination against the Indigenous and those persons considered to be racially mixed. There is no official recognition of *mestizaje* and its alleged ideals in Colombia, and as a result, prejudice can be overt and transparent in that country's media and elsewhere as noted by William García, one of the contributors to this book in his internet postings. See:

http://latinousa.org/2016/05/20/painting-out-blackface/ among other postings.

Argentina and also Uruguay are probably the best examples in Spanish America of how the ideology of white supremacy and privilege operate for these populations on the U.S. mainland in contrast to the experiences of Caribbean Latinos. The Indigenous population of Argentina [subjected to near total genocide in the late 1800s and the Afro-Argentine population once proportionally substantial prior to the 1860s] are considered so small that Argentina is considered a white country. This was the result of a massive and state sponsored migration from Italy, Spain and other European countries after the 1860s; however, there has been an increased migration of the Indigenous and especially mixed race *mestizos* to Argentina in recent decades from neighboring Bolivia, Paraguay and Peru, but this migration has not changed the perception and definition of Argentina as a white nation state. At the same time, Argentinian immigrants in the United States are often mystified by how they may be defined as Latinos and not white in U.S. society and culture. They note that they are automatically defined as white in Argentina where the issue tends not be discussed and are shocked to learn that their white privilege is raised in the U.S. as noted in a number of internet postings (Also, see Chapter 7).

Another issue not necessarily discussed in this volume is the persistence of the older anti-Latino prejudices and patterns of discrimination that date back to the early twentieth century and persist in some sectors of our economy, society and culture which are based on surnames, competency in spoken English without an accent and other factors. At one point, I made reference to my plans to publish this edited volume with a close friend and his son who can "pass" for white. Both were initially mystified or in disbelief that this kind of privilege was an issue because of the prejudice and discrimination they experienced or had seen as white Puerto Ricans. The son, who had recently become a firefighter in the New York City Fire Department, made reference to the racism against Latinos and African Americans in that department. And of course, both the FDNY and the New York City Police Department have been known for their racial diversity problems and racism according to academic studies and media reports published in recent decades. These problems are of course worse in the whiter New York City suburbs and across the country.

The problems as noted by my friend's son and others, are rooted in the hiring practices which still emphasize recruitment in the whiter suburbs. There also is the old, unofficially institutionalized ethnocentric and racist culture of the FDNY which also persists in the Police Department. African Americans, Latinos and other "minorities" who are hired in both departments are subject to a training regimen in their academies designed to encourage, or compel them to accept or be acculturated to the old mostly Irish and Italian American prejudices that still prevail in the cultures of these departments despite some sensitivity training in ethnic and racial diversity. We also should not be surprised by the negative attitudes and the abusive behaviors seen among too many African American and Latinos police officers and even among some firefighters. Many of these individuals were already imbued with negative and even racist attitudes towards their own people when they were initially hired by these departments which works to reinforce the old ethnocentric and racist culture.

However, there are also "minority" organizations that resist and actively struggle against the culture and hiring practices that have prevailed in these departments. These include the African American Guardians Association and the Latino Officers Association in the Police Department, and the Vulcan Society and its Latino equivalent in the Fire Department. Some progress has been made in the hiring and promotion practices in both departments in recent years, but largely as a result of lawsuits, court cases, and decrees issued by the courts. There are also still the grumblings of the mostly dying or retiring breed of white old timers in both departments, and the persistence of the old cultures in many specific police precincts and fire houses. However, a hopeful evolutionary process of progress may also be taking place in these pockets of resistance..

Focusing attention on the book itself, it is the opinion of this editor and writer that the emphasis on the Spanish-speaking Caribbean and its Diaspora is very important because it seems like the issue of white Latino privilege is more easily discussed and defined in this context than in others as a result of the complex racial diversity of the African, the Indigenous [very exaggerated], the European, and the others that are seen in these societies. There is also the idealistic rhetoric of *mestizaje* that tries to promote the idea that two of these societies [Cuba and Puerto Rico] are racial democracies where racism and discrimination does not exist at the same time that it clearly does. This kind of complexity and more importantly, the discourses connected to them are not seen to the same degree if at all in the other societies of Spanish America in my opinion.

The Afro-Latinos in the Spanish-speaking Caribbean and especially in their Diasporas on the U.S. mainland have also played a very important role in highlighting the issue of white Latino privilege in public—especially in social media and on the internet in general. The focus in this book on chapters by persons who mostly identity as Afro-Latinos has been placed in certain areas of importance, such as education, academia, family relations, dating, housing, politics, government, Hollywood, television, advertising, marketing, other media, and also on the viewpoints and assumptions pro-and-con that are made by Caribbean Latinos themselves.

U.S. based African Americans and Afro-West Indians should acknowledge (as many do) but not gloat over the internal colorism and racism that is seen among Latinos [I have had experiences with these attitudes], because internal colorism is also seen among African Americans and other Blacks in U.S. society. I was personally shocked back in 1997 when I first saw Kathe Sandler's documentary, *A Question of Color*—a scathing critique of colorism and its impact among African Americans during those years, which still continues up to the present. I had naively assumed at the time that this sort of thing was passé having lived through the "black is beautiful" and black nationalist movements of the late 1960s. The documentary emphasized the continued importance of labels such as "high yellow," "yellow," "redbone" [etc.] which is also seen among Latin Americans and Latinos when they use labels for non-whites such as *trigueño, jabao* and *mulato*—each of which have their own set of privileges on a sliding scale based on skin complexion, hair texture, facial features, geography and other factors that range from the relatively privileged (light *trigueño* and *jabao*] to denigrated and worse (*negro* and especially "*prieto*"—the blackest]. See the following:

https://www.kanopystreaming.com/product/question-color

The internet currently has many postings with debates that deal with this problem which include these three:

http://www.forharriet.com/2016/01/black-women-who-benefit-from-colorism.html#axzz4wrf0EMDwts

https://www.jstor.org/stable/3090169?seq=1#page_scan_tab_contents

http://www.racismreview.com/blog/2011/03/26/african-americans-still-victims-of-colorism/

It is hoped that this volume will provide some enlightenment and insight on these issues for the reader.

Gabriel Haslip-Viera, New York City, December 29, 2017.

CHAPTER 1

WHITE PRIVILEGE AND THE IDEOLOGY OF WHITE SUPREMACY IN THE SPANISH-SPEAKING CARIBBEAN, ITS DIASPORA AND LATIN AMERICA, 1492-PRESENT

BY GABRIEL HASLIP-VIERA

At the time of their first arrival in the Americas in the 1490s, educated Spaniards generally accepted and promoted the prevailing view of ethnic categorization articulated in the Biblical texts and other more secular writings dating back to the ancient Greeks. Coincidently, the word *raza* [race] also emerged for the first time during this period and was incorporated into the European languages at this time. At first, the word simply referred to pedigree or lineage as in breed, family or people of common descent. There were references to pedigree or lineage in the Biblical texts, especially in the *Book of Genesis*. But there was no indication that these references were connected to skin color, hair texture or other physical, mental or emotional attributes connected to the word race as we understand it today despite claims that were made by later writers—especially with regard to the descendants of the biblical Ham, Shem, and Japhet. Physical and mental attributes were nevertheless connected to specific populations in the writings of the ancient Greeks as transmitted and adopted by educated Romans, Byzantines, "Arabs," Iranians, and also by the Spaniards, Portuguese and other peoples of Western Europe during the Middle Ages.

The ancient Greeks connected variations in alleged physical and mental attributes to geography and environment and divided their known world into extremely damp, cold geographic environments to the north as opposed to extremely hot, dry environments to their south with a more agreeable blended environment in the "middle of the earth" [from the Mediterranean region to India and China] where Greece and other so-called "civilized" societies and cultures were situated. Plinius Secundus [Pliny], the first century Roman naturalist, summarized this concept best when he contrasted the peoples of the Mediterranean from the Germanic and other "barbarians" to the north and sub-Saharan Africans [Ethiopians] to the south by noting that:

> "It is beyond question that the Ethiopians are burnt by the heat of the heavenly body near them, and are born with a scorched appearance, with curly beard and hair, and that in the opposite region of the world, the people have white frosty skins, with yellow hair that hangs straight. While the latter are fierce owing to the rigidity of their climate, the former are wise because of the mobility of theirs…in both regions men's stature is high, owing in the former to the pressure of the fires and in the latter to the nourishing effect of the dampness; whereas in the middle of the earth, owing to a healthy blending of both elements, there are tracts of land that are fertile for all sorts of produce, and men are of medium bodily stature, with a marked blending even in the matter of skin complexion. Customs are gentle, senses clear, intellects fertile and able to grasp the whole of nature; and they also have governments, which the other peoples have never possessed—being quite detached and solitary on account of the savagery of the nature that broods over their regions" In other words, the ancient Greeks and Romans did not see themselves as "white" (Plinius Secundus 1938-1997).

Plinius also made a brief reference elsewhere to the peoples of India when he said that in:

> "In the region to the south of the Ganges the tribes are browned by the heat of the sun to the extent of being colored, though not as yet burnt black like the Ethiopians.

> The nearer they get to the Indus the more color they display" (Plinius Secundus 1938-1997).

Hippocrates, the ancient Greek physician, was much less benign in his description of the northern barbarians [Scythians] four centuries earlier whom he described as follows:

> "In Europe, there are the Scythians, called Sauromatae, who are different from all other peoples." They "have a peculiarity of shape, and do not resemble any of the others. The same observation applies to the Egyptians, only that the latter are oppressed by heat and the former by cold.... Winter may be said to be always present with them; or, if they have summer, it is only for a few days, and the heat is not very strong.... They all equally use the same food and same clothing summer and winter, respiring a humid and dense atmosphere, and drinking water from snow and ice; neither do they make any laborious exertions, for neither body nor mind is capable of enduring fatigue when the changes of the seasons are not great. For these reasons their shapes are gross and fleshy, with ill-marked joints, of a humid temperament, and deficient in tone: the internal cavities, and especially those of the intestines, are full of humors; for the belly cannot possibly be dry in such a country. With such a constitution and in such a climate; but owing to their fat, and the absence of hairs from their bodies, their shapes resemble one another, the males being all alike.... The Scythians are tawny from the cold, and not from the intense heat of the sun, for the whiteness of the skin is parched by the cold, and becomes tawny" (Hippocrates 1881).

These ideas and others which were similar, evolved and changed somewhat in their details during the centuries that followed, but the basic premise that physical and mental attributes were determined by geography and environment remained the same and were accepted or assumed as the reality by the Spaniards and the Portuguese when they first embarked on their journeys of exploration, trade and settlement in Africa and Asia in the middle of the 1400s. They also soon began to apply these ideas to the mysterious and previously unknown peoples they encountered in the Americas after it was concluded that they were not East Asians, nor the descendants of the lost tribes of Israel, or others, which was part of the array of speculation—religious and otherwise—that emerged at that time.

In the beginning, the Spaniards divided the population of their Caribbean colonies of Santo Domingo, Cuba, Puerto Rico, and Jamaica into three broad categories—"Spaniards" or "Europeans," the Indigenous erroneously called "Indians," and sub-Saharan Africans or "*negros*" who were brought to the Caribbean as either persons of free or enslaved status. However, it was legal and religious status that was considered more important than people's physical and mental attributes. Greater consideration was given to whether individuals were slave or free, foreign or subjects of the Crown, or whether they were Catholic Christians as opposed to being Jews, Muslims or pagans. However, attention to physical and mental attributes also became increasingly important as a result of the rapid decline of the Indigenous population in the Caribbean and all other areas where the Spaniards and Portuguese established their colonies. In the Caribbean, "Indians" were soon judged to be physically less robust as workers and disproportionately prone to epidemic disease requiring protection by the Royal government in contrast to sub-Saharan Africans, who were judged to be physically more robust and more suitable as workers for employment as slave laborers on Spanish enterprises. The importance of physical attributes also began to take root over legal and religious status as part of the effort to determine who was European, Indian, or sub-Saharan African and also to determine the precise nature of the persons of mixed background that soon began to emerge in significant numbers as an important factor in the evolving demography of both the Spanish and Portuguese colonies.

In the Spanish colonies, a complex, highly structured, social hierarchy based on physical characteristics and legal status began to emerge in Mexico, Central America and South America during the course of the sixteenth century. The three core groups of Europeans, Africans, the Indigenous, and their surviving descendants were still seen as most important, but new emergent peoples of mixed background were identified and legally defined by the later part of the sixteenth century. These were called *mestizos* [half indigenous and half European], *mulatos* [half African and half European], and *zambos* [half Indigenous and half African]. All three groups were initially seen as deviant and a growing problem because the Royal government had issued decrees to keep the three original core groups segregated from one another [especially the "protected" Indigenous] as part of the model of governance that the Spaniards wished to impose. However, the emergence of the mixed population was eventually acknowledged and a legal and social hierarchy of status was created for all the groups that had been identified and defined by the later part of the sixteenth century. The pattern that emerged in most mainland colonies [*sociedad de castas* or "society of castes"] placed the Spanish born and their white "creole" descendants at the top, *mestizos* below the creoles, *mulatos* below the *mestizos*, with sub-Saharan Africans and their descendants at the bottom. The Indigenous were also at the bottom but separate from the other groups [1]. An elaborate and ever increasing set of ideologically based laws, rules and regulations were created to enforce this hierarchy of status. By the late eighteenth century, new groups came to be identified in Mexico, Central America [the Viceroyalty of New Spain] and South America [the Viceroyalty of Peru—also New Granada after 1717 and La Plata after 1776] and legally placed in the hierarchy of social status. They included in Mexico and Central America, the *castizos* [three quarters Spanish or white creole and one quarter indigenous], *moriscos* [three quarters Spanish or white creole and one quarter African], *albinos* [mix of Spanish and *morisco*] and even a category called *salto atrás* [jump back], which was at times employed against the white creole descendants of the Spanish-born who were suspected of having some Indigenous or [more importantly] African "blood" despite their so-called European appearance and status (Mörner 1967).

Differences in labelling [e.g.: *cholo*, *genizaro*, *lobo*, *zambaigo*, etc.] and differences in certain details with regard to the categorizations employed became part of the *sociedad de castas* as it evolved in different parts of the Spanish Empire. However, the whole effort to categorize the different possible mixtures that had emerged by the late eighteenth century overwhelmed the authorities and as a result, they collapsed all the "mixed race" groups into a single category called *castas*. The use of the term *casta* continued after the wars of independence and the creation of the nation states, but the application of the older labels such as *mestizo*, *mulato* and their variants also continued as part of the vernacular of the popular culture and are still used throughout Latin America to this day. In some countries, the idea of race and race categorization changed as a result of revolution or changes in political policy during the nineteenth and twentieth centuries. In Mexico, a new ideology [*la raza cosmica*, or "the cosmic race"], which venerated the Indigenous and idealized the *mestizo* or race mixture more generally, took root after the revolution of 1910-1920 and was also adopted in different ways in other Latin American countries. However, the old categories, prejudices and patterns of discrimination, especially against the Indigenous, persist in Mexico to this day at the same time that the elites have remained mostly white [*güeros*] to a significant degree—at least in the mind set of most people. These ideas and the attitudes connected to them have also been transferred or have become part of the discourse of Mexican Americans in the United States with variations seen in California that differ from those in Texas and other states. A more idealized ideology that favored a mixed Indigenous or *mestizo* identity emerged in the late 1960s and early 1970s as a result of the Chicano movement and its politics, but there has been criticism in recent years that the older ideas have returned including the idea in some quarters that all Mexican Americans in the U.S. should be defined officially as "white" (Mörner 1967; Wade 2000; Applebaum et al. 2003; Minority Rights Group 1995; Vasconcelos 1997; Haney López 2003a, b). There is even a group called "The National Association for the Advancement of Caucasian Hispanics" [NAACH] but it's not clear how large its membership or influence might be.

In contrast to what happened in the mainland areas of Latin America, a completely different reality emerged on the islands of the Spanish Caribbean. Most notably, the Indigenous peoples of Hispaniola, Cuba and Puerto Rico did not survive the initial contact with the Spanish settlers as identifiable populations in the sixteenth century. Labor exploitation, epidemic disease and war decimated the indigenous to such an extent that Spanish officials ceased to count persons of Indigenous background by the middle of the sixteenth century. This was in contrast to the mainland colonies where the indigenous peoples were also decimated but nevertheless survived to a significant degree as defined groups and even began to increase in numbers by the eighteenth century. Overall, the populations of Cuba, Santo Domingo and Puerto Rico remained quite small and were generally ignored during the entire period from the mid-1500s to the later part of the 1700s. Except for their strategic military importance in protecting the trade and revenue producing networks between Spain's mainland colonies and Europe, little attention was paid to the economic and social development of the islands during this long period. The official Spanish presence was largely limited to the fortified port towns of Havana [Cuba], Santo Domingo [Hispaniola], San Juan [Puerto Rico] and a few other localities.

A relatively small and largely ignored peasant population evolved in the rural interior of all three islands during this period which consisted of the remnants of the Indigenous population, escaped Africans slaves [*cimarrones*], Africans of free status, their descendants, and impoverished Spaniards and other Europeans not connected to the military and commerce of the port towns. This population was seen as a thoroughly mixed population that was difficult to define by the early and middle decades of the seventeenth century; however, they also came to be seen mostly as the mixed descendants of Africans and Europeans [*mulatos*] who migrated into the interior rural areas and became the dominant element in the demography of the islands. This was clearly the view of Fray Iñigo Abbad y LaSierra in Puerto Rico in the 1770s when he observed that:

> "The *mulatos* who constitute the majority of the population of this island are the children of whites and blacks" (See Abbad y LaSierra 2002: 365-7, 495. Also, see Fradera and other relevant chapters in Palme and Scarano 2011).

In contrast to Puerto Rico and also Cuba, the peasant population of Spanish Hispaniola began to play an increasingly important role in the economy of that island after it was divided between France [Saint Domingue] and Spain [Santo Domingo] in the seventeenth century. The French established a profitable and dominant sugar plantation economy on their side of the island that quickly required the importation of food and other necessities to feed its population of mostly enslaved Africans and their slave and free descendants. The peasant population and most of the medium to large landowners on the Spanish side of the island fulfilled this need with exports of food and other products which were sent to the French colony on the other side of the island. This relationship prevailed until the late eighteenth century when the successful Haitian slave uprising and the establishment of the Haitian republic changed the relationship as a result of the Haitian withdrawal from the plantation economy and its commerce (Moya Pons 1998; Cassá 2006; Franco 2012, 2015; Buscaglia Salgado 2003).

All during this period, the alleged social, political and cultural hegemony of the Spaniards and other Europeans was maintained. The ideological basis for race categorization also evolved in various ways throughout Latin America and also in the Caribbean. Most notably, a so-called scientific basis for race categorization emerged and began to replace the genealogies of the Biblical texts and the ancient ideas that geography and environment determined physical and mental attributes. The change began during the eighteenth century "Enlightenment" when pre-Darwinian ideas of evolution were combined with ideas on the importance of geography and the environment. By the later part of the nineteenth century, misinterpretations of Darwin's theory of evolution [Social Darwinism] were applied to racial categorizations based on physical stereotypes and their alleged connection to mental and emotional attributes. The superiority of whiteness in Europe over all other groups was allegedly confirmed through this new scientific research. They were also adopted by the social, cultural and political elites of Latin America and the Spanish Caribbean, but many of the older ideas and categorizations continued to be important in the popular culture and even in official records. Terms such as *mestizo* and *mulato* and their variants continued to be used in Mexico, Central America, South America and the Caribbean as well as black and white well into the twentieth century and continue to be applied up the present time (Wade 2000; Applebaum et al. 2003; Minority Rights Group 1995; Stepan 1991).

CUBA

As noted above, white privilege and the ideology of whiteness in the Spanish-speaking Caribbean began to evolve in a different manner during the sixteenth century. The ideology of white supremacy in Cuba also began to diverge from those in the other two islands in the years that followed, especially during the nineteenth century [2]. This change was rooted in historical trajectories that took place on each island with changes in thinking by the white creole elites who were forced to deal with major events in Santo Domingo, or in the case of Cuba and Puerto Rico, a rethinking of their status as royal subjects under Spanish rule. In Cuba, a major change began in the middle of the nineteenth century among those within the white creole elite who called for independence or autonomist self-government. At one point, the advocates for independence adopted a part Indigenous Native American [*Indio*] identity to separate themselves from the Spanish regime and its supporters. In time, they also became more politically progressive when they called for the abolition of slavery in addition to independence. Several plots, including an 1850 invasion led by exile leader, Narciso López, were suppressed by the Spanish authorities before the movement finally took off during the rebellions against Spanish rule that broke out in 1868-1878 [the "Ten Years War"], 1880 [*La guerra Chiquita* or "Little War"], and the War of 1895 which continued until the U.S. intervened and occupied Cuba in the aftermath of the so-called "Spanish-American War" [1898-1903] (see Pérez 2011; Ferrer 1999; de la Fuente 2001; Schmidt-Nowara 1999).

Afro-Cubans became important participants in these wars as soldiers and commanders in the rebel military forces. The commanders included generals Antonio and José Maceo, and others, such as Flor Crombet, "Perico" Pérez, José Quintín Bandera, and Isidro Acea Gil. Important Afro-Cuban social and political leaders also emerged during this period including most notably, Juan Gualberto Gómez [1854-1933], Martín Morua Delgado [1856-1910], and Rafael Serra [1858-1909] among others. Cuban liberation leader, José Martí also supported the Afro-Cubans before his death in battle at the start of the War of 1895. However, he also called for a society free of racism and rejected the race categories and identity politics of both whites and blacks in Cuban society as being problematic and divisive. Martí's race free society was to be based on a human fusion and not on the idea of race or the Spanish *casta* system which he did not mention in *Mi raza*, his most quoted statement on this issue. With events and thinking like this, the important and even crucial contributions to Cuban independence by the Afro-Cuban leadership and Afro-Cubans in general could not be ignored in the aftermath of the War of 1895 and earlier conflicts. It also could not be ignored because the Afro-Cubans became much more politically and socially organized in Cuba in contrast to their brethren on the other islands by the time Cuba became politically independent under U.S. influence if not total control in 1903. The Afro-Cubans created social clubs, published newspapers, organized protests, ran for public office, and became a force that the white creole establishment had to contend with (Helg 1990, 1995, 1997; de la Fuente 2001; Ferrer 1999, 2014; Guerra 2003; Doherty 2011; Martí 1893).

However, starting during the U.S. military occupation [1898-1903] and later during the "First Republic" [1903-1933], the U.S. actively supported the white creole elites and their Hispanophile ideology and identity, or the U.S. variant of white identity and supremacy that some of the white Cubans also adopted based on social and "scientific" Darwinism. The U.S. acted to suppress Afro-Cuban political organizations and military power during its initial period of occupation. In 1899, the U.S. authorities disbanded the Cuban revolutionary army and created a "rural guard" that was commanded by white officers. This change limited blacks and *mulatos* in military enforcement to the non-commissioned ranks of sergeant, corporal and below—a policy that was continued by the independent Cuban government during the years of the first republic. The Cuban government also effectively banned Afro-Cubans from positions in government at the national, provincial and local levels after 1903, and even banned Afro-Cubans from joining the ranks of Havana's newly created police force. The only concessions that were granted to Afro-Cubans and other non-whites were the laws included in the U.S. inspired constitution of 1901 that gave them "equality [without specifying race, sex, place of birth or religion] and universal male suffrage." However, the independent Cuban government controlled by elite white creoles failed to follow-through on these laws and also failed to institute policies by the U.S. military authorities that encouraged the establishment of public education for all Cubans regardless of race (Helg 1995; de la Fuente 2001; Guerra 2003).

The U.S. military and Cuban governments also instituted new laws (1902, 1906) that restricted emigration to Cuba to families from "Norway, Sweden, Denmark, northern Italy and the Spanish Canary Islands." Curiously and in contrast to what happened in Puerto Rico, the migration of Spaniards [the former enemy] increased dramatically during the years of the first republic in Cuba. Approximately 900,000 Spaniards and Canary Islanders migrated to Cuba between 1900 and 1929 as the sugar and related sectors expanded. This was a significantly larger migration in terms of numbers than for any other European group that came to Cuba during these years. It turns out that Fidel Castro's father was one of these immigrants.

In addition to laws and policy decisions, the white creole intelligentsia of Cuba also articulated ideas that promoted whiteness and served as the ideological basis for the suppression of Afro-Cuban political power and influence during the early years of the first republic. Francisco Figueras, a politician writing in 1907, claimed that "Cubans were still in the process of 'formation,' but [were] already a physical type close to that of the Spaniard." He also claimed that blacks were a "race vegetating in childhood" who brought their "musical sense, their exhibitionism…lasciviousness, and their lack of foresight." However, the elitist intelligentsia had hopes for the future. According to Figueras and others, "natural selection would eventually lead to the absorption of the blacks by the superior race." Fernando Ortíz, who is known for his denunciation of race as unscientific, nevertheless saw Afro-Cubans and Africans in general as culturally and morally inferior. According to him, "Africans" were inferior "because of their lack of integral civilization and morals." He also said that Africans were "lascivious lovers, given to polygamy which resulted in families that were disordered and lacked cohesion. Additionally, he denounced the religious practices of Africans and Afro-Cubans [*Santería*, etc.] which according to him led to human sacrifice, cannibalism, and the most brutal superstitions and criminality (de la Fuente 2001; Helg 1995, Guerra 2003).

Afro-Cubans reacted to these ideas and the attacks on their rights and status with active resistance during the early years of the first republic but apparently not during the earlier U.S. military occupation. One tactic used by the Afro-Cubans during this period was to claim that they were different and were not to be equated with the "primitive" peoples of the African continent. This claim was based on the limited or distorted knowledge about Africa that prevailed at that time which was rooted in racialist anthropology, social Darwinism and other ideas connected to the "science" of Europe and the United States. Some Afro-Cubans also became advocates for racial progress based on "merit, education and work" within the social system and culture. Juan Risquet noted in his book *La cuestión politico-social en la isla de Cuba* [*The Political and Social Question on the Island of Cuba*] published in 1900, that Afro-Cubans were not "Hottentots, but lucid, free beings, civilized men, who know how much they have done," but others also called for collective action against racism and discrimination that would actively challenge the social order perhaps with violence if necessary. In 1907, Rafael Serra called for the establishment of organizations that would defend the rights and interests of Afro-Cubans. He also called for the expansion of the Afro-Cuban *bourgeoisie* which in his mind, would advance the economic and social status of blacks, *mulato*s and other non-whites in Cuba. Soon after the elections of 1908 which resulted in the failure to elect a single non-white candidate, an Afro-Cuban political party, *el Partido Independiente de Color* ["Independent Colored Peoples Party"] was created under the leadership of Evaristo Estenoz. The political program and goals of this group are perhaps best summarized by Aline Helg as follows:

> "Compulsory free education from eight to fourteen years, free technical, secondary and university education, state control of private schools, abolition of the death penalty, reform of the judicial and penitentiary system, and the eight hour workday. It [the program] also advocated an end to racial discrimination, priority for Cubans in employment, black access to higher positions in public service and the diplomatic corps, and an end to the ban on nonwhite immigration" (Helg, 1990: 55).

The *Partido Independiente de Color* claimed 60,000 members in 1910 and the leadership also called for the Party to challenge the two establishment parties which dominated Cuban politics at that time and in the upcoming 1912 elections. The white creole elites in control of the government moved to destroy the *Partido* especially after the creoles were victorious in the 1912 election. At first, the *Partido* and its supporters were accused of advocating "color racism." This was followed by the passage of an electoral law that prohibited political parties from representing a single race or group of races. Afro-Cubans who were mostly concentrated in Oriente province in Eastern Cuba had also lost some of their lands and other properties through unfair expropriations and other means in the years leading up to the elections of 1912. This led to major protests which turned violent in the aftermath of the elections and became known as the "Little War of 1912." The government employed the military, militias, and a newly created secret police to violently suppress the revolt which resulted in some 4,000 Afro-Cuban deaths and additional casualties. The U.S. also intervened with resources and military support in the suppression of this revolt. The year 1912 saw the beginning of the end of Afro-Cuban political influence and power which was to last until an opportunity manifested itself during the revolution of 1933. In the meantime, the ideology of white supremacy continued to evolve during the remaining years of the first republic and this enabled the white creole elites to maintain and even enhance their power.

For example, a significant proportion of the elite adopted a new nationalist ideology during the years of the first republic which was in part in opposition to U.S. influence and its direct interference in Cuban politics and society as mandated by the Platt Amendment which established the independence of Cuba in the first place. The Platt Amendment and other provisions of the treaty between the two countries allowed the U.S. to actively challenge election results and even occupy the country for periods of time which happened with considerable frequency. The U.S. occupied Cuba in 1906–09 [to impose a government friendly to the U.S.], 1917–22 [To protect sugar plantations and preserve the political order] and also as noted, in 1912 [against the Afro-Cubans in Oriente province]. These interventions were rightly seen among most political factions in the country as an abusive intrusion into Cuba's national sovereignty by the 1920s even though the 1912 intervention benefitted the creoles as a group. What also emerged by the 1920s was another anti U.S. idea that claimed that Cubans were a single race—"*La raza Cubana*," which was based on *mestizaje* or race mixture as an ideal through the appropriation of Cuba's African heritage and those of other non-white Cubans into the ideology of white supremacy. This idea was also connected to the assertion that there was no such thing as racism in Cuba in comparison to what prevailed in the U.S. However, these ideas would not result in a more democratized class based hierarchy free of racism. As articulated, it meant the actual reinforcement of the racial hierarchy based on *mestizaje* with the white creole elites still on top and seen as biologically and culturally superior. Racism in Cuba against Afro-Cubans, West Indians, the Chinese and others was obfuscated or denied as part of the false assertion that there was no racism in Cuba, but it continued in reality—often as virulently as ever, and as a result, the possibility of an Afro-Cuban resurgence did not materialize again until the early 1930s when opposition to the government and dictatorship of Gerardo Machado led to his overthrow in the revolution of 1933 (de la Fuente 2001; Pérez 2011).

The revolution of 1933 ushered in a period of political instability that lasted until 1936. The abusive, corrupt Machado dictatorship was overthrown in August of 1933 by various political factions which included most notably, the lower level military of mixed racial orientation led by sergeant Fulgencio Batista, a person defined as *mulato* with significant Chinese ancestry. However, the revolutionary government was quickly overthrown as a result of U.S. interference in a deal between the U.S. and Batista, who became a colonel several months later in January 1934. Afro-Cubans had hoped to reclaim their human rights and even perhaps the political influence they had lost in the previous decades but this was not about to happen despite Batista and certain political factions that came to support the Afro-Cubans. In actuality, most of the so called "progressive" elements of the revolution, along with the conservatives, opposed the goals of the Afro-Cubans, sometimes violently. Attacks on Afro-Cubans and the bombings of their clubs and organizations increased in cities and towns throughout Cuba during the period of the revolution and its aftermath.White creoles also organized a "Ku Klux Clan Kubano" modeled on its U.S. counterpart in September 1933. This group terrorized the Afro-Cubans in Oriente Province and elsewhere during the period of instability that followed the overthrow of Machado. Active and consistent support for Afro-Cubans only came from the small Cuban Communist Party [PCC], the International Comintern, and other fringe groups on the political left. Afro-Cuban membership in the PCC increased and a number of Afro-Cubans took leadership positions in the party. At one point [1934-1935], the PCC became advocates for the establishment of a separate independent Afro-Cuban republic in Oriente Province where Afro-Cubans were said to constitute half the population, but this proposal came to be seen as politically and racially divisive. In the meantime, Batista came to be accepted by the white creole elites, however reluctantly, with U.S. support. He was even racially redefined at this point when it was claimed that he also had Indigenous "Indian" ancestry (Guridy 2010; de la Fuente 2001; Pérez 2011).

Batista preferred to exercise his influence or control over Cuban politics and the country from behind the scenes. He effectively manipulated Cuban electoral politics to his benefit and those of his supporters most of the time. He never gave up his control or influence over the military, his power base, until his overthrow in 1959. He was actually elected president of Cuba in what was judged to be an honest election in 1940 after he aligned himself with "progressive" factions in Cuban politics which also included support from the Communists and the Afro-Cubans who voted for him. The Afro-Cubans had also increased their influence and even some power through the support they received from the Cuban Communist Party which also augmented its power and influence when it became the dominant force in the labor movement through its *Confederación Nacional Obrera* ["National Workers Confederation"]. Afro-Cubans were again appointed to leadership positions in the PCC and became members of the Cuban legislature. They and the PCC also received support from the government during the years of Batista's first presidency [1940-1944] and for a few years after that, but overall, the status of Afro-Cubans remained low. Poverty, overall lack of opportunity and discrimination continued without let-up and increased during the presidencies of Ramón Grau San Martín [1944-1948] and Carlos Prio Socarras [1948-1952]. The power and influence of the Communists along with that of the Afro-Cubans also began to decline rapidly by the end of the 1940s and into the early 1950s when the government withdrew its support and rival political factions made significant inroads into the labor movement (de la Fuente 2001).

However, when Batista came to power again as president after a military coup in 1952, efforts were made once again to include Afro-Cubans in the political system. Batista entered into agreements with social organizations and labor groups that included or represented Afro-Cubans. Two Afro-Cubans became ministers in Batista's first cabinet [Justice and Minister without Portfolio]. Several were appointed to Batista's main advisory group, the Consultative Council, and a number of others were appointed as directors of national and local agencies and bureaucracies [e.g.: the state radio and street cleaning in Havana]. In general, Afro-Cubans did not oppose Batista's coup during the early years of his regime. However, by the late 1950s, Batista's priorities were increasingly devoted to the suppression of the Cuban insurgency led by Fidel Castro in eastern Cuba. There was a crackdown on the Communist Party and other leftist groups in an effort to neutralize or generate support from the anti-communist U.S. government. Groups of Afro-Cubans also began to support the insurgency because of the government's increasingly repressive methods, and also because the actual overall economic and social status of Afro-Cubans had not improved in any meaningful way. The white creole elites were thus able to maintain their dominance of the Cuban economy and its politics all during these years as they had during previous decades. Nothing much had changed by the time Batista was overthrown by Castro and fled the country on New Year's Day, 1959 (de la Fuente 2001).

On March 22, 1959, three months after coming to power, Fidel Castro gave a speech in which he denounced racism and sexism in general and discrimination against blacks in Cuba in particular and called for the following:

> "[We] are going to put an end to racial discrimination at work centers by waging a campaign to end this shameful practice—to end this hateful, repugnant system with a new slogan: work opportunities for every Cuban, without

> discrimination for race or sex. Let there be an end to racial discrimination at work centers; let whites and blacks all get together to end hateful racial discrimination at work centers. In this way we will gradually build the new fatherland" (Castro 1959).

In actuality, Castro made no reference to Afro-Cubans and their status in speeches during the insurgency against Batista, but after he came to power, he instituted policies to promote "real equality" and end discrimination against Afro-Cubans and other marginal groups in Cuban society. A "Movement of National Integration" was created along with policies that desegregated recreational facilities such as beaches, parks, hotels, private clubs, and private schools which were nationalized when necessary. There was the literacy campaign and the mandated lowering of rents which made housing more affordable. There was also the lifting of racial barriers in occupations that had been traditionally closed to blacks and *mulatos*. Most blacks and *mulatos* benefitted materially from these changes—especially when it came to the redistribution of income and resources; however, there was considerable resistance from those Cubans who had benefitted from the ideology of white supremacy. The white upper class, some sectors of the middle class, the mostly white *petit bourgeoisie*, and even some workers opposed the elimination of racial barriers in entertainment, tourism and elsewhere.

According to Alejandro de la Fuente, the idea that blacks and whites would dance together in clubs and other facilities had generated the strongest opposition. One salesperson was quoted as saying at one point that the "black man should be given opportunities 'of the economic type so that he can enjoy a job and have his home' but not social ones" (de la Fuente: 265), but there was also resistance from workers in the areas of employment where progress on the race issue was supposed to evolve quickly. The protests by white Cubans and others who benefitted from white supremacy were condemned by the government as "counter-revolutionary" and as a reflection of U.S. style prejudice, discrimination and its influence. However, there was also some backtracking by the revolutionary government in the name of unity which was a particular concern of Castro in the face of U.S. hostility to his regime when he said:

> "I did not say that we were going to open the exclusive clubs for blacks to go there to dance or entertain themselves. I did not say that. People dance with whomever they want and... socialize with whomever they want" (de la Fuente 2001: 265. Also, see Morales Dominguez 2013; Spence Benson 2016).

A mostly non-confrontational approach was employed when it came to the assault on racism and discrimination in the years that followed the establishment of the revolutionary government. Eventually, the government also attempted to impose a silence on the controversial race issue at the same time that it established an ideal that Cuba had become or was becoming a non-racist society. This was a repeat of assertions that were made in previous decades. At times, there was an admission that racism and discrimination would not wither away overnight. It was therefore seen as preferable to impose a silence on the issue as progress was made. Silence was imposed in the government controlled press and surviving Afro-Cuban organizations and clubs were told to allow, or to open their doors to Cubans of all colors.

However, again as in earlier decades, there was also the promotion of Afro-Cuban folklore in the arts and music which was to be integrated into the national culture, but this integration did not include *Santería* and other similar and mostly Afro-Cuban religious beliefs of Catholic/Afro-polytheistic orientation and practice which were seen as counter-revolutionary forms of primitive superstition and "pathological behavior" ["opiates of the people"] which would be replaced by the secularism of Marxist ideology through education and other means. The hostility towards *Santería* was part of the larger opposition to Catholicism and religion in general which waxed and waned over the years. Despite contradictory policies and their actual inconsistent implementation over time, the status of blacks, *mulatos* and working class Cubans in general actually improved by the early 1980s. Overall health and life expectancy rose to the level of the world's developed countries, illiteracy was eliminated for all practical purposes, inequality in education was erased at all levels, and there was increased equality in the occupational structure of the country. The percentage of persons defined as blacks and *mulatos* in non-agricultural labor, sales, the professions, and as "others," was equal to that of defined whites according to the

1981 census. However, inequalities were still seen in the service sector, in media, in access to housing, in the prison population, in levels of poverty, and in management—especially in government at the municipal, provincial and national level which was 72.5% white according to the 1981 census. The ruling elite in government also remained white for all practical purposes as it had been before the revolution. This was clearly seen in public [e.g.: on TV] when it came to Castro's inner circle despite the official rhetoric, but worse was yet to come (de la Fuente 2001; Morales Dominguez 2013; Spence Benson 2016).

Cuba began to experience a period of economic stagnation perhaps as a result of unwise "reforms" that further centralized the management of the economy in the later part of the 1980s. The stagnation subsequently and unexpectedly turned into a full-fledged economic crisis with the collapse of the Soviet Union and its empire in 1989. The subsidies that Cuba was accustomed to receive along with the trade that prevailed with the Soviet Union and its "satellite" countries disappeared by the early 1990s. Cuba's gross national product declined by forty percent between 1989 and 1993. Jobs were lost, unemployment and competition for work increased and the impact of the depression fell disproportionately on blacks and *mulatos*. Market oriented policies were subsequently instituted by the government during this "special period" in an attempt to stimulate the economy. These included the opening of the Cuban economy to foreign corporate investment, an increase in private self-employment, and the use of U.S. dollars as a legal alternative currency to the Cuban *peso* among other measures.

All of this resulted in increased inequality as the Cuban economy became increasingly fragmented with some sectors becoming more lucrative for workers than others. The increased use and desirability of U.S. dollars was inclined to benefit white Cubans because of the remittances that they received from the mostly white Cubans who lived in Florida and other parts of the U.S. mainland. Black and *mulato* employment also declined in tourism which was seen as the most dynamic sector in the Cuban economy. Private foreign corporations were allowed to discriminate against Afro-Cubans in upscale hotels, clubs and other enterprises connected to tourism and also in other sectors of the economy because blacks and *mulatos* allegedly lacked a "pleasant aspect" and other aesthetic and cultural criteria. The official government silence and avoidance of a discourse on race exacerbated the increased decline in the status of Afro-Cubans. According to Alejandro de la Fuente:

> "What disappeared from the public discourse found a fertile breeding ground in private spaces, where race continued to influence social relations among friends, neighbors, co-workers, and family members. Supposedly harmless racist jokes reproduced traditional negative images of blacks. Racial ideologies were reproduced within the family and enforced in multigenerational households" (de la Fuente 2001: 322).

The ideology of white supremacy and the old negative stereotypes applied to blacks and *mulatos* continued unabated during the late 1980s and into the 1990s despite the government's official anti-discriminatory and egalitarian social policies and the rhetoric of racial integration and inclusion. An overwhelming eighty-five percent of respondents to a 1994 survey believed that racial prejudice was rampant on the island. Sixty-nine percent believed that blacks did not have the proper cultural values and sixty-eight percent also opposed interracial marriage. In reality, nothing much seemed to have changed with the traditional racism reverting back to patterns seen earlier in the century. Cubans in general and defined white Cubans in particular, continued to see blacks and *mulatos* as "lazy, inefficient, dirty, ugly, uncivilized, inherently less intelligent" [despite their educational achievements], "and prone to criminal activity," with the government unable to counteract these views (de la Fuente 2001; Morales Dominguez 2013; Spence Benson 2016).

Afro-Cubans reacted to the increase in racism, discrimination and its increased transparency during the 1990s with resentment, resistance, and demands for justice that included street protests which were ignored or obfuscated in the official media. There was the "*Malecón* [street] riot" of August 1994 along with increased organizational activity which included the creation of a *Cofradía de Negritud* [Fraternity of Blackness] in 1999 along with other similar entities, but in reality, nothing much changed during the next twenty years as Cuba recovered slowly from the crisis of the "special period." In July 2015, the administration of U.S. president Barack Obama announced an agreement with the Cuban government that re-established direct diplomatic ties and a possible rapprochement between the two countries for the first time since 1961. Before this happened and soon after, a number of articles appeared in the U.S. media which focused on the race issue in Cuba. A March 23, 2013 article with the exaggerated headline, "For Blacks in Cuba, the Revolution Hasn't Begun," appeared in the *New York Times*. This article focused on the status of Afro-Cubans at that point and confirmed the problems which had emerged in the 1990s and their continued persistence. It was reported that the private sector created in the 1990s enjoyed "a certain degree of economic liberation," but that blacks were "not well positioned to take advantage of it." It also noted that structural inequality and racial prejudice continued to "exclude Afro-Cubans from the benefits of liberalization." However, the article also reported on government efforts to diminish if not end racism and discrimination in the economy—especially in the tourism sector, and that these efforts had met with some success. In the meantime, the old prejudices and practices connected to white supremacy and its ideology continued to persist among Cuban Americans in Florida and elsewhere on the U.S. mainland (Zurbano 1997; Cave 2016; Morales Dominguez 2013; Spence Benson 2016).

This prejudice and its connection to discrimination against Afro-Cubans was revealed in a September 13, 1997 *New York Times* article by Mireya Navarro titled "Black and Cuban American: Bias in 2 Worlds." In this article, it was shown that Afro-Cubans were not only subjected to prejudice, segregation and discrimination in Miami and within other elitist white dominated Cuban communities, they were also not necessarily accepted by African Americans—especially those in leadership positions who felt that they should rightfully be the ones to be elected or appointed to influential positions in government and elsewhere because of their long-term history in U.S. society which Afro-Cubans as recent arrivals did not share. There was also the very long and sad June 5, 2000 *New York Times* article by Maria Ojito titled "Best of Friends, Worlds Apart." This article told the story of Joel Ruíz, defined as black, and Achmed Valdés, defined as white, who were the best of friends growing-up in Guanabo, Cuba, and how they became increasingly separated in Miami as a result of the racial politics prevalent among Cuban Americans in that city (Zurbano 1997; Ojito 2000). There was also the slightly earlier and tumultuous Elián González controversy of 1999.

Elián González was a five-year old boy who was picked-up floating in a tire inner tube by two Anglo-American fisherman off the east coast of Florida soon after his mother, her boyfriend and others had drowned in a boat after leaving Cuba. The boy was eventually turned over to maternal relatives living in Miami who decided to keep him despite the fact that Elián's natural father lived in Cuba and demanded his return. A major public controversy emerged in the U.S., especially among conservative and Republican Party politicians, over whether the boy should be returned to his natural father in Cuba or be allowed to stay and be raised by his relatives in Miami. Many Republicans and cultural conservatives called for the placement of the boy with his Miami relatives despite their then strong political advocacy for "family values" and the rights of parents when it came to the custody of their children. The Cuban American community and its leadership also actively rallied in favor of the boy's relatives and against the natural father who lived, according to them, in a godless and undesirable communist Cuba. The discourse at times reached absurd levels when false claims were made that Elián was encircled by dolphins that protected him from sharks as he floated in the water (Aja 2016).

A very contentious public legal process followed which also involved protests and demonstrations by elements of the Cuban community as well as by the relatives, but the Cuban community also quickly learned that despite what most assumed, they were not necessarily seen as a "model minority" that would easily assimilate into U.S. society and culture but merely as just another group of Latinos. Elián González was eventually seized in the house of the Miami relatives by federal agents with firearms drawn on orders of then attorney general, Janet Reno, and returned to his natural father. Latino cynics in the know about racism among Cuban Americans also noted at the time that the Miami Cubans would not have made a big deal about Elían González if he had been a black or *mulato* child. The anti-black ideology of white supremacy emerged in its ugliest form during the course of the controversy. Elena Freye, the director of "Cubans for Democracy" noted at the time that Elián was "not some ugly black kid from Haiti" but an "adorable-looking boy, very photogenic." There was also Nivaldo Fernández and Arianne Horta, an inter-racial couple that survived the drownings along with Elián. The darker complected Nivaldo reported at one point that he found himself "unwelcome" at the same time that Arianne's Miami aunt noted with a sigh that "For us, it's a very big thing. He [Nivaldo] is the first black person in our family.... We accept him...because he is a good, hard working man. What can we do?" In the meantime, Latino critics of Cuban racism laughed when it was revealed through photographs that Elián's father had tightly coiled "African" or "bad hair" [*pelo malo*] which made him a non-white *jabao* [passing for white except for the hair texture] (See Aja 2016: 151, 152).

In addition to the stories and events of the 1990s and the early 2000s, a July 2012 article titled "The Colors of the Cuban Diaspora: Portrayal of Racial Dynamics among Cuban-Americans" by Diana Fulger [Universität Bielefeld, Germany] provided a good summary of the history of racism and discrimination within the Diasporic Cuban American communities in all its complexity. Her conclusions strongly suggested as noted elsewhere, that their view towards race and it social construction remained rooted in Cuba and its ideology of white supremacy, and not on those of the U.S. The question that arises at this point is whether the younger generations of Cuban Americans have changed their view towards race.

The answer to this important question remains speculative, but there are suggestions that a change has taken place. Thirty-five percent of the generally conservative Cuban Americans voted for Barack Obama in 2008, but his figure rose dramatically in the 2012 election when the vote for Obama reached 47%. More importantly, Obama handily won the vote of Cuban Americans between ages 18 and 50 in both the 2008 and 2012 elections. A December 17, 2015 Bendixen and Amandi International survey reported that 54% of Cuban Americans ages 18-49 had a favorable opinion of Obama. This was in contrast to the 44% for Cuban Americans aged 50-64, and 39% for Cuban Americans aged 65 and over. Although about 85% of Cuban Americans self-identified as white in the 2010 census, there seems to be an increased change in views towards race and its social construction by younger U.S. born Cuban Americans that may be less racist and discriminatory than has been the case for Cubans who came to the U.S. mainland in the 1960s and 1970s. Nevertheless, the degree to which the ideology of white supremacy remains important even for younger Cuban Americans is not known at this point (Fulger 2012; Bendixen & Amandi 2015).

THE DOMINICAN REPUBLIC

In contrast to Cuba and the rest of Latin America, the ideology of white supremacy in the Dominican Republic evolved in a most unique way during a complex historical and political process that eventually led to independence in 1844. Colonial Spanish Santo Domingo came to an end after a long drawn-out and tortuous period in the years between 1795 and 1821. It was first ceded to France as a result of the 1795 Treaty of Basel which ended a war between France and Spain. It was subsequently invaded by Haitian revolutionaries in 1801 but then re-occupied as a colony by the French until 1809 when the local population and those who thought of themselves as Spanish "subjects" rebelled and re-established Spanish control with British help from 1809 to 1821. At this point, it was again invaded and occupied by Haiti—now an independent republic—which unified the island until 1843 when there was another uprising of the local population that resulted in the establishment of the Dominican Republic as an independent nation state.

It is said that the utter brutality of a failed 1805 Haitian invasion of Santo Domingo led by Jean Jacques Dessalines set the stage for the emergence of a unique ideology of whiteness based on anti-Haitianism as well as anti-blackness. Those who opposed the Haitians along with Hispanophile "patriots" exploited this ideology during the Haitian occupation or unification period between 1821 and 1843 and again during subsequent efforts by Haiti to unify the island through invasion under various Haitian leaders, especially under president and then "emperor," Faustin Soulouque, from 1849 to 1856 (Sagas 2000: 18; Moya Pons 1998; Cassá; Franco 2009, 2012, 2015; Rodríguez Demorizi 1955).

A major unresolved problem that emerges at this point is the inability to determine the actual number and ethnic breakdown of the Dominican population during the period of political turmoil and Haitian rule from 1795 to 1843 and also during subsequent decades. Claims have been made that only a small number of Haitian entrepreneurs, soldiers and government officials established residence on the Dominican side of the island during the period of Haitian rule. Others claim that there was no significant movement of Haitians into the Dominican side of the island—even along the traditional border areas between the two countries. Curiously,

Dominican scholar and former president, Joaquín Balalguer, contradicted these claims when he wrote that Dominican ethnicity and culture was first corrupted by blacks and Haitians after the Treaty of Basel in 1795. According to Balaguer, Santo Domingo was a Christian Spanish community of European families, and descendants of conquistadors which became filled with African slaves after it was turned over to the French in 1795. This view seemed to be based in part on a distortion of assertions made by Dominican essayist, politician and president of the short-lived [1821-1822] "Republic of Spanish Haiti," José Nuñez de Caceres, who claimed that Santo Domingo had a population of 80,000 in 1795 which included European descendants, *mulatos*, a few black slaves and freedmen. This was in contrast to the much larger population of French Haiti or Saint Domingue which totaled 570,000 in 1789 with 30,000 whites [5.2%], 40,000 free colored [7.0%], and 500,000 slaves [87.8%] (see Balaguer 1947; Franco 2009, 2012, 2015; and Hidalgo at:

(<http://haitiintheamericas.tumblr.com/post/101872634573/dennis-hidalgo-searching-for-an-american-dream> and

<https://www.academia.edu/9083491/It_Happened_in_Saman%C3%A1_The_Bay_of_Rinc%C3%B3n_the_Cig%C3%BCayos_and_Columbus_Party>

A more recent speculative assessment suggests that the Dominican population had reached 160,000 by 1789 and was composed of about 35,000 whites [21.9%], some 95,000 free colored [59.4%] and about 30,000 slaves [18.7%] [3]. These figures if more or less accurate would begin to provide an insight into the subsequent historical demography of the Dominican Republic and why the genetic breakdown of its population differs significantly from that of Cuba and Puerto Rico. Both Cuba and Puerto Rico went through what would be called a "blackening" process in the early nineteenth century as a result of increased economic development, especially in the sugar sector which was connected to an increase in the importation of African slaves. This was especially true of Cuba where the slave population reached forty percent of the total in the 1840s. The two islands then went through a subsequent "whitening" process in the later part of the nineteenth century as a result of further economic development in the sugar, tobacco and coffee sectors which also resulted in increased European, Middle Eastern and Asian immigration after slavery came to an end in the 1870s and 1880s (Palme and Scarano 2011). These kinds of changes did not begin to take place in the Dominican Republic until the very end of the nineteenth century. There were some European, Middle Eastern and other immigrants who came into the country because of increased economic development under president and dictator, Ulises Heureaux, in the 1880s and 1890s, but not to the degree experienced by Cuba and Puerto Rico. It can be assumed that Haitians were also migrating into the country especially along the border regions, and there were also some African Americans who arrived on the Dominican side of the island during the period of Haitian rule, but there seems to have been no significant overall blackening or whitening process in the Dominican Republic during this period [4]. According to studies led by geneticists Katarzyna Bryc (2010) and Ani Manichaikul (2012), the average "African" contribution to the current Dominican population is from 41.8% to 43%. This percentage is twice as high as those for the other islands which on average are 20% to 21% for Cuba and from 20.0%, to 21.2% or 23.6% for Puerto Rico (see Marcheco Teruel 2014 and Via 2011 among other sources) [5]. The difference between the Dominican Republic and the other two islands suggest that the demographic characteristics recorded for Santo Domingo at the end of the eighteenth century may have remained relatively unchanged until the next census in 1920 and up to the present [6].

However and regardless of its true nature and historical evolution, the African contribution to the Dominican Republic and its population has been consistently distorted or obfuscated by the purveyors of anti-Haitianism and the unique Dominican brand of white supremacy. Prior to 1844, the ideology of whiteness was specifically articulated against French culture as practiced in Haiti, along with the claim that the Dominican elites were white despite probable mixture, and the view that the former Haitian slaves and their descendants were mostly primitive "*bozales*" [brought directly from Africa] as opposed to Dominican slaves and freedmen who were seen as longterm "*Ladinos*" or creole inhabitants of Spanish culture in Santo Domingo and thus somewhat more "civilized" and assimilated. These claims were supported and re-enforced by the Catholic Church which instilled white Hispanic values among the black and *mulato* lower classes and also denounced Haitian voodoo and other similar practices of part African origin (Sagás 2000: 24-25; Franco 2009, 2012, 2015).

After 1844, the ideology of white supremacy was revised to some degree and now included the view that Haitians and their descendants in the new republic were a potential "fifth column" that would actively support the re-establishment of Haitian rule. This view was especially influential during the period of repeated Haitian invasions from 1844 to 1856 but began to fade afterwards. Other ideas included the view that non-white Dominicans could not possibly be black, that the peasants of the Cibao were primarily white, that the *mulato* skin complexion had its origin in the pre-Columbian Indigenous population, and there was also the hope that the country would be able to attract European immigrants. Such ideas were articulated by important elements of the elite creole intelligentsia which included poets, essayists and others who also advocated for the adoption of an Indigenous identity for non-white Dominicans. They included most notably, Manuel Jesús Galván, who wrote the epic *Enriquillo* (1882), which glorified the Indigenous past and the heroic resistance of the Indigenous population to Spanish colonialism. They also included the poets Salomé Ureña de Henríquez and her *Anacaona* (1880) and José Joaquín Pérez and his *Fantasias indigenas* (*Indigenous Fantasies*, 1877). These works encouraged the adoption of an "Indian" or part Indian ancestry for all non-white as well as white Dominicans (Sagás 2000: 32, 34-35; Franco 2009).

Anti-Haitianism and anti-blackness also continued to be the basis for the ideology of white supremacy and its articulation throughout the later part of the nineteenth century. There were poets such as Félix María del Monte and his 1875 *Cantos Dominicanos* and Juan Antonio Alíx and his 1876 *Dialago Cantado*. Also notable for his anti-Haitianism and anti-blackness was Eugenio María de Hostos, the Puerto Rican educator influential in the Dominican Republic during this period who wrote disparagingly of the Afro-Dominican president and dictator, Ulises Heureux [1882-1884, 1887-1899], as "that blackener of Quisqueyanismo" [another name for the Dominican Republic]. These kinds of writings from the educated creole elites continued unabated into the early decades of the twentieth century with no apparent correction or contradiction. In actuality, there was an increase in the number novels, short stories and poems in the early 1900s that contrasted Dominican traits and Hispanic values with alleged Haitian and African superstitions and customs. There was José Gabriel García, Francisco Henríquez y Carvajal, Tulio Cestero, Gregorio Billini [among others] and most notably, there was Amerigo Lugo, considered the most important Dominican intellectual of the early twentieth century who promoted the idea of a superior Latin culture, Spanish language, Hispanic traditions, and the Catholic religion as a reaction to the U.S. military occupation of the Dominican Republic [1916 to 1924]. Attitudes towards Haitians also changed somewhat during this period. Haitians were no longer necessarily feared the way they were in the mid-nineteenth century but were now increasingly seen as pathetic, desperately poor, illiterate and diseased migrants and workers worthy of Dominican contempt. However, an important change took place soon after Rafael Trujillo established his fascist dictatorial regime in 1930 (Sagás 2000: 38, 39-40; Franco 2009).

Anti-Haitianism, anti-blackness and the ideology of white supremacy was adopted as official state policy to be imposed by the regime in all its institutions and society in general. What had been a generally unorganized set of ideas articulated by elitist white creoles was transformed into a full-fledged state based ideology by Trujillo, a lower class, light complected *mulato* and his advisors, who saw Haitians as an inferior race, a threat to Dominican culture, and once again, as irreconcilable enemies of the nation. This ideology became the basis and justification for some of the brutal anti-Haitian policies and actions that followed Trujillo's coming to power which culminated in the 1937 massacre of an estimated 20,000 to 30,000 Haitians living in the border region between the two countries. Trujillo also recruited Dominican intellectuals who were all too often willing to promote the state ideology. These included most notably, the future Dominican president, Joaquín Balaguer, Church leaders such as Antonio López de Santa Anna, and two prominent historians—Manuel Peña Batlle and Emilio Rodríguez Demorizi. In Balaguer's case, the claim was made that Dominicans had an inalienable right to defend their Christian Hispanic culture and way of life in the face of the alleged Haitian threat. Balaguer was also a not so subtle apologist for the brutality of the Trujillo regime, claiming that Trujillo had to be seen as a savior of the Dominican nation. Supplementing these ideas, historian Peña Batlle romanticized and idealized the earlier Spanish colonial regime, defended Hispanic culture, claimed that slavery in colonial Santo Domingo was benign, and argued that Dominican society was free of race and class based bias, tensions and conflicts. He was also an apologist for Trujillo claiming that the regime's authoritarian methods were justified because democracy was a luxury that the Dominican Republic could not afford because of an alleged Haitian threat which required a strong leader to defend the nation. Leftist and revisionist historian, Emilio Rodríguez Demorizi also glorified the colonial past which in his view instilled the preferred Hispanic character and culture on the Dominican people (Sagás 2000: 44-45, 46-68). He also called for a crackdown on Haitian migration into the country, saw Haitians as the permanent enemy and described Haitians as:

> "Negroes in their totality, almost naked, illiterate, usually famished and sick, nomadic tribes without anything—dark caravans that brought with them misery, superstition, amorality, voodoo, and Africanization" (Rodríguez Demorizi 1955: 46. Also see Sagás 2000; Howard 2001).

Trujillo made every effort to impose his state based ideology during his long thirty-one years in power [1930-1961] through the education system, the censorship of books, imposed dominance over the press and other media, and in every other conceivable way which included the recruitment of conservative Catholic priests and bishops and their religious based schools in their efforts to also suppress the supposed pernicious influences of godless communism [7]. Overall, Dominicans were educated and "conditioned" through their schools and family networks to believe that [a] they were the proud descendants of Catholic Spanish settlers and conquistadors, [b] that they were descendants of brave "Indians" if they were not white, and [c] that they were people of Hispanic culture and its moral values seen as superior to that of Haitian [8]. Dominicans were also educated and conditioned to believe that Haitians were an inferior people—the descendants of African slaves who where ferocious savages, sorcerers and cannibals, who had evolved into an illiterate, poorly dressed, indolent, slothful, malnourished, disease-ridden mass that believed in voodoo and other allegedly non-Christian and pagan superstitions, but were nevertheless prolific—reproducing to a greater degree than Dominicans (Sagás 2000: 46-68; Balaguer 1947; Franco 2009; Howard 2001).

The Trujillista ideology of anti-Haitianism and white supremacy persisted after Trujillo's assassination in 1961 but it was no longer imposed as official state policy even during the years of Joaquín Balaguer's semi-authoritarian presidencies [1966-1978, 1986-1996]. However, Balaguer and others continued to promote the Trujillista ideology in their writings, speeches and also in their political activities which generated a substantial following. In 1983, Balaguer published *La isla al revés* [*The Island in Reverse*], which was a follow-up and update of his earlier *La realidad dominicana* (1947). In the meantime, school curricula, textbooks, museum displays, monuments, beauty pageants, and the media in general continued to emphasize the white Hispanic Catholic culture and its values. At times, this emphasis on whiteness or whitening reach absurd levels. For example, there was the effort to whiten important but non-white historical figures, such as Gregorio Luperón, the Afro-Dominican leader of the 1865 War of Restoration against the Spaniards, who was whitened and his facial features made less "African" in official portraits [see comparative photos on the next page] and even on the currency [9]. At the same time, non-white Dominicans continued to be identified and encouraged to self-dentify as some type of "Indian" depending on skin complexion in official documents and the ID cards carried by all Dominicans [*Cédula de Identidad y Electoral*]. These physical types included "*Indio oscuro*" ["dark complexion"] *Indio canela* ["cinnamon colored"], and *Indio claro* ["light complexion"] among others (see Sagas 2000).

The official whitend Gregorio Luperón (see Google Images)

The real Gregorio Luperón (see Google Images)

A virulent and very public anti-black and anti-Haitian politics emerged in the Dominican Republic during the 1994 and 1996 presidential elections when Afro-Dominican, José Francisco Peña Gómez, the leader of one of the major political parties with a very dark complexion, came very close to becoming president of the country. Peña Gómez was subjected to all sorts of crude and defamatory accusations and insults as a black man with alleged or suspected Haitian origins in newspaper articles, cartoons, flyers, posters, music, on TV, and in other media during both campaigns. However, a counter-narrative against anti-Haitianism and anti-blackness had emerged in the three some-odd decades before the 1994 and 1996 elections resulting in a vote for the otherwise popular and politically progressive Peña Gómez of 1.2 million or 48.7% in 1996. A counter narrative also emerged among Dominican intellectuals and academics on the island and also in the Diaspora on the U.S. mainland which had grown dramatically since the early 1960s. The end of the pre-1961 Trujillista censorship allowed scholars such Roberto Cassá, Franklin Franco, Rubén Silié, Ernesto Sagás, Ginetta Candelario, and Silvio Torres Saillant [among others] to publish critiques of anti-Haitianism, anti-blackness and the ideology of white supremacy. Human Rights organizations, the Organization of American States and the United Nations also took notice of the anti-Haitian, and ant-black racism seen in the Dominican Republic, especially after it had emerged so publicly and virulently during the 1994 and 1996 election campaigns. The United Nations issued a scathing critique of the "profound and entrenched problem of racism and discrimination against blacks in general and Haitians in particular" in a 2007 report. This was followed by a call to eliminate the "*Indio*" race category on the Dominican ID cards and other official documents which was implemented in 2011 when legislation was approved to replace the *Indio* category with *mulato*; however, the current ID cards established in 2014 make no reference at all to race or skin color (Sagás 2000: 105-115, 125-126, 138-140; United Nations 2007; Howard 2001).

Despite pressure from international organizations, Dominican intellectuals and others, the anti-Haitian and anti-black issue grew worse in a most unexpected and dramatic manner in 2013 when as one source put it:

> "The Dominican Republic's highest court retroactively revoked the citizenship of all persons born without at least one Dominican parent since 1929.... Since then, the Dominican Republic has violated international law and the United Nations Declaration on Human Rights and has withdrawn from the Inter-American Court of Human Rights to uphold its citizenship revocation.... While individual international leaders have commented on the possible ramifications this massive statelessness could cause, the international community has failed to hold the Dominican Republic accountable for its human rights violations" (Reed 2016. Also see *Tribunal Constitutional* 2012 and Morris 2014).

This created a major controversy among Dominicans on the island and in the Diaspora. In August of 2015, Dominican president, Danilo Medina in "a full-throated defense of his government's controversial changes to citizenship" declared that "No foreign country can change [the] Dominican Republic's immigration laws" at the same time that there was some effort to minimize the impact of the decree (Medina 2015). But in June 2016, Amnesty International reported that in addition to Haitians, the Dominican government "unlawfully expelled hundreds of Dominicans to Haiti who have been caught in the middle of a wave of returns and deportations of more than 100,000 people in recent months" after it…ended a moratorium on deportations on 18 June 2015." Quite a number of Dominicans in the Diaspora have attacked this decree with some calling it "ethnic cleansing" in the style of Trujillo, but there has also been considerable support for the decree and its implementation among many of the Islanders and also among Dominicans in the Diaspora, demonstrating as in case of Cubans, how the Trujillisa-Balaguerista ideology of white supremacy was transported to the U.S. as an important part of the thinking of Diasporan Dominicans. Systematic survey research is needed to demonstrate how many Dominicans actually support and its implementation, both in the Republic and in the Diaspora. Otherwise, the controversy on Haitians and stateless Dominicans and the impact of the decree continues as of this writing (Amnesty International 2016; United Nations 2015; Pina 2007; and Planas 2015. The race issue in the Dominican Republic and its Diaspora is aso discussed in Eison Simmons 2011; Mayes 2014; Eller 2016; Garcia Peña 2016; Paulino 2016; and Ricourt 2016).

PUERTO RICO

As in the case of Cuba and the Dominican Republic, the ideology of white supremacy and white privilege evolved in Puerto Rico in its own way as a result of historical circumstances. As in Cuba, the difference was rooted in the positions first taken by the white creole elites who were advocates for autonomous self-governance or the independence of Puerto Rico and the end of slavery in the middle years of the nineteenth century. Like their brethren in Cuba, many initially adopted a part Indigenous Native American [*Indio*] identity in an effort to separate themselves from the Spaniards, peninsular officials, and the creole supporters of the Spanish regime. Some of these individuals even acknowledged their part African roots. However, unlike their counterparts in Cuba, they were not able to launch an on-going or successful rebellion against the authorities in 1868 which was supposed to take place in coordination with the Cuban uprising (Pico 2006; Scarano 2015; Schmidt Nowara 1999; Rodríguez-Silva 2012).

In the years leading up to the 1868 uprising, Ramon Emeterio Betances [1827-1898], the most important of the leaders in Puerto Rico, had travelled to Cuba, Haiti and Santo Domingo/Dominican Republic and made contact with the revolutionary leaders in those societies including Afro-Cubans and Afro-Dominicans. In addition to plans for coordinating the rebellion in Cuba with that of Puerto Rico, he apparently adopted the ideas that motivated the rebellion against Spain in the first place and these were independence, the abolition of slavery and the struggle for the civil rights of Afro-Cubans and Afro-Dominicans which were also applicable to Afro-Puerto Ricans. Years later in a mostly forced exile in Paris, where he spent most of his life, he admitted that there was an African component in his background despite the fact that he was defined as white. He also supposedly believed that Puerto Ricans were part of a "*raza Americana*" [American race], a people of mixed background that was kind of a precursor of José Vasconcelos and his idea of "*la raza cosmica*" or "cosmic race." However, the meaning of *La raza Americana* was open to interpretation with just about all of the Puerto Rican elites adopting the view that *La raza Americana* nevertheless preserved the racial hierarchy and the superiority of whiteness despite *mestizaje* or race mixture [10].

Betances was the exception to this. He saw *la raza Americana* as a true social and political mixture of the races—a society that would be based on the ideals of racial equality with its ideological and political origins seen in the struggle for freedom and independence by the Haitians during the Haitian revolution. His writings in praise of the Haitian revolution and its leaders included "*Toussaint Louverture*, *Les Deux Indiéns* (1852) and *Washington Haitiano* [an essay about Haitian president, Alexandre Pétion] (1871, Also See Arroyo, 2011 among others).

And as he noted at one point:

> "[T]he African blood from these sons of the desert [Haitians], just like the Latin blood from the French, ended up planting the seeds of freedom on American soil; a freedom which the United States denied for so many years, and which Spain continues to deny to that race which is capable of so much sacrifice. The more oppressed a nation is, the more blood is required to conquer its freedom. As opposed to the Puerto Ricans, who remain silent and complacent, Cuba is proving to the whole world the reality of this formidable, yet indispensable principle: the ignominy of tyranny can only be washed away with man's blood; only through effort and sacrifice, can we, as men, take back from heartless hands, the independence of the fatherland" (as quoted in Suárez-Díaz 2005).

But as noted in its aftermath by Betances, the rebellion of 1868, centered in the interior town of Lares, was quickly suppressed by the Spanish authorities in contrast to what took place in Cuba where the uprising begun in the town of Yara led to the "Ten Years War." The failure of the uprising in Lares eventually led to a mostly peaceful opposition to the Spanish regime that was largely limited to an advocacy for self-governance under Spanish rule, and this was especially the case after slavery was abolished in 1873 [11]. In contrast to the ideas articulated by Betances, most of the liberal elites in Puerto Rico began to minimize the importance of racial *mestizaje* by emphasizing that the lower levels of the population should be seen as free laborers [*jornaleros*] which would also include the former slaves after emancipation. However, there emerged an on-going debate about the racial composition of this population and whether blacks would be able to peacefully assimilate or be a disruptive or even conflictual element given what was happening in Cuba before and after emancipation. Conservatives were of course, opposed to these liberal ideas and continued to be advocates for the Spanish caste system. There were; however, liberal optimists, who saw a peaceful transition that would lead to a working class population characterized by harmonious relations between the races (Rodríguez-Silva 2012).

The historian, Salvador Brau [1842-1912] was one of these optimists. He described a Puerto Rican population that was *mestizo* and a product of the long-term interaction between the Indigenous, the Spaniards and the Africans. He noted at one point that Puerto Rico:

> "was open to all races. *Latinos*, Saxons, Africans, Indians, slaves, Germans and Scandinavians" and that these groups "mixed in our soil, modifying the generic character of each of them as well as their [physical] complexion" (as quoted in Rodríguez-Silva 2012: 83).

Brau was convinced that racial harmony would prevail among all these different elements in Puerto Rico's working class, but he also accepted the prevailing racial hierarchy that placed the Spanish or white creole elite at the top of society and the non-white population at the bottom (Rodríguez-Silva 2012: 77, 80).

A scientist, Dr. Francisco del Valle Atiles [1852-1928], was also very much concerned about the different elements in Puerto Rico's *mestizo* population which was seen by him as problematic and not racially harmonious. He nevertheless developed a hopeful view in his mind of what would happen in the future based on his own medical research, and also on the scientific theories popular at that time—most notably social Darwinism and eugenics, one of its off-shoots. Del Valle Atiles saw the black element in Puerto Rico's *mestizo* population in a negative light as biologically and culturally inferior. He divided the island population into "mixed bloods, blacks and rural white folks" and proceeded to single-out the allegedly superior but impoverished "white" peasant population of the island's interior with the claim that "there are several natural dispositions—especially among *jibaros de la raza blanca* [highland peasants of the white race] whose brains are better organized" (Rodríguez-Silva 2012: 85, 86). He also claimed that:

> "The dominant element in the ethnic constitution of the Puerto Rican is the white man because of his larger population number and most developed civilization.... The groups of people born out of backward, inept, decadent races and for which their vices and indolence work as deterrent forces cannot fulfill the physical and mental activities the law of progress demands" (as quoted in Rodríguez-Silva 2012: 209).

This was typical social Darwinist racism, and it led del Valle Atiles to call for increased immigration to Puerto Rico from Europe and restrictions on immigration of blacks and *mulatos* from other islands in the Caribbean and elsewhere. With other members of the elite, he also called for the implementation of an aggressive hygiene initiative and other programs to improve the population. Based on his social Darwinistic beliefs, he saw Puerto Rico's *mestizo* population as merely a stepping stone to whiteness. According to the prevailing theory, the inferior non-white elements in a mixed population would eventually fade away naturally because of the alleged biological superiority of the white race. As a result, Del Valle Atiles proposed to accelerate the so-called "inevitable" process by encouraging European immigration and discouraging or stopping non-white immigration altogether (on del Valle Atiles in general, see Rodríguez-Silva 2012: 83-88 and passim).

The ideas of Brau and especially del Valle Atiles were challenged most notably by a small group of Afro-Puerto Rican intellectuals that emerged in the late nineteenth century. These included most notably, Sotero Figueroa, a "*mulato*" artisan typesetter, journalist and playwright [1851-1915] who participated in the 1887 founding of Puerto Rico's autonomist liberal *Partido Autonomista* which favored self-government under Spanish rule. However, he left this group two years later in 1889, came to New York City, and joined the Cuban separatist movement led by José Marti and became a senior member of the Puerto Rican Section of the *Partido Revolucionario Cubano* [or Cuban Revolutionary Party]. As an advocate for the independence of both Puerto Rico and Cuba, Figueroa adopted the social, political and cultural ideas advanced by José Martí but also articulated variations of his own. He collaborated with his friend, the Afro-Cuban intellectual, Rafael Serra, in their radical advocacy for a classless society without racism. After the U.S. intervened in the Cuban war of 1895 and occupied Puerto Rico in 1898, Figueroa did not return to Puerto Rico but went to Cuba and established residence there. He apparently preferred to live in Cuba after it became independent as opposed to Puerto Rico which was turned into a colonial possession of the U.S. In the years that followed, he continued to be an advocate for the civil rights of Afro-Cubans and Afro-Puerto Ricans and for Puerto Rico's independence from his residence in Cuba until his passing in 1915 (Figueroa 1977; Doherty 2011; Huffnung-Garskof 2011).

In addition to Figueroa, there was José Celso Barbosa [1857-1921] who emerged as perhaps the most important spokesperson for black and *mulato* Puerto Ricans during the late nineteenth and into the early twentieth century, but was also problematic as an advocate. A "*mulato*" physician by training and practice who experienced hostile racial prejudice and institutional obstacles as a young man, Barbosa also joined the liberal *Partido Autonomista* during the final years of the Spanish regime. After the U.S. takeover in 1898, Barbosa broke with the *autonomistas* and co-founded the *Partido Republicano* [Republican Party] which called for the incorporation of Puerto Rico into the union as a state. Barbosa also actively collaborated with the U.S. government and became a member of the executive cabinet of Charles H. Allen, the first U.S. appointed civilian governor. He also continued to be a member of this cabinet during the governorships that followed from William Henry Hunt in 1901 to Arthur Yager in 1917. In 1917, Barbosa ran and was elected to the Puerto Rican legislature as a senator and continued in this capacity until his death in 1921 (on Barbosa, see especially, Jiménez Román 1998).

An avid reader who was familiar with the writings and the politics of Booker T. Washington and W.E.B DuBois among others, Barbosa came to the conclusion that blacks and *mulatos* in Puerto Rico would fare better if the island became a state of the union despite its racism and discriminatory practices because the U.S. had a modern, progressive, political and economic system. He was clearly opposed to the interests and status of the traditional white creole elite on the island and especially those he called upstarts, dwarfs, pretenders to whiteness and "quasi whites," but he also claimed that race mixture [*mestizaje*] would resolve any problems that might exist with "true" whiteness [the acknowledged superior race] as the inevitable and ultimate goal. In this sense, he and del Valle Atiles were not all that different. Adopting the social Darwinist ideas of the time, including the assertion that the black race would eventually disappear, Barbosa claimed that:

> "The race problem does not exist here [in Puerto Rico]. This problem is resolving itself through the evolution of the black race. Here, the black race has been mixing with the other races, and today, every man of color in Puerto Rico is a conglomerate of blue blood [i.e.: white], Indian blood, and African blood through evolution, depending on the predominance of those parts and the fading pigment. Blacks have evolved from black, to mixed, *mulato* or white, and the black continues to disappear. Evolution will continue, and the problem will be resolved" (Barbosa de Rosario 1937).

Barbosa also seemed to adopt many of the accommodationist ideas and positions of Booker T. Washington for blacks living on the U.S. mainland. He insisted preliminarily that blacks and *mulatos* in Puerto Rico had nothing to fear from the United States and that Puerto Ricans would insure that race prejudice would not become a problem through the application of justice and the law. He advised blacks and *mulatos* to adopt a respectful "stay in your place" mentality of self-improvement based on merit. He insisted that separation and segregation, including segregation in housing, was logical and natural. He even made excuses for the summary justice and lynching of blacks in the U.S. which was rampant in the southern states during this period—claiming that it was defensible if a woman was insulted or assaulted by the man who was lynched. With thinking like this and a lack of real alternative voices, the ideology of white supremacy and its promotion of social Darwinism and hierarchical *mestizaje* monopolized the discourse in the immediate decades that followed the U.S. takeover. Blacks and *mulatos* were expected to accept a hierarchical *mestizaje* that led to whiteness in the name of ethnic and cultural unity. Otherwise, they would be accused of fomenting racial tensions and divisiveness in an island society that was supposedly free of racism. This was the position also taken by important politicians, such as Rosendo Matienzo-Cintrón, and also by the charismatic union leader, Santiago Iglesias Pantín, who headed the *Federación Libre de Trabajadores* [The Federation of Free Workers] which had many black and *mulato* members. In a fiery1902 speech, Iglesias reminded union members that "True union means we cannot allow the antagonisms of race and color. We all, blacks and whites, young and old, workers and the wealthy, should be in union." Blacks and *mulatos* were thus silenced from several quarters and became invisible at the same time they were subjected to continued prejudice and discrimination (Jiménez Román 1998; Rodríguez-Silva 2012: 147-148).

However, the call for unity did not last very long in the complex political reality that emerged in the immediate aftermath of the U.S. takeover. An on-going economic crisis gripped the island in the years after 1898 which nevertheless favored U.S. based economic interests at the expense of Puerto Rico's people and its white creole elite. This was followed in 1930 by the economic and social catastrophe of the "Great Depression," which further diminished the status of the white creole elite. The result was a re-appraisal of Puerto Rico's status within the U.S. political and economic system by creole intellectuals that also included a re-assessment of island culture, *mestizaje*, the ideology of whiteness, and what it meant to be Puerto Rican [12]. In contrast to the "yankeephile" Barbosa at the beginning of the century, the target of criticism became the United States with a concurrent and romanticized nostalgia for Spain and Spanish culture. The old concept of the *mestizo* "*raza Americana*" returned, but this time, it was transformed into "*La raza Iberoamericana*" [the Iberian-American race] which erased white North America. This opened the discourse to white creole Hispanophiles and their ideas about Spain and against *mestizaje* which was always lurking in the background.

In 1934, a university professor, Antonio S. Pedreira [1899-1939], published *Insularismo: Ensaysos de interpretación Puertorriqueña* [*Insularism: Puerto Rican Interpretive Essays*] a book which glorified Spain and Spanish culture and lamented the backwardness of Puerto Rico and its people because of its history of racial mixture. This was not only an attack on the U.S., it was also an attack on the ideas behind *mestizaje* as articulated earlier by Puerto Rican intellectuals based on social Darwinism and evolution theory. Tomás Blanco, another white creole and literary figure [1896-1975], soon published two books against Pedreira titled *Prontuario histórico de Puerto Rico* (*Historical Handbook for Puerto Rico*, 1935) and *El Prejuicio Racial en Puerto Rico* (*Racial Prejudice in Puerto Rico*, 1942) which defended the race mixture that Pedreira denounced. However, although Blanco wrote commentaries along with the poet Luís Palés Matos [e.g. the poem "*Tun tun de pasa y griferia"*] that focused on the African contribution to Puerto Rican culture, he nevertheless claimed that Puerto Ricans were essentially white, Catholic and Spanish and that Spanish culture was superior to U.S. culture. Tomás Blanco justified this view by claiming that Spain had treated its slave population more humanely, had allowed a significant amount of racial mixing, was culturally benign in comparison to the U.S., and that it was for these reasons that there was no race problem in Puerto Rico (Pedreira 2005; Blanco 1970 1983; Rodríguez-Silva 2012: 187-193; Ayala and Bernabe 2007: 117-135).

The ideas of Tomás Blanco and similar ones articulated by others became the consensus view of race and race relations in Puerto Rico in the decades that followed. Even nationalist leader, Pedro Albizu Campos, influenced by the ideas of Vasconcelos and his *raza cosmica*, adopted a variant of the ideas advanced by Blanco which could be used against "yanqui tyranny," but also like Blanco, Albizu was still a Hispanophile who lauded Spain's superior culture, Catholic mores, and its sense of honor which he saw as being rooted in the people at the bottom of the social hierarchy and not imposed by education and other means by the white creole elite at the top. However, and more importantly, *mestizaje* also became official state policy with the establishment of the commonwealth government under Governor Luís Muñoz Marín and a dominant Popular Democratic Party at the beginning of the 1950s.

Muñoz Marín's government soon eliminated the race category from the census and other official records. Puerto Ricans were to be taught that they were the mixed descendants of Spaniards,

Indians and Africans. This view was to be promoted by the educational system with support from important cultural institutions—most notably the Institute for Puerto Rican Culture which adopted an official three headed symbol that prominently placed the Spaniard in the center with the Indian and African on either side of the Spaniard. Working class Puerto Ricans might have interpreted this tripartite symbol as illustrating the equality of races under the concept of *mestizaje*. This was certainly the way it was understood by many in the mainland Diaspora, but as historian Ileana Rodríguez-Silva and others have noted, the symbol and *mestizaje* itself continued to be seen as hierarchical by the political and cultural elite with the white Spaniard said to be on top, followed by an idealized and romanticized Indian, with the African or black relegated to a distant bottom. In the meantime, the reality of prejudice and discrimination against blacks and *mulatos* in Puerto Rico continued unabated during the 1950s with little or no opposition (Albizu Campos 1974; Maldonado Denís 1973; Rodríguez-Silva 2012: 224; Ayala and Bernabe 2007: 208-219).

Hierarchical *mestizaje* and the practices associated with it would not be effectively challenged until the 1960s and 1970s, when the impact of the civil rights and black power movements in the U.S. mainland would result in writings and publications that would challenge the supposed consensus on the race issue promoted by the island's creole elite with Puerto Ricans in the Diaspora playing a significant role in the challenge. In the Diaspora, there were the writings and positions taken by the mostly young radicals in their mainland political organizations that defined Puerto Ricans as a non-hierarchical "rainbow people" with criticism of the racism that existed on the island and among mainland Puerto Ricans. There was also the double 1972-1973 article published by the Chicago based "motivational speaker," Samuel Betances, titled The "Prejudice of Having No Prejudice in Puerto Rico," which informed many mainland Puerto Ricans about how prejudice and discrimination functioned among Puerto Ricans—especially on the island (see reference). In Puerto Rico, there was the now mostly ignored or forgotten 1965 article by Juan Rodríguez Cruz titled "*Las relaciones raciales en Puerto Rico*" ("Race Relations in Puerto Rico") and the 1973 book by Martín Sagrera titled *Racismo y política en Puerto Rico: la desintegración interna y externa de un pueblo* (*Race and Politics in Puerto Rico: The Internal and External Disintegration of a People*). There was also the 1980 essay in José Luís González's book *El País de cuatro pisos y otros ensays* (*The Four Story Country and other Essays*, See references).

However, the most important publication which created a major storm of controversy and invective on the island was the 1974 two volume treatise by Isabelo Zenón Cruz titled *Narciso descubres su tresero: El negro en la cultura Puertorriqueña* [*Narciso Discovers his Background: the Black in Puerto Rican Culture*]. A gay university professor of Spanish literature, Zenón Cruz, like Barbosa, was an accomplished intellectual black Puerto Rican—still rarely acknowledged on the island in the 1970s and also at present. He systematically denounced the prejudice, discrimination, stigma, and marginalization of black and *mulato* Puerto Ricans in all areas of the national economy, politics and culture. Initially, there was a strong negative response to his book by the purveyors of hierarchical *mestizaje* and whiteness. There was for example, the 1976 study by Dr. S. Aran Soto titled *Puerto Rico: Sociedad sin razas* [*Puerto Rico: Society without Races*]. However, the writings and complaints against Zenón Cruz, José Luís González and others were also largely ignored [or suppressed?] in the years that followed as hierarchical *mestizaje*, whiteness and the assumption that Puerto Rico had no race problem continued to be the majority consensus view on the island and among Puerto Ricans in the mainland.

The continued dominance of this consensus was made clear during the controversy that engulfed former governor, Rafael Hernández Colón, during his second and third terms [1985-1993], when he was quoted as making a not too careful statement that seemed to support the old Hispanophile ideology of white supremacy at the expense of *mestizaje* and the idea that Puerto Ricans are free of race prejudice. At the time, Hernández Colón was trying to develop a close relationship with Spain which involved incentives for Spanish investment in the island economy, but instead, attention focused on his remarks and he was subjected to virulent and very public criticism from the purveyors of *mestizaje* representing most factions in Puerto Rico's political and cultural elite (Godreau 2015: 127-131).

Despite the consensus on race in Puerto Rico and among Puerto Ricans in general, there have been a number of challenges to the Puerto Rican brand of *mestizaje* and the reality of white privilege on the island and Diaspora in recent years. There have been the continued critiques of hierarchical *mestizaje* by a number of Hispanophile academics and other writers with this view but these have had little impact on the overall consensus. There are also the die-hard Puerto Rican white supremacists who are mostly seen on the internet with their provocative "in your face" racism. However, and more importantly, there has been the growing Afro-Boricua identity movement [usually subsumed under the Afro-Latino movement] which has rightly focused on the real prejudice and discrimination experienced by Afro-Puerto Ricans and other dark Latinos on the island and the mainland. Unlike the very small group of Afrocentric extremists with their smug ideas about black superiority who are also in this group, the Afro-Boricua movement should be seen primarily as a movement for civil rights, social justice, and social equality [13].

A small so-called "Neo-Taíno" movement has also emerged on the island and Diaspora in recent years. These individuals have adopted an exclusive indigenous or "Taíno" identity and alleged pedigree that would deny or minimize the importance of the actual contributions of Africans, Spaniards, and others to the reality of their biological and cultural background. In this regard, the minimalization or denial of the African background is rooted in the acknowledgement that defined blacks are seen as people of low status in Puerto Rico and among Puerto Ricans in general despite the rhetoric of *mestizaje*. Europeans and especially the Spaniards are also rejected because they are seen to have been ruthless, imperialists who decimated the native peoples in the sixteenth century, harshly exploited Africans slaves on the island (when mentioned), and brutalized Puerto Ricans in general during the period of Spanish rule.

Despite these challenges, the consensus on the island and among Puerto Ricans on the U.S. mainland remains the same. Although the overwhelming majority [75.8%] of Puerto Ricans identified as "white alone" in the 2010 U.S. census, there is the recognition articulated in public that Puerto Ricans are people of mixed ethnic and national background based on the concept of

"*La gran familia Puertorriquña*" [the Great Puerto Rican Family] and the particular brand of *mestizaje* that still privileges whiteness which has evolved on the island and Diaspora since the earlier decades of the twentieth century (Haslip-Viera 2001, 2014a and b).

THE DIASPORAS IN THE U.S. MAINLAND

It is clear from the previous discussion that the ideology of white supremacy and *mestizaje* has evolved in different ways in the Spanish-speaking Caribbean largely as a result of differences in their historical trajectories. However, migrants and immigrants from Cuba, the Dominican Republic, Puerto Rico, and the rest of Latin America discover [if they don't know already] that they become homogenized as "Hispanics" or "Latinos" when they establish residency in mainland communities. Their national or island origins tend to be ignored unless there is a large identifiable concentration of these populations in specific localities [e.g.: Cubans in Miami, Puerto Ricans in New York, 1945-1980]. There also is the inclination at least unofficially, to still place Caribbean and other Latinos within the old racial binary of "black" or "white," despite the fact that the binary has been breaking down in recent decades as a result of increased immigration, not only from the Caribbean and Latin America in general, but also from South Asia, East Asia, Africa, and the Middle East, etc. More importantly, there has been an overall reluctance until recently to engage the racism that prevails among mainland Latinos which varies by national origin and location. Up until recently, the public debate in the U.S. has been largely limited to whether Latinos are a race, or an ethnic or regional group with a racial breakdown. The focus has also been on social and cultural stereotypes that are supposedly shared by all or most Latinos. The social and cultural stereotypes include the following [summarized and edited from the originals]:

Latinos in general:

1. are assumed to be foreigners, and mostly undocumented or illegal recent immigrants.
2. refuse to assimilate into U.S. culture.
3. are assumed to be incapable of speaking English or speaking it well without an accent.
4. are found in low level jobs in manufacturing and services when employed.
5. are assumed to be lazy, dumb, school dropouts, gang members, drug dealers, rapists, and are always trying to hustle or get away with something.

6. are assumed to be uneducated and are not interested in schooling especially for their daughters.
7. Latinos will turn America into a third world country.
8. Latinos are criminally inclined.
9. Latinos have big families.

Latinas or Female "Hispanics:"

1, are assumed to be all fiery, as in ill-tempered.
2. walk around strutting their stuff in body-hugging attire 24/7 because they're all curvaceous olive-skinned sexpots with long black hair.
3. are assumed to be great cooks and dancers.

Latinos or Male "Hispanics:"

1. are assumed to be all *macho*, misogynist, patriarchal and expect and enjoy being waited on by submissive women, and may also be inclined to be abusive and even violent towards their wives and other women.
2. are assumed to be all jealously paranoid and possessive of their women and everything else.
3. are assumed to be homophobes.
4. are assumed to be bad, absent, or negligent dads.
5. are assumed to be great dancers and obsessed by sports. (See for example Esteves 2016; Singh 2015)

This is only an abbreviated list of social and cultural stereotypes. There are plenty of others. Latino media to some degree has tried to combat these stereotypes but they almost never engage the race issue or the racism that prevails within the Latino communities or within Latino media. This is seen in the comment above that makes reference to the assumption that Latinas are "olive-skinned sexpots with long black hair" and the subsequent failure to engage or acknowledge that this stereotype is connected to the social and political construction of race in the U.S., the Spanish-speaking Caribbean, and among other Latin Americans. The reluctance to engage the race issue is also seen in some of the survey research that has been completed in recent years by the better known think tanks. For example, the Pew Research Center recently published a short and quite inadequate summary of "multiracial Americans" by Ana González-Barrera and Mark Hugo López that focused on whether Latinos are a race or an ethnic group. This report was connected to concerns about what the Census Bureau would institute in the 2020 census. The Bureau and the U.S. government in general has been dissatisfied with the results of earlier census enumerations in which large numbers of Latinos do not respond to the race question leaving the question blank. This has resulted in a controversial and on-going debate over whether all Latinos should be crudely lumped together as a single race or whether the Census Bureau should continue to enumerate Latinos in a two-part question as an ethnic group that is subdivided into racial groups.

To give the Pew Research Center some credit, Ana González-Barrera also co-authored with Gustavo López, a report on a recent survey completed by the research center on Afro-Latinos (López and González-Barrera 2016). It was noted in this survey that:

> "In the U.S., Latinos with Caribbean roots are more likely to identify as Afro-Latino or Afro-Caribbean than those with roots elsewhere [34% versus 22%, respectively]. Those who identify as Afro-Latino are more concentrated on the East Coast and in the South than other Latinos [65% of Afro-Latinos live in these regions vs. 48% of other Latinos]. They are also more likely than other Latinos to be foreign born [70% vs. 52%], less likely to have some college education [24% vs. 37%], and more likely to have lower family incomes."

However, the following was also noted— raising questions about the methods employed by the research center in their survey.

> "higher shares of Afro-Latinos identified as white alone or white in combination with another race [39%] or volunteered that their race or one of their races was Hispanic [24%]. Only 9% identified as mixed race."

Afro-Latinos have been in the forefront in the effort to expose the racism and discrimination that prevails against part African descended and other non-white Latinos in the U.S., the Spanish-speaking Caribbean and the rest of Latin America. Journalist Audra D.S. Burch reported on the emergence of self-identified Afro-Latinos and an Afro Latino movement in the

Miami Herald back in 2007, but academics have also been focusing on this issue dating back, for example, to 1947 if not earlier, when Renzo Sereno published "Cryptomelanism: a study of color relations and personal insecurity in Puerto Rico" in the journal *Psychiatry*. For many years, the focus was on the islands of the Caribbean and Brazil and then later, the rest of Latin America with the United States finally included in the discourse in the 1990s. However, except for a number of superficial references, the issue of whiteness and white Latino privilege has emerged as part of a focused discussion only in very recent years. The writings of Arlene Dávila, Yeidy Rivero and others have been notable examples in this regard among academics. These authors have elaborated in general and also specifically on how Latinos of a darker appearance have been relegated to subordinate roles as gardeners, maids, school dropouts, criminals, and gang members on prime time English and Spanish language television and movies along with an overall "whitewashing" that takes place as a result of industry and ethnic prejudices. They also note that marketers, politicians and even scholars are complicit in this whitewashing which in some cases can result in white Latinos acting in white roles [e.g.: Mackensie Vega in the TV series, *The Good Wife*]. These writers also note that this whitewashing is seen in other areas such as advertising, in music and in the music business in general. It is hoped that the essays that follow in this book by mostly younger Caribbean Latinos will give readers an insight into the evolving thinking on these issues as we head towards the third decade of the twenty-first century (Burch 2007; Sereno 1947; Dávíla 2008, 2012; Dávila and Rivero 2014; Rivero 2005).

Notes:

[1] Sub-Saharan Africans were seen as inferior at this time because most of them were said to be of enslaved status. This was not the case during the previous European middle ages, when the view towards sub-Saharan Africans was more complex with powerful empires and kingdoms acknowledged to exist in Mali, Ethiopia and other places.

[2] Jamaica ceased to be a Spanish colony when it was taken over by the British in 1655.

[3] According to Franklin Franco, the Dominican population may have declined to 103,000 five years later in 1794 (See Franco 2015: 57 and also Hidalgo in references).

[4] This issue admittedly needs to be studied in a more systematic and rigorous manner.

[5] Figures vary because of differences in the methods employed and differences in the genetic data sets which continue to evolve.

[6] Unfortunately, the demographics of the Dominican Republic from the pre-independence period of 1789 and 1794 and up to the census of 1920 remains a blank.

[7] The clergy in the Dominican Republic at this time was overwhelmingly Spanish, very conservative and virulently anti-communist. Trujillo also signed a concordat with the Vatican in 1954 which provided the Catholic Church with certain privileges and enhanced status..

[8] Although admitting that non-white Dominicans were mixed, the clergyman, Antonio López de Santa Anna, claimed that "Borderland Dominicans were Indians because of their 'greater facial angle, caucasoid cranium, straight and abundant hair, delicate hands, small teeth, less height and muscular development than Africans'" (Sagas 2000: 60.).

[9] It was also seemingly impossible to do this kind of whitening for the very dark complected [etc.] former Afro-Dominican president and dictator, Ulises Heureux [1882-1884, 1887-1899]. A protégé Luperón and a military commander during the War of Restoration, his image is not often shown (see next page).

[10] It was discovered in 1840 that the members of the Betances-Alacán family were defined as "negros y bastardos" in the parish records for the family [blacks and bastards]. However, Betances' father, Felipe, who was said to be a plantation owner [*hacendado*]

Ulises Heureux, President of the Dominican Republic (1882-1884, 1887-1899), in Military uniform.

A thinner perhaps younger Heureux as a civilian.

was able to redefine the family on his death certificate as white and free of tainted blood [*limpio de sangre*—perhaps through purchase which was not uncommon]. In his biography, Luis Bonafoux Quintero (1970) describes Betances as "racially ambiguous"—more "Arab than Roman" and more "Indian than African," but still with an image close to a bust of some Roman patrician. Bonafoux also insisted that Betances did not see himself as "Spanish."

[11] The opponents who favored independence including Betances, were forced into exile or otherwise eliminated by the Spanish authorities in Puerto Rico.

[12] This has been called *La generacíon del treinta* or the "Thirties generation."

[13] Afrocentrism is a complicated phenomenon; however, the extremists in the group believe sub-Saharan Africans and blacks in general are biologically, psychologically and culturally superior. They believe that the first Europeans, Asians and Americans were black Africans, and employing reverse Eurocentric ideas with regard to race, they claim that black Africans were the founders of all the world's major civilizations including those of Egypt, India, China, Mexico, Central America and South America. See the writings of Frances Cress Welsing, Ivan Van Sertima, Clyde [Ahmad)Winters, and David Imhotep among others.

References:

Abbad y Lasierra, Iñigo. 2002 (1776, 1866). *Historia geográfica, civil y natural de la Isla de Puerto Rico*, 3rd edition. Madrid and San Juan, PR: Editorial Dos Calles and Centro de Investigaciones Históricas.

Albizu Campos, Pedro. 1974. *La conciencia nacional puertorriqueña: Selecciones*, ed. Manuel Maldonado–Denis. Mexico, DF: Siglo Veintiuno.

Amnesty International. 2016. "Haiti/Dominican Republic: Reckless deportations leaving thousands in limbo," *Amnesty International News*, June 16: https://www.amnesty.org/en/latest/news/2016/06/haiti-dominican-republic-reckless-deportations-leaving-thousands-in-limbo/.

Andrews, George Reid. 2008. *The Afro-Argentines of Buenos Aires, 1800-1900.* Madison: University of Wisconsin Press.

_____. 2010. *Blackness in the White Nation: A History of Afro-Uruguay.* Chapel Hill: University of North Carolina Press.

_____. 2016. *Afro-Latin America: Black Lives, 1600-2000.* Cambridge, MA: Harvard University Press.

Applebaum, Nancy P., Ann S. Macpherson and Karen Alejandra Rosemblatt, eds. 2003. *Race and Nation in Modern Latin America.* Chapel Hill: University of North Carolina Press.

Aran-Soto, S. 1976. *Puerto Rico: Sociedad sin Razas.* San Juan: Asociación Médica de Puerto Rico (Many thanks to independent scholar, Miriam Jiménez Román, for this reference.).

Arroyo, Jossianna. 2011. "Revolution in the Caribbean: Betances, Haiti and the Antillean Confederation:" http://www.habanaelegante.com/Spring_Summer_2011/Invitation_Arroyo.html.

Ayala, César and Rafael Bernabé. 2007. *Puerto Rico in the American century: a history since 1898.* Chapel Hill: University of

North Carolina Press.

Balaguer, Joaquín. 1947. *La realidad dominicana: semblanza de un país y de un régimen*. Buenos Aires: Ferrari Hermanos.

______. 1983. *La isla al revés : Haití y el destino dominicano*. Santo Domingo, DR: Fundación José Antonio Caro.

Barbosa de Rosario, Pilar, ed. 1983 (1937). *La Obra de José Celso Barbosa*, 3 vols. San Juan, PR: Imprenta Venezuela.

Bendixen & Amandi International. 2015. *Survey of Cuban-Americans: One Year After the Normalization of United States-Cuba Relations*. December 17: http://www.miamiherald.com/latest-news/article50333010.ece/binary/Read%20the%20full%20survey.

Benson, Devyn Spence. 2012. "Owning the Revolution: Race, Revolution, and Politics from Havana to Miami, 1959–1963," *Journal of Transnational American Studies* 4(2): http://escholarship.org/uc/item/5sb9d392.

_____. 2016. *Anti-Racism in Cuba: The Unfinished Revolution*. Chapel Hill: University of North Carolina Press.

Betances, Samuel. 1972. "The Prejudice of Having No Prejudice in Puerto Rico, Part I," *The Rican* 2: 41-54.

_____. 1973. "The Prejudice of Having No Prejudice in Puerto Rico, Part II," *The Rican* 3: 22-37.

Tomás Blanco. 1985 (1942). *El prejuicio racial en Puerto Rico*, 3rd ed. Río Piedras, PR: Ediciones Huracán.

_____. 1970. *Prontuario histórico de Puerto Rico*. San Juan, PR: Instituto de Cultura Puertorriqueña.

Bonafoux y Quintero, Luis. 1970 (1901). *Ramón Emeterio Betances*. San Juan: Instituto de Cultura Puertorriqueña..

Bryc, Katarzyna, Christopher Velez, Tatiana Karafet, Andrés Moreno-Estrada, Andy Reynolds, Adam Auton, Michael Hammer,

Carlos D. Bustamante, and Harry Ostrer. 2010. "Genome-wide patterns of population structure and admixture among Hispanic/ Latino populations," *PNAS (Proceedings of the National Academy of Sciences)*: http://www.pnas.org/content/107/Supplement_2/8954.full.

Burch, Audra D.S. 2007. "Afro-Latin Americans: A rising voice," *Miami Herald*, June 10: http://media.miamiherald.com/multimedia/news/afrolatin/part1/index.html.

Buscaglia-Salgado, José. 2003. *Undoing Empire: Race and Nation in the Mulatto Caribbean*. Minneapolis: University of Minnesota Press.

Candelario, Ginetta E. B. 2007. *Black behind the ears: Dominican racial identity from museums to beauty shops*. Durham: Duke University Press.

Castro, Fidel. 1959. *March 1959 Speech*: http://lanic.utexas.edu/project/castro/db/1959/19590323.html.

Cassá, Roberto. 2006. *Historia social y económica de la Republica Dominicana*. 2 vols. Santo Domingo, DR: Editora Alfa y Omega.

Cave, Damien. 2016. "Cuba Says It Has Solved Racism: Obama Isn't So Sure," *New York Times*, March 23: https://www.nytimes.com/2016/03/24/world/americas/obamaurges-raised-voices-incubas-husheddiscussions-ofrace.html?_r=0.

Dávila, Arlene M. 2008. *Latino spin: public image and the whitewashing of race*. New York: New York University Press.

_____. 2012. *Latinos, Inc: the marketing and making of a people*. Berkeley and London: University of California Press, 2012.

Dávila, Arlene M and Yeidy M. Rivero, eds. 2014. *Contemporary Latina/o media: production, circulation, politics*. New York: New York University Press.

De la Fuente, Alejandro. 2001. *A nation for all: race, inequality, and politics in twentieth-century Cuba*. Chapel Hill : University of North Carolina Press.

Doherty, Kyle. 2011. "Afro-Cuban Intellectuals and the Doctrine of Martí: The Discursive Battle for *Cuba Libré's* Soul." MA Thesis. University of Florida.

Dominican Today. 2011. "Legislation eradicates Dominican 'Indians,'" *Dominican Today*. November 11: https://dominicantoday.com/dr/local/2011/11/11/Legislation-eradicates-Dominican-Indians/.

Duany, Jorge. 1985. "Ethnicity in the Spanish Caribbean: Notes on the Consolidation of Creole Identity in Cuba and Puerto Rico, 1762-1868." In *Caribbean Ethnicity Revisited*, Stephen Glazier, ed., pp. 15-39. New York: Gordon and Breach.

_____. 2006. Racializing Ethnicity in the Spanish-Speaking Caribbean. *Latin American and Caribbean Ethnic Studies* 1(2): 231-248.

Eison Simmons, Kimberly.2011. *Reconstructing Racial Identity and the African Past in the Dominican Republic* (New World Diasporas). Gainesville, University Press of Florida.

Eller, Anne .2016. *We Dream Together: Dominican Independence, Haiti, and the Fight for Caribbean Freedom*. Durham, NC: Duke University Press.

Esteves, Geraldine. 2016. "10 Latino Stereotypes We've Heard All Our Lives That Are Completely False," *Latina Magazine*, March 23: http://www.latina.com/lifestyle/our-issues/latino-stereotypes.

Ferrer, Ada. 1999. *Insurgent Cuba: Race, Nation, and Revolution, 1868-1898*. Chapel Hill: University of North Carolina Press.

_____. 2014. *Freedom's Mirror: Cuba and Haiti in the Age of Revolution*. New York: Cambridge University Press.

Figueroa, Sotero. 1977. *La verdad de la historia*, Carlos Ripoll, ed. San Juan, PR: Instituto de Cultura Puertorriqueña.

Fradera, Joseph. 2011. "The Caribbean Between Empires: Colonists, Pirates and Slaves," In *The Caribbean: A History of the Region and Its People*, Stephen Palme and Francisco Scarano, eds. pp. 165-176. Chicago IL: University of Chicago Press.

Franco, Franklin J. 2009. *Las ideologías políticas dominicanas en síntesis*. Santo Domingo, DR: Cuesta-Veliz Ediciones.

_____. 2012. *La población dominicana: razas, clases, mestizaje y migraciones*. Santo Domingo, DR: Editoria Universitaria.

_____. 2015. *Blacks, Mulattos, and the Dominican Nation*. New York: Routledge.

Fulger, Diana. 2012. "The Colors of the Cuban Diaspora: Portrayal of Racial Dynamics among Cuban-Americans," *Forum for Inter-American Research*. 5(2): http://interamerica.de/volume-5-2/fulger/.

Garcia Peña, Lorgia. 2016. *The Borders of Dominicanidad: Race, Nation, and Archives of Contradiction*. Durham, NC: Duke University Press.

Godreau, Isar P. 2015. *Scripts of Blackness: Race, Cultural Nationalism, and U.S. Colonialism in Puerto Rico*. Urbana: University of Illinois Press.

González, José Luís. 1980. *País de cuatro pesos y otros ensayos*. San Juan: Editorial Edil.

González-Barrera, Ana and Mark Hugo López. 2015. "Is being Hispanic a matter of race, ethnicity or both?" *Pew Research Center*, June 15: http://www.pewresearch.org/fact-tank/2015/06/15/is-being-hispanic-a-matter-of-race-ethnicity-or-both/.

Guerra, Lilian. 2003. "From Revolution to Involution in the Early Cuban Republic: Conflicts over Race, Class and Nation, 1902-1906," In *Race and Nation in Modern Latin America*, Nancy P. Applebaum, Ann S. Macpherson and Karen Alejandra Rosemblatt, eds. pp. 132-162. Chapel Hill: University of North Carolina Press.

Guridy, Frank Andre. 2010. "War on the Negro: Race and the Revolution of 1933," *Cuban Studies* 40: 49-73.

Haney-López, Ian F. 2003a. *Racism on Trial: The Chicano Fight for Justice*. New York: Cambridge University Press.

_____. 2003b. "White Latinos," *Harvard Latino Law Review*: http://scholarship.law.berkeley.edu/cgi/viewcontent.cgi?article=2910&context=facpubs.

Haslip-Viera, Gabriel. 2001. *Taino Revival: Critical Perspectives on Puerto Rican Identity and Cultural Politics*. Princeton, NJ: Markus Wiener.

_____. 2009. "Changed Identities: A Racial Portrait of Two Extended Families, 1909-present," *Centro, The Journal of the Center for Puerto Rican Studies* 21(1): 37-51.

_____. 2014a. *Race, Identity and Indigenous Politics: Puerto Rican Neo-Tainos in the Diaspora and the Island*. New York: Latino Studies Press.

_____. 2014b. *Thieves of Civilization: Afrocentric Attempts to Appropriate the Cultural Heritage of Native Americans and Latino Indo-Mestizos in America*. New York: Latino Studies Press.

Helg, Aline. 1990. "Race in Argentina and Cuba, Theory, Policies, and Popular Reaction: 1880-1930." In *The Idea of race in Latin America, 1870-1940*, Richard Graham, ed. pp. 37-69. Austin: University of Texas Press.

_____. 1995. *Our Rightful Share: The Afro-Cuban Struggle for Equality, 1886-1912*. Chapel Hill: University of North Carolina Press.

_____. 1997. "Race and Black Mobilization in Colonial and Early Independent Cuba: A Comparative Perspective," *Ethnohistory* 44(1): 53-74.

_____. 2005. "Race and Politics in Cuba," In *Contemporary Caribbean Cultures and Societies in a Global Context*, Franklin W. Knight and Teresita Martínez-Vergne, eds. pp. 183-210. Chapel Hill: University of North Carolina Press.

Hidalgo, Dennis. nd. *Searching for an American Dream: The Run-away Free Blacks Who Left for Hayti*. University of Alabama Press. Forthcoming.

_____. "It Happened in Samaná: The Bay of Rincón, the Cigüayos and Columbus' Party" at: https://www.academia.edu/9083491/It_Happened_in_Saman%C3%A1_The_Bay_of_Rinc%C3%B3n_the_Cig%C3%BCayos_and_Columbus_Party

Hippocrates. 1881. *Hippocrates on airs, waters, and places: the received Greek text of Littré, with Latin, French, and English translations by eminent scholars*. London, Wyman & Sons.

Howard, David. 2001. *Coloring the nation: race and ethnicity in the Dominican Republic*. Boulder, CO: L. Rienner.

Hoffnung-Garskof, Jesse. 2011. "To abolish the law of castes: merit, manhood and the problem of colour in the Puerto Rican liberal movement, 1873-9," *Social History* 36(3): 312-342.

Jiménez Román, Miriam. 1998. "Un hombre (negro) del pueblo: José Celso Barbosa and the Puerto Rican 'Race' Toward Whiteness," *Centro: The Journal of the Center for Puerto Rican Studies* 8(1-2): 8-29.

López, Gustavo and Ana González-Barrera. 2016. "Afro-Latino: A deeply rooted identity among U.S. Hispanics," *Pew Research Center*, March 1: http://www.pewresearch.org/fact-tank/2016/03/01/afro-latino-a-deeply-rooted-identity-among-u-s-hispanics/.

Loveman, Mara. 2007. The U.S. Census and the Contested Rules of Racial Classification in Early Twentieth-Century Puerto Rico. *Caribbean Studies* 35(2): 79–113.

Loveman, Mara and Jeronimo O. Muñiz. 2007. How Puerto Rico Became White: Boundary Dynamics and Intercensus Racial Classification. *American Sociological Review* 72: 915–39.

Maldonado Denís, Manuel. 1973. *Semblanza de cuatro revolucionarios: Albizu, Martí, Che Guevara y Camilo Torres*. Rió Piedras, P.R.: Ediciones Puerto Rico.

Manichaikul, Ani, Walter Palmas, Carlos J. Rodriguez, Carmen A. Peralta, Jasmin Divers, Xiuqing Guo, Wei-Min Chen, Quenna Wong, Kayleen Williams, Kathleen F. Kerr, Kent D. Taylor, Michael Y. Tsai, Mark O. Goodarzi, Michèle M. Sale, Ana V. Diez-Roux, Stephen S. Rich, Jerome I. Rotter, Josyf C. Mychaleckyj. 2012. "Population Structure of Hispanics in the United States: The Multi-Ethnic Study of Atherosclerosis," *PLOS Genetics*: http://journals.plos.org/plosgenetics/article?id=10.1371/journal.pgn.1002640.

Marcheco-Teruel, Beatríz, Esteban J. Parra, Evelyn Fuentes-Smith, Antonio Salas, Henriette N. Buttenschøn, Ditte Demontis, María Torres-Español, Lilia C. Marín-Padrón, Enrique J. Gómez-Cabezas, Vanesa Álvarez-Iglesias, Ana Mosquera-Miguel, Antonio Martínez-Fuentes, Ángel Carracedo, Anders D. Børglum, and Ole Mors. 2014. "Cuba: Exploring the History of Admixture and the Genetic Basis of Pigmentation Using Autosomal and Uniparental Markers," *PLOS Genetics*: http://journals.plos.org/plosgenetics/article?id=10.1371/journal.pgen.1004488#pgen-1004488-g001.

Marti, José. 1893. *Mi Raza*: http://www.historyofcuba.com/history/race/MyRace.htm.

Mayes, April J. 2014. *The Mulatto Republic: Class, Race, and Dominican National Identity*. Gainesville: University Press of Florida.

Minority Rights Group, ed. 1995. *No longer invisible: Afro-Latin Americans today*. London: Minority Rights Publications.

Montinaro, Francesco, George B.J. Busby, Vincenzo L. Pascali, Simon Myers, Garrett Hellenthal, and Cristian Capelli. 2015. "Unravelling the hidden ancestry of American admixed populations," *Nature Communications*: http://www.nature.com/articles/ncomms7596.

Morales Dominguez, Esteban. 2013. *Race in Cuba: Essays on the Revolution and Racial Inequality*. New York: Monthly Review Press.

Mörner, Magnus. 1967. *Race mixture in the history of Latin America*. Boston, Little Brown.

Morris, Addison. 2014. "Dominican Republic leaves Inter-American Court of Human Rights," *Jurist Twenty*. November 6: http://www.jurist.org/paperchase/2014/11/dominican-republic-leaves-inter-american-court-of-human-rights.php.

Moya Pons, Frank. 1998. *The Dominican Republic: a National History.* Princeton, NJ: Markus Wiener Publishers.

Navarro, Mireya. 1997. "Black and Cuban-American: Bias in 2 Worlds, *New York Times*, September 13: http://www.nytimes.com/1997/09/13/us/black-and-cuban-american-bias-in-2-worlds.html.

Ojito, María. 2000. "Best of Friends, World's Apart," *New York Times*, June 5: http://www.nytimes.com/2000/06/05/us/best-of-friends-worlds-apart.html.

Palme, Stephen and Francisco Scarano. 2011. *The Caribbean: A History of the Region and Its People*. Chicago IL: University of Chicago Press.

Paulino, Edward. 2016. *Dividing Hispaniola: The Dominican Republic's Border Campaign against Haiti, 1930-1961*. Pittsburg: University of Pittsburgh Press.

Pedreira, Antonio Salvador. 2005 (1934). *Insularismo: ensayos de interpretación puertorriqueña*. New York: Ausubo Press.

Pérez, Louis A. 2011. *Cuba: between reform and revolution*. New York: Oxford University Press.

Pew Research Center. 2015: http://www.pewresearch.org/fact-tank/2015/06/15/is-being-hispanic-a-matter-of-race-ethnicity-or-both/.

_____. 2016: http://www.pewresearch.org/fact-tank/2016/03/01/afro-latino-a-deeply-rooted-identity-among-u-s-hispanics/.

Pico, Fernando. 2006. *Historia general de Puerto Rico*. San Juan, PR: Ediciones Huracán.

Pina, Diógenes. 2007. "Dominican Republic: Gov't Turns Deaf Ear to UN Experts on Racism," *Inter-Press Service*, October 31: http://www.ipsnews.net/2007/10/dominican-republic-govrsquot-turns-deaf-ear-to-un-experts-on-racism/.

Planas, Roque. 2015. "No Foreign Country Can Change Dominican Republic's Immigration Laws, President Says," *Breaking News* (also *Huffington Post*), February 27 and March 3: http://www.breaking2news.com/no-foreign-country-can-change-dominican-republics-immigration-laws-president-says/.

Plinius Secundus (Pliny). 1938-1997. *Natural History*, Book II, no. 80, Book VI, no. 22. Boston: Loeb Classical Library.

Reed, Ketura T. 2016. "Dominican Republic violates int'l law in canceling citizenship," *North Carolina Journal of International Law*, January 26: http://blogs.law.unc.edu/ncilj/2016/01/26/dominican-republic-violates-intl-law-in-canceling-citizenship/.

Ricourt, Milagros. 2016. *The Dominican Racial Imaginary: Surveying the Landscape of Race and Nation in Hispaniola*. New Brunswick, NJ: Rutgers University Press.

Rivero, Yeidy M. 2005. *Tuning out blackness: race & nation in the history of Puerto Rican television*. Durham: Duke University Press.

Rodríguez Cruz, Juan. 1965. “Las relaciones raciales en Puerto Rico,” *Revista de Ciencias Sociales* 9(4): 373-386.

Rodríguez Demorizi, Emilio. 1955. *Invasiones Haitianos de 1801, 1805 y 1822.* Ciudad Trujillo, DR: Editora del Caribe.

Rodríguez-Silva, Ileana M. 2012. *Silencing Race: Disentangling Blackness, Colonialism, and National Identities in Puerto Rico.* New York: Palgrave/MacMillan.

Sagás, Ernesto. 2000. *Race and politics in the Dominican Republic.* Gainesville: University Press of Florida.

Sagrera, Martin. 1973. *Racismo y política en Puerto Rico: La desintegración interna y externa de un pueblo.* Rio Piedras, PR: Editorial Edil.

Scarano, Francisco. 2011. “Imperial Decline, a Colonial Interpretation,” In *The Caribbean: A History of the Region and Its People*, Stephen Palme and Francisco Scarano, eds. pp. 177-189. Chicago IL: University of Chicago Press.

_____. 2015. *Puerto Rico: Cinco Siglos de Historia.* 4th Edition. New York: McGraw-Hill.

Schmidt-Nowara. Christopher. 1999. *Empire and Antislavery. Spain, Cuba, and Puerto Rico, 1833-1874.* Pittsburgh, PA: University of Pittsburgh Press.

Sereno, Renzo. 1947. “Cryptomelanism: a study of color relations and personal insecurity in Puerto Rico,” *Psychiatry* 10(3): 261-269.

Singh, Kyll. 2015. “21 Stereotypes About Latino Men That Latino Men Want To Dispel,” *Huffington Post*, September 23: http://www.huffingtonpost.com/entry/stereotypes-about-latino-men-dispelled_us_56003629e4b00310edf7db88.

Stepan, Nancy Lays. 1991. *The Hour of Eugenics: Race, Gender and Nation in Latin America*, 5th Edition. Ithaca, NY: Cornell University Press.

Suárez Díaz, Ada. 2005. *El doctor Ramón E. Betances y la abolicíon de la esclavitude*. San Juan: Instituto de Cultura Puertorriqueña.

Tribunal Constitucional, Republica Dominicana. 2012. "Sentencia TC/0168/13," July 10 and September 23: http://www.refworld.org/docid/526900c14.html.

United Nations. 2007. "UN experts find 'profound and entrenched' racial bias in Dominican Republic," *UN News Centre*. New York: UN News Centre, October 30: http://www.un.org/apps/news/story.asp?NewsID=24468.

_____.. 2015. "Dominican Republic: UN experts warn against deportations, racial profiling of people of Haitian descent." *UN News Centre*. New York: UN News Centre, July 28: http://www.un.org/apps/news/story.asp?NewsID=51512#.WNSjQbhXuvB.

Vasconcelos, José. 1997. *The Cosmic Race: a Bilingual Edition*, translated and annotated by Didier T. Jaén. Baltimore, MD: Johns Hopkins University Press.

Via, Marc, Christopher R. Gignoux, Lindsey A. Roth, Laura Fejerman, Joshua Galanter, Shweta Choudhry, Gladys Toro-Labrador, Jorge Viera-Vera, Taras K. Oleksyk, Kenneth Beckman, Elad Ziv, Neil Risch, Esteban González Burchard, Juan Carlos Martínez-Cruzado. 2011. "History Shaped the Geographic Distribution of Genomic Admixture on the Island of Puerto Rico," *PLOS One*: http://journals.plos.org/plosone/article?id=10.1371/journal.pone.0016513.

Peter Wade. 2010. *Race and ethnicity in Latin America*. London, New York: Pluto Press.

Zenón Cruz, Isabelo. 1974. *Narciso descubre su trasero. El Negro en la cultural Puertorriqueña*. San Juan: Editorial Furidi.

Zurbano, Roberto. 2013. "For Blacks in Cuba, The Revolution Hasn't Begun," *New York Times*, March 23.

CHAPTER 2

WHITE PRIVILEGE AND THE EFFACEMENT OF BLACKNESS: PUERTO RICO AND ITS DIASPORA IN THE EARLY 21ST CENTURY

BY WILLIAM GARCÍA

It was August of 2009 when I returned to Puerto Rico to begin my studies at the University of Puerto Rico in Rio Piedras and first encountered the amalgamation of a new kind of Puerto Rican, the *guaynabitos/blanquitos*. Most impoverished and working-class people in Puerto Rico call them *guaynabitos* or *guaynabichos*, derivatives of the word *blanquito*, meaning white Puerto Ricans with money. These wealthy, privileged white Puerto Ricans were quite different from the working-class whites I remembered from my childhood years in the Toa Baja *barrio* of Candelaria and my teenage years in New York City. I first heard the term *guaynabito* while in the *barrio* of Sabana Seca in Toa Baja and somebody started yelling, "*En poco le rompo la cara al guaynabito pendejo ese…*" [I almost broke that idiot *guaynabito's* face]. Shortly afterward, I heard someone else remark about a college student, "*Ese es un blanquito de la YUPI.*" [That's a little white one from the University of Puerto Rico]. I wondered what could a *guayanabito* or *blanquito* be? I noticed most of the people being labeled as *guaynabitos* or *blanquitos* were dressed in different styles: some were dressed like hipsters, others like yuppies, some looked like California surfers, while others were dressed in the latest European fashions. One thing all of these people had in common was that they were the whitest Puerto Ricans I had ever seen in my life. Another important thing I noticed was that these *blanquitos* were quite the exclusive bunch. It was immediately clear to me that these *blanquitos* had no problem taking pride in their whiteness and only associated with other *blanquitos*. While many of the *blanquitos* were wealthy, socio-economic status was not the most important determinant of whether or not one could permeate this group. At the University of Puerto Rico, there were *blanquitos* with no money as well as those who came from outside the metropolitan area. It became clear to me that the most important factor in gaining entry into the *blanquito* group was whiteness and money. The formula was clear as long as your skin was not darker than singer/songwriter, Luis Fonsi, you drank *Medallas*, listened to the "rustic reggae" band, *Cultura Profética*, and revered the light-blue Puerto Rican flag, you were in. It was also very clear to me that this was a group that my too-brown *mulato* Nuyorican self would never enter..

Many of them spoke English very well, but unlike New York Puerto Ricans whose speech was more tied to black urban vernacular, *blanquitos*, startlingly, spoke like white Americans with the "bro," "totally," and "dude" colloquialisms. I'd notice, moreover, how they uttered the words, "like," and "*loca*," in the same sentence every time they spoke. I was impressed by the way they were speaking in Spanglish with an Anglo-American twist, because it was these people who were supposed to hate Nuyorican Spanglish and be patriotic "Spanish only" Puerto Ricans whenever convenient. They behaved very similarly to U.S. hipsters who talked disparagingly about hipsters but never admitted they were the very hipsters they criticized. These hipster *blanquitos* also criticized upper-class politicians without looking in the mirror. I would also hear them claim to be hard-core activists in search of social justice while never bringing up racial inequalities on the island.

The reality was that this elite group actually enjoyed more privilege than white Americans on the mainland thanks to the myth of Puerto Rican *mestizaje*, the false notion that all Puerto Ricans come from the same ethno-racial "recipe" of European, indigenous, and African blood. The myth of *mestizaje* encourages the racial cleansing process of *blanqueamiento*, the eugenic "whitening" of the race through selective white breeding, which allows *blanquitos* to enjoy their teeming white privilege in a judgment-free zone wherein claims of racism against black Puerto Ricans are silenced. The principle on which *blanquitos* stand is that if all Puerto Ricans are mixed with the same blood, racism cannot exist—and if it does, it is nowhere near as bad as racism in the United States.

In her book, *Imaging The Great Puerto Rican Family* (2014) Hilda Lloréns points out that whiteness in Puerto Rico has always been understood to be a fact by both white elites on the island and White Americans. She notes that:

> "Eighteenth and Nineteenth-century scientific literatures promoted the notion that these whites [Tropical Whites], if not biological and culturally generated, were different from European and American whites, as a result of living in latitudes naturally unsuited for white habitation...some held a scientific belief in the biological degeneracy of the white body as it suffered from a type of maladaptive acculturation to the tropical climate. But this was distinct from the cultural degeneracy that gave birth to 'tropicalized cultural whiteness'—a result of living far away from the center of [pure] white culture for extended periods."

Furthermore, throughout her book, *Scripts of Blackness* (2015), Isar Godreau suggests that after the U.S invasion of 1898, white Puerto Rican elites dichotomized highland and coastal Puerto Ricans arguing that those in highland regions preserved the European purity of Puerto Rican identity [for example the myth of the *Jíbaro* as white] while those on the coast carried the burden of blackness and degenerate mixing.

Most of my professors at the University of Puerto Rico refrained from talking about blackness, stateside Puerto Ricans, or anything that questioned their privileged gatekeeping, and protected intellectual superiority. I spent five more years defending the Puerto Rican diaspora and contemporary blackness in those classrooms, and my fact-based claims were usually rebutted by a simple silent treatment from the professor and students. I would hide behind my old New York Yankees fitted baseball cap, a long white t-shirt, and my crusty Nike sneakers. My brown skin covered in tattoos wanted to disappear into thin air like Chevy Chase in the *Invisible Man* movie. It was obvious they enjoyed a good chunk of white supremacy and privilege and didn't mix with Puerto Ricans of darker hues even if Puerto Rican nationalism stressed we were all mixed. One could tell many of the professors at UPR-Rio Piedras came from the same *blanquito/guaynabito* stock, who probably did not think much of me either—even though they never gave me an unfair grade and even to this day I am grateful for that. It might have been because they had the privilege of being color-blind.

It was surprising for me to see white-privileged Puerto Ricans listen to and dance *plena*, *bomba*, and *salsa* music considering those are Afro-diasporic derived musical inheritances of resistance [1]. This usurpation of Black culture frustrated me because I knew black Puerto Rican culture was more than listening to *salsa* while getting drunk off *Medalla Lights* on the Juan Ponce de Leon Blvd. I noticed what acclaimed Afro-Puerto Rican scholar, writer, and researcher, Isar Godreau, argued was right: —"There is a selective celebration of blackness in Puerto Rico. A selective blackness that was folklorized and distanced and does not require critically assessing the inner-workings that contribute to racial inequity and injustice" [2]. In these academic spaces, most black Puerto Ricans seem to be more interested in being accepted as Puerto Rican first before embracing their blackness and never speak about racism and white supremacy—always reinforcing racial harmony.

Felipe Luciano's publication "A New Deal Between State-side and Island Puerto Ricans: The View From a New York Rican" (2012) predicted the problems with the ongoing smug institutional racism in Puerto Rico. He comments:

> "We've noticed that your professional class has been coming in droves to America, many with their *bourgeois* attitudes on class and race, their inability or unwillingness to deal with black people and their occupation of top level positions in our cities based on their educational attainment. In the main they've done well, but, now, they've got to take a back seat. They're hurting us" [3].

Nowhere was the reality of Luciano's comments more visible to me than at the university—the pinnacle of institutional racism that so happens to be filled with *blanquitos*.

One of the most well-documented and researched works on gated communities in Guaynabo City is Carlos Suarez,Carrasquillo's Ph.D. dissertation "Marketing and Gated Communities: A Case study of Guaynabo, Puerto Rico" (2014), which examines the emergence of surveillance and luxury-gated communities and their relationship to race and class. He notes that:

> "Homogeneity can be accounted for in these communities in the Puerto Rican context which is dominated by income, and not surprisingly, the spheres of power that belongs for the most part to white Puerto Ricans. A clear example is how the term *guaynabito* has been gaining more prominence in popular conversations. This in my opinion is certainly an off-spring of the term *blanquito* which is how whiteness has been defined in the Puerto Rican context that not only includes race but income as well" [4].

Shockingly, over the past ten years, white middle-class Puerto Rican migration to the United States has been on the rise because of the very serious and on-going economic crisis [now a financial disaster—especially in the aftermath of hurricane María in 2017] and it continues to change the landscape of the Puerto Rican diaspora. The massive population decrease in Puerto Rico and the alarming population reconfigurations of popular Puerto Rican migration destinations such as Florida and the Midwest require an examination through an Afro-Latino lens and epistemology if we are to condemn black racism and continue to support anti-racist organizations that began in Latin America and the Caribbean in the 1970s. The term Afro-Latino was coined in the United States within a transnational framework that engaged the United States, Latin American, and the Caribbean. This movement challenges anti-blackness within Latino communities themselves which tends to stress a propensity to uphold *mestizaje* while keeping blackness at the bottom of the racial hierarchy.

What effect does the mass-production of *blanquitos* at Puerto Rican universities have on the way transnational Puerto

Rican-ness is constructed? Are these *blanquito*s going to stand in solidarity with marginalized black folks in the U.S., or will their engagement with blackness be limited to listening and dancing to Afro-created *bomba* and *plena* music on holidays? Will stateside *blanquitos* intermix with darker-skinned people, or will they continue to reproduce only with their own kind?

The lack of sustained academic attention to the racial stratification and dynamics of this new wave of Puerto Ricans is worrisome. Puerto Rican racial politics is deeply connected to the whitewashing of Latinos in the United States. Despairingly, the significant academic and cultural politics of Nuyorican and Afro-Latino artists like Tato Laviera, Miguel Piñero, Mariposa [María Teresa Fernández], Pedro Pietri and studies by scholars such as Juan Flores, Miriam Jiménez Román, Jossiana Arroyo, among others, are under scrutinized by the many ivory towers in Puerto Rico and the United States. This reminds us that racially-conscious Latinos of African descent have a strong base and that our presence cannot be ignored, especially in mainland territory. The Afro-Latino movement is on the rise and would benefit from analyzing the constructions of Puerto Rican whiteness in recent migrations. My concern is that the increase of mostly middle class white Puerto Rican migration into mostly white American spaces—integrated with an already racist Puerto Rican culture—will continue to efface the Afro-diasporic linkages of Puerto Rican cultural heritage.

According to the late, much admired Puerto Rican scholar, Juan Flores, more than just economic remittances result as part of the circular migration that arises between countries of origin and the United States. Flores coined the term "cultural remittances" as the process that results from the cultural exchanges, interactions, and experiences that Puerto Ricans have had in the ebb and flow of migrations resulting in a fluid reconstruction of Puerto Rican identity. When Puerto Ricans arrive stateside, they not only bring with them cultural elements such as language, arts, and cuisine, they also bring their racist belief systems rooted in the Puerto Rican foundational myth of *mestizaje*—the myth that all Puerto Ricans are mixed with the same recipe of African, Indigenous, and European blood. This foundational myth of *mestizaje* allows white Puerto Ricans to enjoy their white privilege unbridled while pretending Puerto Ricans across the entire color spectrum have the same opportunities and are treated equally. What does this do for non-white Puerto Ricans who are buying these ideas? Many of my own black family members have come to believe that these ideas make them feel that they are part of "the Puerto Rican nation on the move" [the title of Jorge Duany's book]. Often-times, we fear giving up these beliefs in order to avoid feeling displaced or uprooted.

I predict that white middle class Puerto Rican migrations toward predominantly white spaces in the U.S. will create centrifugal cultural remittances that will rapidly increase the already racist establishment in both Puerto Rico and the mainland. Racism and white supremacy in the U.S. can also become part of "cultural remittances" affecting Puerto Rico. Conversely, the racist baggage Puerto Ricans bring with them is also worrisome. Most of the scholarship on blackness in Puerto Rico centers on the historical underpinnings of slavery and a few notable black descendants. However, there is a dearth of scholarship on the legacy of slavery and its socio-cultural impact on present-day race relations. In Puerto Rican culture, blackness does not exist outside the framework of nationalism. To defy institutional racism in Puerto Rico is to reject the accepted definition of Puerto Rican essentialism, thereby renouncing one's Puerto Rican identity.

Strangely, the scholarship that does exist on present-day racial topics in Puerto Rico and the Diaspora focuses on blackness without acknowledging the supremacy of whiteness. Puerto Rican academics writing about blackness in Puerto Rico and the United States don't always discuss the reality of white identity and privilege maintained by white supremacy. White supremacy has increased exponentially in Puerto Rico in the years of increased economic crisis, severe population decrease, and increased talk about statehood. The same way social media around the globe creates groups of movements of resistance, so has social and corporate media propagated the construction of *blanquito* identity in Puerto Rico. Ironically, stateside Puerto Ricans have chosen to defy U.S. assimilation by upholding a nationalistic discourse that is not only anti-black but is also pro-white *blanqueamiento*. The process of whitening the population through selective *blanquito* breeding, is alive and well and promoted by most Puerto Ricans.

Construction of White Puerto Rican Identities on the Island

During the second annual Arturo Alfonso Schomburg Symposium in 2014 at The University of Puerto Rico-Rio Piedras, Isar Goudreau argued: "Taino culture is explained thoroughly while black history starts in slavery without mentioning powerful African nations and cultures prior to resistance, capture and slavery." Indeed, very seldom do Puerto Ricans in general ask the question: were *plena* and *bomba* invented for all Puerto Ricans or for just black people in Puerto Rico? Does blackness always have to be examined through a national lens? In this sense, has black consciousness consisted of simply imitating the United States or has black consciousness been hijacked by some mythical tri-racialized nationalism? If this is the case, then, many pro-black advocates in Puerto Rico and abroad who also embrace Puerto Rican nationalism have been embracing the very same ideology that subjugates black Puerto Ricans. We have seen the matter in which nationalism and communism has not eradicated racism in Cuba despite claims of a racially mixed *Cubanidad.* Why do we keep believing that Puerto Rican nationalism and anti-U.S. sentiment is the antidote for anti-blackness?

Anti-blackness has been swept under the rug by a ruling white middle class and elite who habitually accuse those advocating for black rights of being a "*vende patria*" [sellout] or a "*Boricua de embuste*" [fake Puerto Rican] whenever one claims a right to exist and be recognized as black bodies. There is a white Puerto Rican history. It is called Puerto Rican history. There is white Puerto Rican poetry. It is called Puerto Rican poetry. Puerto Rican culture has been unable to shepherd our people out of the wilderness of racism and inequality. White racialized homogeneity excludes black and low-income people in general. Guaynabo City is a microcosm and paradigmatic example of the future new waves of white Puerto Ricans that are migrating to the United States.

During the 1970s, while the development of gated communities or "*controles de acceso*" [controlled access] were on the rise, so to were low-income government housing projects. Institutions like El Instituto de Cultura, Department of Tourism and the University of Puerto Rico among other prestigious institutions and government agencies were in part responsible for making sure that the politics of black exclusion within island society went unmentioned. The universities very seldom teach black Studies, African diaspora studies, or courses on the Puerto Rican Diaspora and migration, which would further emphasize how Puerto Ricanness should be envisioned. This gap in university studies is another product of white supremacy on the island. While university students protest and demand public education, the end of corruption, gender rights, independence, where's the fight for racial equality? After years of Puerto Ricans' blatant dissociation with stateside Puerto Ricans for not being "real" Puerto Ricans, it has now become a reality for many of them as they leave the crisis-ridden island for the U.S. mainland in the aftermath of the financial crisis and the devastation left by hurricane María.

Massive Population Decrease 1990s-Present

Puerto Ricans on the island have been an important presence in the more recent migrations to areas of the U.S. that have not had previously established Puerto Rican communities, which some analysts read as brain drains and as a drastic population decrease. Puerto Rico has been experiencing a massive population decrease in the last fifteen years with a new type of Puerto Rican moving from the island to the U.S. mainland. Although many are poor working-class Puerto Ricans who are seeking a better life, an abundant white middle class Puerto Rican population is also migrating to the United States. Unlike poor working-class Puerto Ricans, many *blanquitos* have strong academic backgrounds, are able to enjoy white privilege in U.S. society, continue their studies, and thrive amongst their mostly white neighbors, while working-class Puerto Ricans may benefit from their whiteness in certain situations but not in others. Many of these white middle-class Puerto Ricans have their counterparts among the growing number of other white Latin American immigrants as noted by Arlene Davila in her book *Latino Spin: Public Image and the Whitewashing of Race* (2008):

> "In dispute is whether Latinos will mongrelize America, or become the new group on the route to whiteness, the new Italians or Irish Americans; or whether they will become the new 'mainstream,' or perhaps, the new base

for the Republican Party" [6].

In the last decade, various racist videos on YouTube have been posted by Puerto Ricans from the island attacking mainland Puerto Ricans such as "*Boricuas vs. Nuyoricans, The Truth!*" which stress the difference of white and sophisticated islanders in comparison to the alleged ghetto, uneducated stateside Puerto Ricans [7]. In her article "*Boricuas vs. Nuyoricans–Indeed!*" (2008), Miriam Jiménez Román responds:

> "It is to this white identity that our amateur video-maker pays homage citing census figures and mitochondrial-DNA studies of University of Puerto Rico biologist Juan Carlos Martínez Cruzado to 'buttress' his argument that 'real' Puerto Ricans owe their genetic and cultural *mestizaje* to European and Indigenous peoples. And it is this understanding of a de-Africanized *mestizaje* that many Puerto Ricans cling to when they first arrive to the United States" [8].

The perils and advantages of these attacks underscore that not identifying as white is a clear indication that white Puerto Ricans want to continue to enjoy white privilege in the U.S. while also claiming Puerto Rican identity through a racist agenda. Stateside Puerto Ricans who refuse to acknowledge their whiteness at the same time that they articulate defiance of white Anglo supremacy also do a disservice to Puerto Rican equality because of their failure to acknowledge their own white privilege and because they also ignore the multi-dimensionalities within Puerto Rican identity. This indoctrination has been ingrained in Puerto Ricans since birth with hopes that black history, African slavery, black resistance, black consciousness, black identity, and the contributions of black culture to Caribbean culture can be ignored.

Many recent Puerto Rican migrants have settled in locations that tend to be predominantly inhabited by Anglo-Americans. According to research on migration to the Orlando area of Florida by Jorge Duany and Félix Matos Rodríguez, the media has falsely portrayed Puerto Ricans from the island as educated, middle-class, white collar, and from the suburbs, while they also admit that many may come from working-class backgrounds as well. Yet the report states:

> "In particular, Puerto Rican communities in Orlando differ significantly from their counterparts in other major U.S cities, such as New York, not only in their historical origins and settlement patterns, but also in their mode of economic, political and cultural incorporation. Economically, Puerto Ricans have been more successful in Central Florida than elsewhere, as measured by their income, occupational, residential and cultural incorporation" [9].

The analysis of data from the 2000 census by Duany and Matos Rodríguez also highlighted the following:

> "More than two thirds classified themselves as white, the highest proportion of all states. Inversely a smaller proportion of Puerto Ricans identified themselves as black or some other race. According to the census, Island-born Puerto Ricans are more likely to describe themselves as white and less likely to describe themselves as black than mainland-born Puerto Ricans" [10].

This research still valid eighteen years later is helpful but does not address white privilege and discrimination in the Puerto Rican communities of Central Florida. The U.S. census considers white Puerto Ricans as racially white, allowing these "tropical white" Puerto Ricans to adhere to their national identity without racial accountability. Also, there is a possibility that due to living in the southern U.S., a region known to be extremely racist, Puerto Ricans may identify as white as a protective measure. This also shows that although not all Puerto Ricans are identifying as white in the United States and prefer the option of "Puerto Rican" or "other" in the census, it tells us that discussions of race are still an unspoken issue in the Puerto Rican culture of the Diaspora. They will likely hide under the "Latino" nomenclature while continuing to mix with Anglo-Americans as I have previously observed.

In September 2014, writer, activist, film, and video director, Cesar Vargas, published an article: "The Privilege of the White Hispanic II, Facts, Stats and Cognitive Dissonance" arguing that white Latinos enjoy more privileges than black or Afro-Latinos and have more opportunities for upward mobility [11]. This particular article was a continuation of his first posting titled

"The Privilege of White Latinos: Leaving Out the Rest" which infuriated many white, mixed and black Latinos when it went viral on the internet [12]. This exemplifies the extent to which white supremacy and so-called "racial harmony" obstructs any real discussion or pathway toward racial equality.

Puerto Rican Diaspora research needs to take on white supremacy on the island, along with the uncritical celebration of "Latino middle class" desires that are masked by the continuous mainstreaming of the color-blind ideology, the false racial invention of the homogenous pan Latino, and the racism that prevails in the Latino media. Arlene Davila's research on the controversial transformations in the leadership and focus of New York's El Museo del Barrio and other Latino institutions which she discusses in her book, *Latino Spin* (2008), exemplifies how the gains of the Afro-Latino movement have begun to falter as a result of the emergence of white Latino establishments that are obsessed with "Latinizing" [read: whitewashing] or erasing our black identities.

Conclusion

Afro-Puerto Rican scholar and writer Yolanda Arroyo Pizarro published a short article suggesting that Africana studies courses and programs be established for students in Puerto Rico [15]. However, many Afro-Puerto Rican scholars refuse to deconstruct white supremacy and white privilege. Although return to Puerto Rico migrants in the 1970s and at present are often treated harshly, our loyalties to our national identity obligate us to give white Puerto Ricans a break and a right to be as racist as they want to be simply because we are all colonial subjects. Sympathetically, matters of national belonging and a fear of becoming completely invisible and unaccounted for is the space of liminality that black Puerto Ricans live in.

The options are limited: black Puerto Ricans on the island either confront white supremacy straight-on using their voice and risk being completely obliterated from belonging to a Puerto Rican nationhood, or not take the risk and continue to enjoy a small piece of belonging within a liminal space. It is a space of having a social life in a very limited and marginal space. We need to explore the space of liminalities in national identity in order to understand their fears of confronting an identity that attempts to erase them completely. How do people make the best out of this space of liminality? What does it allow us to do? How can we position ourselves as black bodies in order to have some agency? It goes back to strategic exceptionalisms. If we are to unite against the U.S., it will not be by upholding a flag that represents white supremacy.

As a colonial territory, there is little thought given to criticizing our own people while achieving autonomy and belonging. Many black subjects that seek independence on the island are often supported by many white middle-class *blanquitos/guaynabitos* who want the same thing, but this results in the placement of race in the back seat for another discussion that never gets discussed. As a U.S colony there is a fear of eroding any hopes of achieving independence; hence the fear of critiquing racism and white supremacy. These multiple positionalities are sometimes in contradiction. I say it's time we continue to explore white supremacy and white privilege in Puerto Rico while understanding our own Afro-diasporic and multiplicities of black consciousness, and not just our African heritage, like *bomba* and *plena*, but our black Afro-Caribbean and diasporic inheritances as well.

Notes:

[1] See Godreau, Isar. 2006. "Folkloric Others: '*Blanqueamiento*' and the Celebration of Blackness as an Exception in Puerto Rico," in *Globalization and Race: Transformations in the Cultural Production of Blackness*, Deborah Thomas and Kamari Clarke, eds. pp. 171-187 Durham: Duke University Press.

[2] Goudreau, Isar. 2015. *Scripts of Blackness: Race, Cultural Nationalism and U.S colonialism in Puerto Rico*. Urbana: University of Illinois Press.

[3] Luciano, Felipe. 2011. "A New Deal between Stateside and Island Puerto Ricans: The View From a New York Rican," *National Institute for Latino Policy Newsletter*, Guest Commentary, March 30:
http://montyandme.tumblr.com/post/6469349094/a-new-deal-

between-stateside-and-island-puerto.

[4] Suarez Carrasquillo, Carlos. 2009. "Marketing and Gated Communities: A case Study of Guaynabo, Puerto Rico," Ph.D. Dissertation, University of Massachusetts-Amherst, p. 179, n. 183: http://scholarworks.umass.edu/cgi/viewcontent.cgi?article=1148&context=open_access_dissertations.

[5] Oh, Sookhee. 2014. "Locked in, locked Out: Gated communities in a Puerto Rican City," *American Journal of sociology* 120(1): 290.

[6] Dávila, Arlene. 2008. *Latino Spin: Public Image and the Whitewashing of Race*. New York: New York University Press: p. 1.

[7] Boricuas vs. Nuyoricans The Truth! https://www.youtube.com/watch?v=WDvMf_DLrbE.

[8] Jiménez Román, Miriam. 2008. "Boricaus vs Nuyoricans—Indeed!," *ReVista, Harvard Review of Latin America:* http://revista.drclas.harvard.edu/book/boricuas-vs-nuyoricans—indeed.

[9] Duany, Jorge and Felix V Matos Rodríguez. 2006. "Puerto Ricans in Orlando and Central Florida, *Policy Report*," Center for Puerto Rican Studies, Hunter College (CUNY) 1(1): http://latinamericanstudies.org/puertorico/Puerto_Ricans_in_Orlando.pdf.

[10] Duany and Matos Rodrígue, 2006: 21.

[11] Vargas, Cesar. 2014. "The Privilege of the White Hispanic II, Facts, Stats and Cognitive Dissonance" (See updated version in Chapter 3 of this book).

[12] Vargas, Cesar. 2014. "The privilege of the White Hispanic: Leaving out the Rest" (See updated version in Chapter 3 of this book).

[13] Jiménez Román, 2008.

[14] Dávila, Arlene, 2008: 18.

[15] Arroyo Pizarro, Yolanda. Nd. "Estamos Listos Para Tener Nuestra Propia Facultad de Estudios Africanos en Alguna Universidad en Puerto Rico?" *Revista Cruce, Critica Socio-Cultural Contemporanea*, Universidad Metropolitana: http://revistacruce.com/politica-y-sociedad/item/1062-estamos-listos-para-tener-nuestra-propia-facultad-de-estudios-africanos.

Other Sources Consulted:

Bonilla Silva, Eduardo. 2010. *Racism Without Racists: Color Blind Racism & Racial Inequality in Contemporary America*. New York: Rowman & Littlefield Publishers.

Betances, Samuel. 1972. "The Prejudice of Having No Prejudice in Puerto Rico, Part I," *The Rican* 2: 41-54.

_____. 1973. "The Prejudice of Having No Prejudice in Puerto Rico, Part II," *The Rican* 3: 22-37.

Chaves, Linda. 1991. *Out of the Barrio: Toward a New Politics of Hispanic Assimilation*. New York: Basic Books.

Duany, Jorge. 2014. *Blurred Borders, Transnational Migration Between the Hispanic Caribbean and the United States*. Chapel Hill: The University of Carolina Press.

Flores, Juan. 2000. *From Bomba to Hip-hop: Puerto Rican Culture and Latino Identity*. New York: Columbia University Press

_____. 2004. "Créolité in the Hood: Diaspora as source and challenge," *Centro, The Journal of the Center for Puerto Rican Studies* 16(2): 282-293: http://wayneandwax.com/pdfs/flores-diaspora-creolite.pdf.

_____. 2009. *The Diaspora Strikes Back: Caribeño Tales of Learning and Turning*. New York: Routledge.

González, Lydia. 1993. "La Tercera Raiz: Presencia Africana en Puerto Rico," Centro de Estudios de La Realidad Puertorriquena del Instituto de Cultura Puertorriquena.

Jiménez Román, Miriam and JuanFlores, eds. 2010. The Afro-latin@ Reader: History and Culture in the United States. Durham, NC: Duke University Press.

La Fountain-Stokes, Larry. 2009. *Queer Ricans: Cultures and Sexualities in the Diaspora*. Minneapolis: University of Minnesota Press..

Kantrowitz, Nathan. 1950. "Algunas Consecuencias Raciales: Diferencias Educativas y Ocupacionales entre los Puertorriqueños Blancos y No Blancos en los Estados Unidos Continentales," *Revista de Ciencias Sociales* 15(3): 387-397.

Lloréns, Hilda. 2014. *Imaging The Great Puerto Rican Family: Framing Nation, Race, and Gender during the American Century*. New York: Lexington Books.

Pabón, Carlos. 2002. *Nación Postmortem: Ensayos Sobre los Tiempos de Insoportable Ambigüedad*. San Juan, PR: Ediciones Callejon.

Rodríguez Olleros, Ángel. 1974. *Canto a la Raza: Composición Sanguínea de Estudiantes de la Universidad de Puerto Rico*. Rio Piedras: Ediciones Colegio de Farmacia, Universidad de Puerto Rico, Recursos Federales, HEW.

Wise, Tim. 2009. *Between Barack and a Hard Place: Racism and White Denial in the Age of Obama*. San Francisco, CA: City Light Books.

CHAPTER 3

THE PRIVILEGE OF THE WHITE HISPANIC: LEAVING OUT THE REST WITH FACTS, STATS AND COGNITIVE DISSONANCE

BY CESAR VARGAS

Part 1: Leaving Out the Rest:

People talk so much about Latinos denying their Blackness, but bring up the term "white Latino" and you will see an extreme reaction, visceral attack from white Latinos themselves. Responses such as [and I'm pretty sure you've read this a lot from racist Americans]: "stop talking about race," "Latinos aren't racist," "white and Black Latinos are still treated the same," and "your language is divisive." They love to pretend they don't enjoy privileges when they identify as Latino or Hispanic.

Embracing Latino or Hispanic has not benefited Indigenous folks, Chicanos, or Afro-Latinos because it has been robbed from the rest of us by white Latinos for their own agenda: money and political pull with brands, sponsors, the government, publications, grants, you name it.

We Afro Latinos or Black Latinos are here to demand to be included in *latinidad* and not just with the identity so we can be targeted for political and monetary gain with positions in the government as brand ambassadors, with positions in both the film industry and TV networks—with jobs.

How can white Latinos—a people who know so little of what it means to be part of a majority in U.S. society represent so many of us? Can you really speak with authority about the lack of diversity and discrimination when you have hardly experienced it yourself? Privilege has a price and that price is having blind spots. You can perhaps legitimately represent yourselves as long as you acknowledge the disparity and relinquish some of your privilege. How do you do that? Recommend a *mestizo* or an Afro-Latino to a job within your industry. Hire a Chicano of color and not just for the low level jobs you may think they're qualified for. Leave your biases behind. Stop thinking that people are comprised of both negative and positive stereotypes, but are fully complex human beings. Stop believing that we don't also fall for the "merit," colorblind, and bootstrap myths when it comes to judging our own.

Until then, I will continue to point out that just being in the workforce, participating in a panel discussion, or having membership in a board full of white Hispanics is not representation for the majority of Hispanics. The Latino representation in the States seems to be a microcosm of the racial and social disparity in Latin America. This only solidifies my point of white Hispanic being ill-equipped to speak for the rest of us—at least when they're the only ones who are considered for jobs with the rest of us becoming victims [or thugs] in a system that white Latinos can milk for their own benefit.

The privileges of identifying as Hispanic are not trickling down to us. I want to see more Latinos in film, TV, publications, the government, getting grants for their orgs, and not just white Latinos.

Part 2: Facts, Stats, and Cognitive Dissonance:

Perhaps I should've written this piece before the earlier one [see above]. Which turned out to be extremely polarizing, and controversial to some [really?], but that was my intention. I expected the outrage from a lot of people. I even wrote it in my original piece. My point was more than proven and I'm glad it received the reaction that helped give exposure to this piece that's more thorough.

So intense was the cognitive dissonance experienced by those who received and opposed my message that it unintentionally made it go viral due to the Streisand effect. I was not the least shocked by the responses. There were many derailing and even downright ridiculous comments made about it: I was accused of being divisive, nonsensical, sexist, Marxist, a bad writer [perhaps the only legitimate indictment], and a terrorist. They should've added Nazi while they were at it so I could've at least invoked Godwin's law. Maybe I should've paid heed to Oscar Wilde and made you all laugh with the truth instead—a truth that is based on undeniable facts.

First, let's get the concept of Latino privilege and struggle out of the way. There are a ton of stories of white Latino struggles taking up precious space in the media. Do you know what's the biggest struggle white Latinos face according to these articles/blogs?—being confused for white and having to prove to other Latinos their *latinidad*. Seriously, if that is your biggest struggle then it would behoove you to reconsider your entire existence and why you think this should supersede any other issue we're facing today. Oh, and the day Indigenous and Afro-Latinos have the same amount of access to the media [not just blogs or Twitter] to speak about their experience, then we can talk. Until then, single experiences [good or bad] about being a white Latino should not be given the same level of credence, space, and time as legitimate gripes or studies about racial discrimination that affect people en masse.

The truth of the matter is that white Latinos enjoy way more privileges and more opportunities for upward mobility. That is a fact. A fact backed up by studies that have been done. The reason you don't think [just like a lot of white Americans, trust me, don't think] that being or identifying as a white Latino has rained down benefits on you is because you don't see the privileges you enjoy that are usually denied to others. Again, you have blind spots.

I am personally an able-bodied man. That's two privileges right there. Living in the United States is a huge privilege. That's three [add numerous more to that, actually]. I am lighter complected than most Afro-Latinos. People don't "confuse" me for Black. Most people think I'm Mexican and I'm completely fine with that. That affords me the privilege of speaking about Latino issues and no one will question me about it. That's four. I had the privilege to get a college education—something millions of Latinos don't have the privilege of attaining. That's five. I have the privilege to have my opinions published in several news outlets. That's six. I could go on. My point is that I use those privileges to bring attention to something that's bigger than my own struggles, and trust me, a lot of people have it worse. Lots of us have the opportunity to speak for the less fortunate and some do [that includes some of you], and others don't. But don't sit there and pretend you don't enjoy any privileges. Because we all do to different degrees and those degrees have a lot to do with our skin color, too.

I know you're annoyed, angry even, but your first reaction shouldn't be so reactionary and extreme. You should first try to at least understand the points I'm presenting. Then do your own research on the matter. There are numerous sources you can tap into. Several things you should've done and taken from this are as follows: [1] It's not the "Oppression Olympics" and to bring up your struggles as a "white Latina(o)" [compare them to what darker Latinos face] tells me that you're self-absorbed; [2] that white Latinos do enjoy more privileges, [3] that this is a huge problem, [4] that you are ill-equipped to be the sole representative of the majority of us when you are not part of the majority of the racial Latino makeup even though you are publicly shown the most, [5] and please, don't get all incriminatingly defensive and froth at the mouth because someone brought all this up, [6] Acknowledge and rectify.

The struggle that lighter complected Latinos face is, again, being confused for a white American so a lot of them go out of their way to prove to other Latinos that they are "down"—or let white folks know that they're Latino. Yes, white Latinos receive some shunning. Yes, that will ultimately lead them to a slight identity crisis [don't we all?], but that's as far as it goes since they don't suffer major discrimination with employment or anything else. In contrast to the white Latinos, darker Latino, the Indigenous and Afro-Latinos receive the same level of discrimination as African Americans. Those are facts—facts corroborated by Dr. Margaret Hunter in "The Persistent Problem of Colorism: Skin Tone, Status, and Inequality," who notes that:

> "Light-skinned or white Latinos have clear significant advantages in income and wealth relative to their darker or black-identified counterparts. Richard Alba, John

Logan, and Brian Stults studied housing access, ownership, and segregation. They found that:

> 'Hispanics who describe themselves as black are in substantially poorer and less white neighborhoods than their compatriots who describe themselves as white. The penalty they absorb in neighborhood affluence varies between $3,500 and $6,000 and thus places them in neighborhoods comparable to those occupied by African Americans.'"

The Alba, Logan, and Stults' study of the immigrant adaptation and spatial-assimilation theory reveals that despite their immigrant status and identity as Latinos, Black Latinos' housing experience more resembles that of native-born African Americans than that of other Latinos. That is, Black Latinos live in more racially segregated neighborhoods with less exposure to non-Hispanic whites and lower property values. This not only socially isolates, but also stunts the opportunity for the accumulation of wealth through home ownership" (See Hunter 2007: 242).

All these things must be taken into account. Yes, there is a pipeline issue. Meaning that sometimes it is difficult to recruit talent of color that's qualified for a job, but that falls on you if you are representing [getting exposure or payment] to find that talent. Most places require a hiring or appointment of people of color, but those people of "color" who get in tend to be of privileged status and it appears others are screened out if they aren't. They get in because they are also apt pupils and champions of the politics of the respectability myth, which only facilitates the perpetuation of the vicious cycle of discrimination. It all starts from the minute we are old enough to be indoctrinated by labels and stereotypes that turn into self-fulfilling prophesies. Add limited resources along with a school system that's been ravaged by [at best] well-intentioned bureaucracies and you've got a recipe for failure—a failure that many teachers see as a herculean task that they can't overcome on their own [because they have their hands tied behind their backs].

However, if you are teaching Black and Latino kids, it falls on you to recognize that they are as capable as anyone else to succeed. It falls on you to help them see that through positive encouragement instead of through destructive criticism and apathy, they are constantly subjected to by society. There are nuances [be it racial, financial, or cultural] that you might not understand because you weren't raised in an environment that has been compared to a war-zone. Again, your privileges have given you blind spots to work with, educate and represent. That is why it is extremely important to not only take cultural and racial sensitivity classes, but most importantly, also refer or hire Indigenous folks and Afro-Latinos to whatever it is you are involved with. Especially if it's representation of a people in any field.

Take the show business field, for instance. If your biggest struggle in Hollywood as a white Latino is that you aren't getting gigs [typecast, really] because you don't look Mexican or Latino enough then consider yourself lucky. You won't play a stereotype for the rest of your career. God knows we don't need more of those roles perpetuating narratives that usually hurt us. By the way, white Latinos do enjoy way more privileges in Hollywood. Yes, there are Afro-Latinos who are famous and "over-indexed" in Hollywood [I hate that the study used that term because it will undoubtedly be used against them], but their *latinidad* is usually erased. They play mostly African American roles. If they did play a Latino, then the reaction would be as you could imagine—hostile. Zoe Saldaña caught a lot of flak for playing a Colombian in the movie, *Colombiana*. Some people did have legitimate concerns about the premise of the film, but most were angry that an Afro-Latina played a Colombian. There are Black folks in Colombia—many of them, actually, but the media in Colombia and both of the Americas in general rarely recognizes that.

If you are a successful Afro or Indigenous Latino, it would behoove you not to use your single experience to make sweeping generalizations about the Latino condition and how to fix it. It's nothing more than a rugged individualism—a rugged individualism that some unscrupulous entities push. No one makes it without the help of others—no one, and no matter how hard they're working to get ahead. To say otherwise would make it a myth. The bootstraps myth. To perpetuate that myth would make you a conduit for suffering and pain. Instead, use your success to give a break to another one of your kind. Yes, it is your responsibility because someone else gave you the opportunity to succeed. You didn't do it all alone. We live in an interconnected world. Don't close the door behind you after someone else helped you get in. One single experience doesn't equal a trend. It's unfortunate that the few successful Latinos we have are used as examples to shame those who've had it rough for not being successful or successful enough without considering the real factors as to why they're not. Instead of just merely being an inspiration for success by simply being successful, why not really make a difference by being a hands-on advocate instead of solely enjoying your glory? Some people are and I commend them, for their compassion and generosity.

Hands-on doesn't even have to mean donating money. It also means dispelling myths, acknowledging publicly that there is a disparity, and rectifying this with actions or a call to action. Not regurgitating self-serving feel good platitudes is important because most people will appeal to authority by referring to you and your false narratives as the preacher and gospel for success. Even though most likely, you got incredibly lucky by being born healthy at the right place, right time, right sex, right gender, right ethnicity, right race, right creed, right sexual orientation—it has to be understood that all of these are unearned privileges that might make you oblivious of how you became successful. Being around the right people to enrich your social capital and therefore increase your odds for upward mobility for each privilege you accumulate [if you're not already there, that is]—has to be also understood as unearned privileges that might make you oblivious of how you became successful. This happens to most wildly successful people. Even to those who did not inherit monetary wealth. That includes "self-made" CEOs that believe they came up from the bottom without any privilege. Trust me, you are sitting at that throne because you had a road paved for you before you started to walk that road—and that road was most likely built through the exploitation of a people who now want to rightfully walk through that road. Since you are the only one allowed to go through it, you have a greater chance to succeed even if you encounter a rock or two. We all do, but others a lot more. There are many obstacles and it takes some Latinos longer to reach their goal. Latinos of color don't even have a road to walk-on and to insinuate that they don't want to walk that road because it's hard work simply makes you a bigot—an oblivious bigot that's unable to represent us.

If you are sitting at a discussion panel, or a board meeting composed of white Latinos who allegedly represent a diverse Latino landscape: [1] You are not an accurate representative [2]. You are not doing enough to promote diversity and be as diverse as you say you are [3]. You are not speaking up enough about this, which also makes you complicit in robbing the Latino name solely for your benefit—a Latino name that is making and giving networks, brands, agencies, politicians, and orgs a lot of money and power. This is money and power that is not trickling down to brown and Black Latinos because white Latinos are hijacking and exploiting that money and power either through obliviousness on your part, or downright maliciousness. Acknowledge and rectify. That should be your mantra as a white Latino representative. It's way easier for you to get these jobs, positions of power, investments, and grants for the obvious reasons mentioned here. So you can't really tell people who have little or no access to opportunities to do it themselves. It is your responsibility if you put on that cape on and take the money. Don't be a wolf in sheep's clothing. Look around you. If you don't have a Latino of color among you, then say and do something about it.

You cannot represent the Latino landscape as a white Latino if you don't admit to the fact that darker Latinos had and continue to have a harder time than you. Yes, all Latino groups experience some kind of discrimination regardless of their appearance, such as being passed over for a job if you have a Spanish surname, but ask any human resources department if knowing someone inside doesn't trump it all. It does. That includes having a Spanish surname. You can't hijack the struggles of the Indigenous and Afro-Latinos and act like you are experiencing the same level of discrimination. According to studies, you're not.

In 2003, social science researchers found that Latinos who identified as white earned about $5,000 more per year than Latinos who identified as Black, and about $2,500 more per year than Latinos who identified as "some other race." A clear hierarchy is evident among Latinos with white Latinos at the top, "others" in the middle, and Black Latinos at the bottom. White Latinos also had lower unemployment rates and lower poverty rates than Black

Latinos. Their findings are consistent with other work in this area. Dark skin results in costs for dark Latinos in terms of income and occupational prestige (See Hunter 2008: 66).

This is wrong and don't even dare say that darker Latinos aren't working as hard or don't have what it takes. That is a myth. The myth of meritocracy. Which has been debunked. Any human being that starts with a clean slate [that includes prenatal and even their parents' good health prior to conception] has the ability to succeed if given the opportunity. That includes people of color, or of any ethnicity.

You can't speak for all us if you don't include us, which you don't. I never said that white Latinos can't represent us. I never said you're not a Latino—and I feel silly for even having to explain that Latino is an ethnicity and not a race, which means that there are several socially and politically constructed races within the Latino ethnicity and that includes white Latinos. Don't play dumb about it. You should represent Latinos by acknow-ledging and rectifying—not by just enjoying the benefits. You can't wish discrimination away by not speaking about it. You just can't think that bringing to light only the good things that Latinos provide to this nation will magically result in the erasure of the prevailing racism in this country. Those are terrible counter-arguments concocted from a place of obliviousness and privilege, but I repeat myself. Those suggestions have been proven to be myths—myths that the African American intelligentsia as well as white and Latino scholars are very familiar with. You ought to be ashamed of yourself for repeating them—especially publicly. Let white America know that there's internal strife. Perhaps white Latinos will pay more attention to the Indigenous and Afro-Latinos as a result. Otherwise, you'll just be used as a dis-traction and a gatekeeper to the very people you're supposed to represent and advance.

My biggest detractor is a male Afro-Latino. I'm not surprised by that either. It's expected from our own kind. Too many have been fed and have accepted the same false narratives. What I am concerned with most is that he says he's a cryptogra-pher who's worked in the Department of State and Defense for both the Bush and Obama administrations but still misunderstood my point. In fact, he had to do a lot of mental flips to write his rebuttal and he still didn't refute my assertions. He just accused me of writing things I did not write. Then proceeded to attack my character. Which smells a lot like libel if you asked me. I'm surprised the *HuffPost Latino Voices* even published it and I question the integrity of the editor who gave it the green-light while passing up this one. If that is the kind of incompetent people the government and the media hire then we are doomed.

I did not intend to divide Latinos by pointing out discrimination within our own ranks. That's ridiculous. I want nothing more than for Latinos to unite. I did not create any divisions. Ask Indigenous and Afro Latinos if they feel included. Ask them! The divisions are already there. If they tell you they don't feel excluded from *telenovelas*, the Latino media in general, and from other areas, they are in denial, oblivious to what's happening, or afraid to speak-up for whatever reasons. If you are a white Latino and deny this, then that's just treasonous. You can't solve a problem without recognizing its existence. The problem is there and talking about it hardly makes it worse. On the contrary, it can and will make people uncomfortable to bring it to light, but there is no progress in comfort. The real consequences of discrimination supersede your feelings.

I do know what people are hating the most about all this. It seems that they think I'm dismissing their individual struggles, which is hardly the case. And then there's the way white Americans feel about their own privileges. They tend to consider only themselves when they act to diminish or take away from others. It has to be understood that we are all struggling, but some more than others. Again, that has a lot to do with race and skin tones. Being Black or Indigenous and having limited resources in any part of the world comes with innumerable challenges. Take poverty, for instance: poor people's brains are literally changed by the constant bombardment of stressors—stressors that lead to making decisions that might be counterproductive in the long run, but seem the obvious choices to make in order to survive no matter how counterintuitive they might seem to those in positions of privilege. Because even poor people of color have blind spots, but for different reasons. By the way, you can't speak about poverty without speaking about race. The two are irrevocably intertwined in today's world. Those are irrefutable realities. You would really have to be self-absorbed, willfully ignorant, and callous to deny them—what we can call the dark triad of privilege.

Let's stop denying that there isn't colorism and racism within the American Latino landscape—a colorism and racism that has real consequences. Our biases did not stop at the border or when our plane landed. They came with us [and continued with those of us born here, too] and we are all guilty of perpetuating and exacerbating them if we don't acknowledge and rectify them. Then and only then can you say that you're a Latino representative, because real representatives lift their brothers and sisters up regardless of how they look. Studies are saying that white Latinos are not doing much of this. Don't be these folks. Be a catalyst of change for the betterment of all Latino peoples—not just of those who look exactly like you. Otherwise, you're just holding us back.

If you ask me—what am I doing to help white Latinos in this regard? I'll tell you, more than enough. I've included you in my efforts to uplift the community when you are doing a lot better than darker Latinos. What are you doing for the others?

References:

Hunter, Margaret. 2007. "The Persistent Problem of Colorism: Skin Tone, Status, and Inequality," *Sociology Compass* (1)1: 237–254.

_____. 2008. "The Cost of Color: What We Pay for Being Black and Brown," in *Racism in the 21st Century: An Empirical Analysis of Skin Color*, Ronald E. Hall, ed. pp. 63-76. New York: Springer.

CHAPTER 4

WHITE PRIVILEGE
HOW "*MESTIZAJE*" IN PUERTO RICO MAKES ROOM FOR RACISM TO FLOURISH

BY DOROTHY BELL-FERRER

"*Somos de tres razas! La blanca, la india, y la negra*!" ["We are three races, the white, the Indian, and the Black!"]. This is a clichéd response you can almost always count on hearing anytime you bring up race or racism in Puerto Rico or in the Puerto Rican Diaspora. It's cute, easy to remember, and also a lie—a lie that is socially and politically constructed.

Not so ironically, the European root, which is most often mistaken as the basis of Puerto Rican culture, is mentioned first. The Indigenous "Taíno" root, which is often recognized strategically [yes, strategically] in front of blackness is named second. Oh, and the third?—African or Black is last but not least!—right? I'd like to think so, but I know better.

The blending of these three races or roots in Puerto Rico are what we refer to as "*mestizaje*," or race mixture [1]. This "*mestizaje*" is what causes Puerto Ricans to believe that we are all racially mixed in equal parts in the exactly same way. Accordingly, there can be no "true" differences because *mestizaje* is seen as the racial essence of all Puerto Ricans and even exists in the genetic heritage of the people [with few exceptions]. However, the way in which *mestizaje* is recognized makes room for racism and white supremacy to flourish in actuality because it gives us a dismissive and false analysis of race that ignores how race in Puerto Rico has been historically constructed.

Where does this *mestizaje* narrative come from? We are all taught, whether in school or through conversation with our elders that Spaniards came to Puerto Rico, encountered Taínos, killed most of them off with diseases and weapons, subsequently brought slaves from Africa [or more accurately, African peoples who were enslaved], and eventually everyone got married and generations later we have what is now referred to as the Puerto Rican racial admixture of African, Taíno, and Spanish. That's the irresponsible and also inaccurate way to tell our history. Let's discuss what is wrong with this because our history is, of course, the foundation for our present state of affairs.

It is a documented fact that Africans first came to *Boriké* [the Indigenous name for Puerto Rico] and other parts of the Americas with the Spanish *conquistadores* as free men. One of the most recognized examples of this was a Black man by the name of Pedro Mejias who reportedly married the *Taína Cacica* [Chief], Yuisa [2]. Supporting this mostly ignored story about race in Puerto Rico means that we need to analyze the history of race and ethnic groups more closely. For those who know about this, the union between Mejias and Yuisa marked the beginning of an Afro-Indigenous relationship in Puerto Rico—specifically in the areas of Loiza and Canóvanas. This Afro-Indigenous identity, while often erased is very much present in the essence of the people and in various traditions to this day. The best example of this tradition can still be seen in the simultaneous use of cooking utensils such as the buren (flat griddle made of clay) which is Indigenous and the *fogón* (a type of stove) which is African.

It also has to be recognized that there was African heritage among the Spanish *conquistadores*. While carrying with them their white supremacist/white savior ideas and biases, many *conquistadores* in fact had African heritage derived directly from North Africa as a result of both African immigration to Spain and the occupation of southern Spain by the Moors beginning in AD 711 [3]. The Moors who first came to Spain in the early eighth century were a racially mixed group that included darker sub-Saharan Africans and lighter complected North Africans [Berbers] and Arabs. Quite a number of the Moors also became, or were whiter through conversion, with blond hair and blue eyes in the centuries that followed because of inter-marriage with northern Europeans who continuously migrated into the peninsula. It therefore has to be understood that the term "Moor" has more to do more with religion than with race as we understand it today.

The first people to become enslaved under Spanish colonial rule in America were the Taínos—not the Africans. But this soon proved unsuccessful because the Taínos being Indigenous to the islands, were either decimated [especially by disease], or they were able to escape to other islands not controlled by the Spaniards. It also has been documented that the Taínos resisted colonialism in a more determined manner [e.g.: 1511-1518 rebellions, etc.] than the Africans because Puerto Rico was their homeland. The enslaved Africans brought to the island were more seemingly, or more easily Christianized and colonized according to this interpretation because they were not in a land they knew and were convinced they could return home to their West African communities [possibly] upon "good behavior" [4].

By 1530, the Puerto Rican gold mines were depleted and many *criollos*, who were European, primarily Spanish descendants born and living in Puerto Rico, left the island and relocated to other newly established Spanish colonies like Mexico and Peru. Puerto Rico became a military outpost as a result with a small population that was mostly Black/Afro-descendant and *mulato*. It wasn't until the late 1700s and especially after 1815, just a few years after the Haitian Revolution, that the population of Puerto Rico began to whiten with an increase in the number of Europeans who came to the island. That year [1815], the Spanish Crown under King Ferdinand VII issued the "Royal Decree of Graces" which encouraged Spaniards, other Europeans, and white *criollos* from other regions in the Americas to populate Puerto Rico as well as Cuba so as not to have a Black rebellion, "Black colony," or "Black nation" like the one that had emerged in Haiti where the French colonizers were defeated by Black rebels [5].

This influx of Europeans is referred to in Spanish and by many Puerto Rican scholars and historians as a process of "*blanqueamiento*" or "whitening" [6]. The white settlers were provided with free land, and even monetary incentives to populate the island. This allowed for the creation or resurgence of *cañaverales* [sugar enterprises], and other cash crop plantations based on African slave labor, especially in the coastal regions of

Puerto Rico like Mayagüez, Ponce, Guayama, Loíza, Arroyo, Vega Baja, Patillas, and Salinas etc [7]. The 1815 Royal decree also restructured the socioeconomic environment of the mountainous regions of Puerto Rico where *mestizos* and non-land owning white people farmed the land. The population of *mulatos*, *cuarterones* [one quarter Black] and whites increased in the mountains and along the coast during these years of increased "*blanqueamiento*" that also led to the abolition of slavery.

Slavery in Puerto Rico was finally abolished on March 22, 1873, but this didn't necessarily "free" Blacks in Puerto Rico and make them equal to their white [or whiter] counterparts. Once "freed," Blacks were forced to work under contracts as *libertos* [most likely doing the same work they did as slaves] for a minimum of three years and were denied political rights for five years [8]. Each municipality has it's own history with how Afro-descendants in respective regions economically developed [if at all] during the post slavery period, but overall, the post-abolition laws allowed for very little upward economic mobility—the effects of which can still be seen today. A large majority of economically and socially marginalized communities in Puerto Rico are said to be made up of Black Afro-descendants as analyzed in a case study that was done at the University of Puerto Rico at Cayey. This study attacks "*las tres razas*" as a viable argument when talking about Puerto Rico because not every Puerto Rican lives the same experience and much of the lived experiences in Puerto Rico are attributed to race in one way or another seen as a physical attribute.

To understand why the *tres razas-mestizaje* concept does not apply to Puerto Rico, we take the historical understanding of race in Puerto Rico and apply it to the present social environment. As cited, the UPR Cayey study has provided empirical data suggesting that racial inequality and racial discrimination are prevalent in Puerto Rico, but if everyone in Puerto Rico is supposedly a single mixed race, the study is seen as completely invalid to be silenced or ignored if not openly denounced. If we deny that racism exists in Puerto Rico when it obviously does, it is impossible for us to see the root of many of the social problems on the island, and as a result, they are left unresolved.

If we pretend, for example, that the reason that Loiza is often dehumanized as violent by the media and people who do not go to

Loiza or in nearby Piñones beyond eating *alcapurrias* or enjoying *toques de bomba* in *Medianía* [sometimes], then the pretense is that the experience of the people living in these communities is rooted in racism—a racism that is rooted in structural racism. If we practice "colorblindness" when it comes to Loiza [or Canóvanas and Carolina], it is nearly impossible to understand that much of the marginalization and social problems experienced by Black people in these communities is motorized by folklorization which suggests that Black people are for cultural consumption and demonization, which also suggests that Black people are dangerous, careless and aggressive or violent. Open the link to this video and connected links with thanks to William García:

https://www.youtube.com/watch?v=bs4trwwtwtA&feature=youtu.be

Additionally, if all Puerto Ricans are one race, the fact that every governor in the 500 year history of Puerto Rico has been a white male is completely disregarded. Puerto Rico is an island of mostly *mulatos* and Black people [though empirical data through the census inaccurately suggests the very opposite] but representation at the government level has not been representative of the population. Such views of race also dismiss the fact that higher academic spaces in Puerto Rico are also dominated by white men and as a result, sway the educational system to the benefit of whiteness and keeps the ability for educational and racial progress to a minimum. To pretend that this is not rooted in the white supremacist structure that exists in Puerto Rico allows for white people to dismiss white privilege, which is an obstacle to social progress because the root of a common social problem is dismissed.

At the lower educational level, schoolchildren in Puerto Rico are taught [brainwashed to believe] from an early age that regardless of their physical appearance, they all individually derive from the same aforementioned roots. Not acknowledging the fact that racism, racial discrimination and a racial construct exists in Puerto Rico allows white privilege, white saviorism, and finally white racism to flourish with this lack of acknowledgement ingrained in schoolchildren from an early age. On another level, the PNP [*Partido Nuevo Progresista* or "New Progressive Party"], a corrupt, pro-U.S. statehood political party with a mostly white leadership, never acknowledges race or the privilege that white Puerto Ricans enjoy [also true of the center-left "Popular Democratic Part" or *Populares*]. They go into municipalities with large, historically Black communities, bribing people for votes in exchange for a household appliance they may need. This behavior is "accepted" because in Puerto Rico, such privileged people are allowed to say "my ancestors were Black" or "but we are all Puerto Rican" and allow them to claim to want to eradicate marginalization and invisibility. There's no limit to what white privilege in Puerto Rico can do when no one acknowledges that it exists. But again "if we're all Puerto Rican, why does color matter?"

Colorblindness is convenient for people when it comes to remembering that we are supposedly one race and can unite over traditions, but it's the easy way out of the "race talk", especially when you factor-in the reality that many of us have *hermanos* or *primos* or even parents and grandparents that are of a totally different "race" [for lack of a better term we can also say color here] than ourselves. It seems easy. A Puerto Rican is a Puerto Rican [yes] but colorblindness doesn't resolve anything when it comes to actual racism and racial discrimination. It simply suggests that Puerto Ricans as a whole live in a false magical utopia [a colony, mind you] of fairness, equality, and justice. Poverty in Puerto Rico isn't colorblind, invisibility in Puerto Rico isn't colorblind, and racial discrimination in Puerto Rico isn't colorblind. So if you choose to not see color, you are responsible for not acknowledging the marginalization and struggle of others —possibly your own struggles. I wouldn't blame any single Puerto Rican or single-out a group of Puerto Ricans for the existence of white supremacy because it began during the time of Spanish colonialism, but I do dare say that anyone who uses *mestizaje* and the "*somos de tres razas, somos iguales*" narrative as a way of silencing conversations on the need to deconstruct white supremacy and racism in Puerto Rico, is an avid supporter and fan of this concept, regardless of color. They may even have an obsession with white supremacy.

Acknowledging that white supremacy is deeply ingrained in Puerto Rican society is not to say that we shouldn't strive for equality, but equality is deeper than how you personally see others.

There is a difference between your indiscriminate kindness [bless your heart], and the system's "kindness." Regardless, we must call the problems in Puerto Rican society for what they are. A large amount of socio-economic inequality is a result of white supremacy that has existed in Puerto Rico since before Puerto Rico became a United States colony. This inequality throughout Puerto Rico is an intersection between both race and class, with race unfortunately being the largest determining factor. Colorblindness may be the way in which you prefer to see things in Puerto Rico, and again I say, colorblind folks are avid supporters of white supremacy, but it doesn't recognize intermittent problems that exist within Puerto Rican society, those problems being racially charged. If true colorblindness existed, race would not exist. Well—but it does.

To be clear, race is a social construct in the Americas that originates with the arrival of the Spaniards. Tribal and cultural differences were part of the mindset of pre-Columbian Native Americans, but not race as we understand it today. In our system, race categorizes and separates people based on physical appearance, mostly by skin color. Unfortunately, as a result of the way that our societies have developed with white supremacy controlling most of the world, race matters and we are forced to deal with it whether we admit to it or not, and whether it's convenient or not. But just to be clear, your race doesn't necessarily define what roots you carry [though it may]. Rather your race defines how the white supremacist system sees you and how the system treats you. Some Puerto Ricans are racially identified as Black and some are not, regardless of what they may mark on the census form. This does not mean you cannot have blonde hair, green eyes, and white skin and have African ancestry and it certainly doesn't mean that you can't have kinky curly hair and darker skin and have white ancestry. You can, but regardless of what roots you truly have, society treats you according to what they see. You can identify as you please but society will treat you according to what you look like. Racial identification is difficult to understand in a country with *mestizaje* so deeply entrenched and when you add the *mulato* representation, it becomes even more confusing. We therefore have to factor-in the "tragic *mulato* syndrome" which matters. The tragic *mulato* syndrome refers to people who really don't know what to call themselves or understand how white supremacist society will treat them. Even if I am half white [*mulato*] or even 75% white [*cuarteron*], I am physically an Afro-descendant with kinky curly hair and *piel de canela* ["cinnamon skin complexion"], and will be treated [or mistreated] as such regardless of what I decide to call myself or mark on a census form.

If the promotion of *mestizaje* in Puerto Rican society is successful in its effort to make it seem as though racism on the island and Diaspora does not exist, I am sure there wouldn't be terms in everyday vocabulary like "*pelo malo*" ["Bad Hair," or sub-Saharan tightly coiled hair]. I am also sure that travel agencies wouldn't tell African Americans who want to see and tour historically Black communities in Puerto Rico like Loíza to stay away because of their alleged violence, and I am absolutely sure Blacks and other historically Black communities on the island would be more proportionally represented in the Puerto Rican Senate and other governmental organizations, but it's not like that and that is an uncomfortable truth that we must understand.

Being intentionally conscious about race in Puerto Rico, and denying the *mestizaje* of the "*somos de tres razas…*" nonsense isn't about having a US American separatist mentality. It is about recognizing the ills which exist in our society and using our own efforts to get rid of them. Talks about racism and book chapters like this one may seem inconvenient, even uncomfortable, but imagine how inconvenient racism is, especially for Black people living in Puerto Rico. One cannot pretend that enough water in life is great because people are not thirsty and can happily ignore the fact that there is a group of people who are dehydrated and also trying to fix the leak because it doesn't affect them. One also can't believe that those of us working to fix the leak have to listen to anyone who refuses to even look at the leak because they are drinking perfectly fine.

Vamos a ponernos claros, El boricua es boricua hasta el más blanco y el más negro ["We are going to make ourselves clear, the Puerto Rican is Puerto Rican from the most white one to the most Black one"], but to ignore the implications and effects of white supremacy in Puerto Rican society, especially through concepts like colorblindness, would be inconsiderate and irresponsible of any Puerto Rican who wishes for Puerto Rico and Puerto Rican communities to thrive and to be the very best they can be. The *mestizaje* of "*somos de tres razas*" silences the work to deconstruct racism in Puerto Rico. It pretends that white privilege does not exist in Puerto Rico, it pretends that everyone is visible, it interrupts movements against anti-blackness, it silences conversations about racial discrimination, and it removes the acknowledgement of white privilege in Puerto Rico thereby allowing for racism, the main component of white supremacy, to flourish.

If you want to understand why advocates for racial equality, like myself, seemingly single-out specific groups as Black—ask not us, but consider the marginalization via white supremacy that has done so.

Notes / References:

[1] Santiago Pérez, William. 2009. "Análisis del mestizaje en Puerto Rico," *Prensa RUM*: http://www.uprm.edu/news/articles/as2009154.html.

[2] elyunque.com. nd. "The Last Taino 'Queen:' Loiza Aldea: Legend of Yuiza. Taino Cacique of Puerto Rico:" http://www.elyunque.com/loiza.htm.

[3] Fletcher, Richard. 2004. *Moorish Spain* 2nd edition. London: Phoenix Press.

[4] Beckles, Hilary McD. and Verene A. Shepherd. 2004. *Liberties Lost: Caribbean Indigenous Societies and Slave Systems*. New York: Cambridge University Press.

[5] Enciclopedia de Puerto Rico. nd. *Real Cédula de Gracia (1815)*: https://enciclopediapr.org/en/encyclopedia/real-cedula-de-gracia-1815/.

[6] Santiago, Tony. nd. "A Brief History of the Afro-Borincano:" http://www.elboricua.com/AfroBorinquenArticle.pdf.

[7] Rodríguez-Silva, Ileana. 2012. *Silencing Race: Disentangling Blackness, Colonialism, and National Identities in Puerto Rico*. New York: Palgrave Macmillan.

[8] Enciclopedia de Puerto Rico. nd. "The Abolition of Slavery (1873):" https://enciclopediapr.org/en/encyclopedia/abolition-of-slavery-1873/.

CHAPTER 5

INDICATORS OF WHITE PRIVILEGE IN LATINX COMMUNITIES

BY JENNIFER LOUBRIEL

A version of this piece was originally published in *Everyday Feminism* [1].

Quote: "I'm Latino, I wish people would stop calling me white." "Aren't all Latinxs people of color?" "If I'm Latina, how can I benefit from white privilege?"

Confusing as hell isn't it? Because even though we often associate the idea of a Latinx person with the image of a "brown person from Latin America," racial identity for Latinxs is far more complex than that. *Latinidad* refers to the cultures of both the folks living in Latin America and those in the Diaspora which encompasses dozens of nations, cultures, and ethnoracial groups. Latin America is one of the most ethnically and racially diverse regions in the world. Each nation has its own specific history of slavery, colonization, and migration that creates different racial make-ups, tensions, and systems of oppression. Because race is a social construct, it is viewed in vastly different ways across the Americas [2]. But what remains the same is that white folks—starting with the descendants of Spanish, French, and Portuguese colonizers—have always been in positions of power. The histories of white supremacy are rooted in the policies and ideologies of many of these countries and in *latinidad* as a whole. Ideas such as *mejorar la raza*—"improving the race"—have praised whiteness and light skin since colonization with rules and racial hierarchies, both in Latin America and amongst U.S. Latinxs [3]. Again, this is not to say that conceptions of whiteness are the same across Latin America and the United States [4]. Each Latin American nation has its own categorizations for race that have to do with ancestry, skin tone, and class that is different than how many of us in the U.S. think about race. But something that is similar in all of *latinidad* is this: that if you are perceived as white, you are someone who benefits the most from prevailing power structures. As Latinxs in the United States, we carry these legacies of white supremacy with us.

In my experience as a mixed Afro-Puerto Rican, I've seen and experienced the ways in which whiteness is upheld because of the way race has been constructed in both Puerto Rico and the United States. This is important. We need to be able to talk about this because of the ways in which white supremacy is a central oppressing force for Latinxs of color both within and outside our communities. And I know it can be difficult to talk about. It's easier to make sweeping statements like, "Talking about race is dividing us!" "We're all one people!" "*Viva la raza!*" But this is not a particularly helpful attitude [5]. It's important to talk about the differences within our communities because of the impact that differences have on specific Latinx subgroups. As a result of the many different ethnoracial identities in *latinidad*, we do not all navigate the world in the same way. Because whiteness is uplifted, both across Latin America and in the United States, folks who are racialized as white have many more advantages and benefits than everyone else. Even though you can be marginalized because you are simply Latinx, it does not erase the systemic white privilege you have because of your race. I know it can be difficult to think about your privileges, especially when it's directly harming your family members, friends, and other folks in your community. It can make you feel defensive or guilty that you benefit from something that you had no choice in. I also know how it can feel how talking about your whiteness will somehow minimize or erase your *latinidad*. I've often seen folks argue, "I'm discriminated against because people don't believe that I'm Latinx." I understand that this kind of personal erasure can be very hurtful. Your race doesn't determine whether you are "Latinx enough" or not [6]. However, your race does determine the kind of advantages that you are given on a systematic level, both within all Latinx communities and throughout the broader United States. It's important to remember that white privilege is about automatically having advantages on multiple levels simply because of your race. Once we as Latinxs really begin to look at the ways in which white privilege deeply and negatively impacts everyone in our communities, we can begin to unlearn all the ideas that being white means—for example, that you're harder working, smarter, more desirable, safer, and just straight-up better than everyone else.

Across Latin America and the United States, there have historically been different policies and ideologies that have centered white populations at the expense of others. Overall, these policies have led to the continued erasure and violence of anyone who isn't white. In particular, Black and Indigenous peoples in Latin America have borne the brunt of white supremacist beliefs. This is a problem because it completely erases how whiteness has been used as a tool of violence in our histories. It completely diminishes the ways that things like colonization, slavery, industrialization, and militarization have protected and upheld white people at the expense of everyone else. The ideas behind these systems and policies still affect Latin Americans today. What follows are a number of examples for how you might benefit from white privilege as a white Latinx:

[1] That most of your relatives were probably never enslaved or colonized. Of the 11.2 million enslaved Black people that were brought to the Americas, only about 450,000 were brought to the United States directly through the Africa trans-Atlantic trade; however, these numbers do not include slaves purchased through the resale market [7]. Haiti, Cuba, Puerto Rico, Panama, and Venezuela have huge populations that are descended from enslaved Africans which is often not acknowledged. At the same time, Brazil has the second largest defined Black population in the world. Since the arrival of the *conquistadores,* Indigenous peoples have been enslaved, brutalized and killed (8). Indigenous activists such as Rigoberta Menchú, have talked about the oppressio that most Indigenous peoples in Latin America still face today.

[2] That racially, there were no government regulations on your choice to have children. It has to be recognized that many countries in Latin America have laws that literally try to make you and the population as white as possible. This means that policies that support *blanqueamiento* [literally, the biological "whitening" of a people] are rampant in Latin America [9]. Particularly in the Caribbean, many governments and families encouraged folks to only reproduce with white or light skinned folks in order to have children that looked as white as possible. Modesto Broco's painting "The Redemption of Ham" directly portrays this idea. In the painting, a Black grandmother praises God because her family becomes whiter with every new generation. It shows that even in Latin American countries as ethnoracially diverse as Brazil, whiteness is valued above all else [10]. Some of these policies were directly caused by U.S. intervention and racist eugenics. In Puerto Rico, mostly poor non-white women were forcibly sterilized through governmental "population control" policies. By the 1980s, over a third of Puerto Rican women underwent *la operación*; although some wholeheartedly consented to the procedure, many others were not fully made aware of what the surgery entailed [11].

[3] That your family probably had little or no problem in migrating to Mexico, Central America or South America at any time in the past. Across Latin America, European immigrants have historically been more welcomed than other immigrants [12]. Nations like Brazil and Cuba not only welcomed European immigrants with open arms, they placed bans on "non-white" immigrants entering the country. In the early 1900s, Cuba spent a million dollars on an immigration law that encouraged European migration. This policy was enacted in order to "whiten" the island, and resulted in hundreds of thousands of Spaniards settling in Cuba [13].

[4] That violent, racist policies have most probably protected your family. Many nations, such as the Dominican Republic, have had rampantly anti-black policies that have led to mass deportations and genocide [14]. Unfortunately, these kinds of laws aren't things of the past. In recent years, the Dominican Republic has continued to deport and abuse Haitian-Dominicans because of their

blackness [15]. In 2015, author-activists Junot Diaz and Edwidge Danticat spoke at length about the anti-Haitian sentiment throughout the Dominican Republic [16]. Asian Latinxs have also faced rampant abuse because of governmental policies. Many Asian migrants, such as Chinese laborers to Mexico, were treated as second-class citizens. They and their spouses didn't receive full rights under the law [17]. Another major example of racist governmental policies occurred in Peru during World War II. Japanese-Peruvians experienced racial violence and some were even deported to the United States to be placed in internment camps [18].

[5] That in all probability, your family has always been counted in population tallies. Some nations have been so eager to only represent white people that many Indigenous and Black populations have been deliberately undercounted or left out in government documents and statistics. It wasn't until 2015 that Afro-Mexicans were even included in the national census. Their most recent census reported that over 1.3 million Mexicans self-identified as being of African descent [19]. Similarly, many Latinxs in the United States have chosen to identify as white racially on the U.S. census, whether they actually are or not. In 2010, over half of Latinxs checked off "white" as their race [20]. This is important because historically, claiming whiteness has been key to assimilation and gaining full access to citizenship [21].

[6] That you benefit from Eurocentric beauty standards—meaning that the more you look white, the more beautiful you are said to be which is a huge problem in Latinx and Black communities in general. Across the board, folks with straight hair, pale skin complexion, slim noses, and light-colored eyes are praised for the ways they look above everyone else. And while this isn't a concept that is seen only within Latinx communities, it is one that is constantly being reproduced in our families, neighborhoods, and through media [22]. The White Latinxs as the epitome of beauty are often the only Latinxs that are accorded a kind of positive representation in media throughout the Americas. Even though Eurocentric beauty standards tend to have a women-centric connotation, the idea of whiteness as perfection affects folks of all

genders in Latinx communities. Benefiting from Eurocentric beauty standards is an aspect of white privilege. One of the strongest examples of uplifting whiteness in *latinidad* is heard in comments about hair—whether or not you have *pelo malo*, or "bad hair" [23]. Folks with longer, straighter and "finer" hair are praised at the same time that those with Afro-textured, very curly, and thick hair are teased and are forced to spend hours trying to make their hair as straight as possible. Straight hair means looking—or being—more white, and is constantly valued in Latinx communities.

[7] That you've probably never been told that you're too dark to be beautiful, successful, or desirable. Along with the actual policies that have been used to physically whiten skin tones in populations across *latinidad*, there are many cultural norms that uplift pale skin complexion above all else. Colorism—or the systemic prejudice against dark-skinned people—is a huge issue in Latinx communities [24]. It's prevalent in every aspect of people's lives, from how beautiful one is perceived to be to how smart or educated one appears to be [25]. Children are still told to not date or marry anyone darker than themselves. Dark skinned Latinxs in the media are often photoshopped or use bleaching creams to appear whiter than they are in actuality [26]. In 2013, there was a national backlash against Nayara Justino, an Afro-Brazilian woman who won the honor of *Globeleza*, all because she was "too dark" [27].

[8] That you've probably been told that you resemble Latinx celebrities who are praised for their good looks. Celebrities like Christina Aguilera, Cameron Díaz, or Bella Thorne are seen as beauty and fashion icons without being exoticized because of their whiteness. And while celebrities like this have been outspoken about their *latinidad*, they seem to be much more accepted by the media in contrast to brown and Black Latinxs [28]. Meanwhile, Latinxs of color, particularly Black Latinxs, receive less praise or recognition for their work [29].

[9] That TV and films depict people who look like you in a more positive light. Within Latin American media, white Latinxs are overly represented. Beauty pageants, *telenovelas*, and news

outlets are over-represented by white Latinxs and almost never show non-white Latinxs in prominent starring roles or in other positive ways [30]. Oftentimes, Latinxs of color, particularly if they are dark-skinned, can only be in roles as background characters [31]. However, this isn't just a problem in Latin America.. Across U.S. media, brown and Black Latinxs are overrepresented as criminals [32]. Hollywood is also no stranger to whitewashing when it comes to Latinx roles. A major issue in U.S. media, both historically and in contemporary films, has been the casting of non-Latinx white actors as Latinx characters [33]. This often happens because of the assumption that *latinidad* is homogenous and mostly light-skinned. But even when Latinx actors get Latinx roles, most of these go to white or light-skinned people. As Gina Torres has pointed out, "When I became an actress, I quickly realized that the world liked their Latinas to look Italian, not like me" [34]. Most of the Latin American cultures are of course rooted in the marginalized traditions and heritages of white supremacy, but white Latin Americans and Latinxs still receive the majority of representations despite the occasional rhetoric that promotes diversity and inclusion in U.S. and the other societies.

[10] West African and Indigenous American traditions are the cornerstone of so many aspects in the art of Latin America. However, these histories are minimized or erased entirely with the traditions divorced from the circumstances of struggle against white supremacy and seen as belonging to everyone in a particular ethnic group. Furthermore, in the United States, the majority of stories that we get about *latinidad* come from white Latinxs. This means that we, and non-Latinxs in the United States, only get a very narrow, specific point of view of *latinidad*. Instead of recognizing that Latinxs come from all different cultures, families, and histories, we continue to learn the same often negative or dismissive narratives about non-white Latinxs. More often than not, those narratives come from white Latinxs who have class privilege. They are the ones who can quite literally afford to put their art out there, and whose works are consumable by mainstream media. Representation in the arts is an example of white privilege because you are more likely to be recognized for your musical and other artistic talents. Despite the fact that many artistic

and specifically musical traditions, such as *bomba*, *plena*, *salsa*, *merengue*, *bachata*, Latin jazz, and the *tango* (etc.) directly stem from the rhythms, beats, and music of enslaved Africans brought to Latin America and their descendants, Black Latinxs are rarely in the spotlight [35]. What often happens is that these Afro-influenced rhythms and dances are hailed as staples of Latin American nations overall. They become national and cultural traditions without much reflection on the oppressive histories behind them. With the exception of artists like Celia Cruz, most of the famous Latinx musicians to break into mainstream U.S. music are white or of light skin. This is even true of religious, musical and dance traditions, such as *candomblé*, whose roots in enslaved Black communities are celebrated. Carlos Paez Vilaro, a white Uruguayan, was world-renowned for his art and music, all of which was influenced by Afro-Uruguayan culture [36].

[11] That you are more likely to be recognized in the visual arts than non-white Latinxs with some exceptions that prove the rule. Famous Latin American artists like Frida Kahlo, while extremely important and inspirational to many Latinxs, also have had protection because of their racial and class backgrounds. Although Frida experienced oppression as a disabled woman in Mexico, she had many privileges because of the wealth of her mostly European family background. She had direct access to education, healthcare, and money because of her whiteness [37]. Frida's art was based on the foundation of Indigenous, post Columbian *mestizo* Mexican and 20th century European art. Frida was able to adapt her art and style based on Indigenous groups that did not have the same access that she had [38]. However, 20th century *mestizo* Mexican artists were able to have access and became successful in the years after the Mexican revolution (after 1920) including Diego Rivera and Rufino Tamayo. These artists and others were also influential among U.S. Latinxs and even U.S. based Anglo American and Black artists. Examples included the many Mexican American and other Latinx muralists across the country and their works seen in various parts of the country since the 1930s. There are also the specific contemporary artists such as Juan Sánchez, Diogenes Ballester, Daphne Arthur, Annette Martínez, and the late Rafael Tufiño (defined as white) among others. These artists can be said

to be Afro-Puerto Ricans or just Latinxs in one way or another. Frida's work is now renowned worldwide after a long period of neglect, but the art of defined Indigenous peoples—many of whom are still around today—has not been acknowledged in recent decades except for their "folk art" highlighted in certain countries.

[12] That you are more likely to be recognized in the literary arts as opposed to non-white Latinxs, again with some exceptions. White Latinx writers, although sometimes racialized as "brown" within the United States, still benefit from their European ancestors and affluence. These Latinxs, even though writing in the Diaspora, have been able to pursue their crafts because of generational wealth based on their education which has been supported by their wealthy white families of Spanish ancestry. Julia Álvarez talks about this a bit in her essay, "A White Woman of Color" [39]. Narratives similar to Julia's—the ones about Latinxs who were wealthy in their homeland, and then faced discrimination in the United States, before ultimately regaining their wealth—are some of the only stories about *latinidad* that's in mainstream literature. This is an issue because it perpetuates the idea that these stories represent all Latin American and Latinx experiences. As Chimamanda Ngozi Adichie said, "the single story creates stereotypes, and the problem with stereotypes is not that they are untrue, but that they are incomplete. They make one story become the only story" [40].

[13] While white Latinxs certainly can—and do—experience xenophobia once folks discover that they are not *gringos*, it is true that white Latinxs are rarely or less targeted when it comes to racist and xenophobic policies. When you listen to the rhetoric and images that are used to stereotype and threaten Latinxs, it is not white Latinxs who are being attacked. Along the east coast of the U.S. it tends to be blackness, especially when it comes to their alleged assumed criminal behavior [41]. We know this both within Latinx communities and outside of it. As folks who are seen as white, you are usually seen as non-threatening in the eyes of law enforcement and the government. This, along with class privileges, also means that white Latinxs experience these kinds of official behaviors and attitudes in the same way that Anglo-American

white folks experience them in contrast to non-white Latinxs, African Americans, other Blacks and other non-whites. Policies that have forcibly sterilized, incarcerated, and deported Latinxs of color have very rarely affected white Latinxs [42]. Whiteness is a visible shield for white Latinxs who are protected against policies that are based on physical appearance [and connected to assumed citizenship status]. For example, police violence is no stranger to Latinx communities, particularly for those of us who are Black and low-income [43]. Specific laws like New York's "stop and frisk" specifically targeted Black and brown folks including non-white Latinxs, but not necessarily white Latinxs, unless they lived in "minority" dominant neighborhood [the hood] defined as problematic and high crime. According to the New York Civil Liberties Union, the police stopped New Yorkers 45,787 times because of stop and frisk policies [44]. Fifty three percent of folks stopped were identified as Black while 27% were identified as Latino. And when data uses "Latino" as a racial identity, chances are that it's speaking about Latinxs with brown and dark skin.

[14] That you are less likely to be viewed as undocumented by law enforcement. Arizona's S.B. 1070 and other laws are largely based on racially profiling folks to determine citizenship status [45]. Again, these kinds of laws specifically target folks who are viewed as non-white. As the American Civil Liberties Union put it, "apart from appearance, it's hard to imagine any way a police officer could suspect that someone was not in the country legally under these rules. The question could be what other factors could they use? Could they use accent and language? Could they use that they're near another person who admits that he or she is undocumented? Could they use alleged "foreign dress" [46]? This doesn't even begin to get into the rampant human rights violations that occur when law enforcement agencies take undocumented folks into custody. Law enforcement officers, such as former Arizona sheriff, Joe Arpaio, were notorious for their abuse of undocumented people—all of which is rooted in xenophobic racism [47].

To summarize, benefiting from white privilege doesn't erase your latinidad. But recognizing the ways in which white Latinxs do experience privilege is important when we think about the ways in which white supremacy functions in our society. it gives us all a more nuanced look into our own histories, cultures, and positions of power. It also helps us all to understand how much power whiteness is systemically afforded across the world. *Latinidad* will never thrive if we continue to praise and uplift only whiteness. Understanding your white privilege means you can begin to actively support the racially marginalized people within *latinidad*. You can use and should use your privilege in order to uplift the voices, experiences, and stories of Latinxs of color.

Notes:

[1] Jennifer Loubriel, "14 Examples of White Privilege in Latinx Communities," *Everyday Feminism*, April 6, 2016: https://everydayfeminism.com/2016/04/latinx-white-privilege/.

[2] This is not a new theory. For more of an introduction on what "race as a social construct" means, see Audrey, Smedley, "'Race' and the Construction of Human Identity," *American Anthropologist*, September, 1998, accessed December, 2017: http://www.jstor.org/stable/682047. For more on why race is central to these conversations, see Melissa A. Fabello, "Yes Race Is a Social Construct – Here's Why It Still Matters," *Everyday Feminism*, February 5, 2015, accessed March, 2016: https://everydayfeminism.com/2015/02/yes-race-still-matters/.

[3] María Alejandra Casale-Hardin, "'*Mejorar la Raza'*: An Example of Racism in Latino Culture," *Huffington Post*, June 15, 2015, accessed March 2016: https://www.huffingtonpost.com/maria-alejandra-casalehardin-/mejorar-la-raza-an-exampl_b_7558892.html.

[4] Kali Holloway, "10 Insidious Ways White Supremacy Shows Up in Our Everyday Lives," *Everyday Feminism*, September 1, 2015, accessed March 2016: https://everydayfeminism.com/2015/09/white-supremacy-everyday-life/.

[5] Jon Greenberg, "13 Things Even More Divisive Than People Who Always Bring Race Up in Discussions," *Everyday Feminism*, February 1, 2016, accessed March, 2016: https://everydayfeminism.com/2016/02/more-divisive-than-race/.

[6] Nicholle LaMartina Palacios, "Being a White Latina: A Reflection on Racial And Ethnic Identities," *Huffington Post*, January 31, 2015, accessed March, 2016: https://www.huffingtonpost.com/nicholle-lamartina-palacios/being-a-white-latina-a-re_b_6238242.html.

[7] "Q&A with Professor Henry Louis Gates, Jr.," *PBS*, November 11, 2015, accessed March, 2016: http://www.pbs.org/wnet/black-in-latin-america/featured/qa-with-professor-henry-louis-gates-jr/164/.

[8] Just one example of the many Indigenous people who have been silenced is Berta Cáceres. She was a Honduran activist and leader who was murdered in her home in March, 2016. For more information see Jonathan Blitzer, "The Death of Berta Cáceres," *The New Yorker*, June 19, 2017, accessed December, 2017: https://www.newyorker.com/news/news-desk/the-death-of-berta-caceres.

[9] Alyssa García, "Blanqueamiento," *The Oxford Encyclopedia of Latinos and Latinas in the United States*, 2005.

[10] All Things Considered, "Skin Color Still Plays A Big Role in Ethnically Diverse Brazil," *NPR*, September 19, 2013, accessed December, 2017: https://www.npr.org/2013/09/19/224152635/skin-color-still-plays-big-role-in-ethnically-diverse-brazil.

[11] Iris López, "The Birth Control Movement in Puerto Rico," *Matters of Choice: Puerto Rican Women's Struggle for Reproductive Freedom*, (New Brunswick: Rutgers University Press, 2008): 3-19.

[12] A. Moore, "5 Nations That Imported Europeans to Whiten the Population," *Atlanta Black Star*, March 10, 2014, accessed March, 2016: http://atlantablackstar.com/2014/03/10/5-black-nations-that-imported-europeans-to-whiten-the-population/.

[13] Henry Louis Gates, Jr., "Black in Latin America: Cuba - The Next Revolution," Directed by Ricardo Pollack, (Arlington, VA: *Public Broadcasting Service—PBS*. 2011): https://search.alexanderstreet.com/view/work/bibliographic_entity%7Cvideo_work%7C2362693.

[14] Michele Wucker, "The Dominican Republic's Shameful Deportation Legacy," *Foreign Policy*, October 9, 2015, accessed March 2016: http://foreignpolicy.com/2015/10/08/dominican-republic-haiti-trujillo-immigration-deportation/.

[15] Jonathan M. Katz, "In Exile," *The New York Times*, January 13, 2016, accessed December, 2017: https://www.nytimes.com/2016/01/17/magazine/haitians-in-exile-in-the-dominican-republic.html.

[16] Associated Press in Miami, "Junot Díaz and Edwidge Danticat condemn deportations of Haitians," *The Guardian*, June 25, 2015, accessed December, 2017: https://www.theguardian.com/us-news/2015/jun/25/junot-diaz-edwidge-danticat-condemn-dominican-republic-haitian-migrants.

[17] Julia María Schiavone Camacho, "The Women Are Neither Chinese nor Mexican," *Chinese Mexicans: Transpacific Migration and the Search for a Homeland, 1910-1960*, (Chapel Hill: University of North Carolina Press, 2012): 105-120.

[18] Jaime González de Gispert, "The Japanese-Peruvians interned in the US during WW2," *BBC News*, February 22, 2015, accessed December, 2017: http://www.bbc.com/news/world-latin-america-31295270.

[19] Yara Simón, "1.38 Million Afro-Descendants Are Identified on the Mexican Census for the First Time," *Remezcla*, December 10, 2015, accessed March, 2016: remezcla.com/culture/afro-mexicans-identified-on-mexico-census-first-time/.

[20] "Afro-Latinos Seek Recognition, And Accurate Census Count," *NBCNews.com*, September 21, 2014, accessed December, 2017: https://www.nbcnews.com/storyline/hispanic-heritage-month/afro-latinos-seek-recognition-accurate-census-count-n207426.

[21] Gene Demby, "On The Census, Who Checks 'Hispanic,' Who Checks 'White,' And Why," *NPR*, June 16, 2014, accessed December, 2017: https://www.npr.org/sections/codeswitch/2014/06/16/321819185/on-the-census-who-checks-hispanic-who-checks-white-and-why.

[22] Maisha Z. Johnson, "10 Ways the Beauty Industry Tells You Being Beautiful Means Being White," *Everyday Feminism*, January 3, 2016, accessed March, 2016: https://everydayfeminism.com/2016/01/when-beauty-equals-white/.

[23] Awilda González, "No More '*Pelo Malo*:' My Love-Hate Relationship with My Hair," *The Body is Not an Apology*, March 28, 2015, accessed March, 2016: https://thebodyisnotanapology.com/magazine/no-more-pelo-malo-my-love-hate-relationship-with-my-hair/.

[24] Alice Walker first defined "colorism" as "prejudicial or preferential treatment of same-race people based solely on their color." See Alice Walker, In *Search of Our Mothers' Gardens: Womanist Prose* (San Diego, CA: Harcourt Brace Jovanovich, 1983).

[25] Raquel Reichard, "11 Examples of Light Skin Privilege in Latinx Communities," *Everyday Feminism*, March 25, 2016, accessed March, 2016:

https://everydayfeminism.com/2016/03/light-skin-privilege-latinxs/.

[26] Nicole Akoukou Thompson, "Skin Color Politics, African Diaspora and Latinos in America and Latin America: Denouncement of Ethnic Identity [SERIES]--PART I," *Latin Post*, March 3, 2014, accessed March, 2016: http://www.latinpost.com/articles/8095/20140303/skin-color-politics-african-diaspora-latinos-in-america-latin-america-denouncement-of-ethnic-identity.htm.

[27] Black Girl with Long Hair, "Brazil Ditched its First Dark-Skinned Carnival Queen for Being Too Black," *Black Girl with Long Hair*, February 13, 2016, accessed March, 2016: http://blackgirllonghair.com/2016/02/brazil-ditched-its-first-dark-skinned-carnival-queen-for-being-too-black/.

[28] Laura Steiner, "Christina Aguilera Addresses 'Not Latina Enough' Criticism, Opens Up About Her Hispanic Heritage and Estranged Father," *The Huffington Post*, February 07, 2012, accessed March, 2016: https://www.huffingtonpost.com/2012/02/07/christina-aguilera-_n_1258067.html.

[29] Carolina Moreno, "9 Famous Faces On The Struggles And Beauty Of Being Afro-Latino," *The Huffington Post*, March 20, 2016, accessed December, 2017: https://www.huffingtonpost.com/entry/9-famous-faces-on-the-struggles-and-beauty-of-being-afro-latino_us_56c3a3cee4b08ffac126ecd9.

[30] Matt Sandy and Morgann Jezequel, "Brazilian soap operas slowly cast black middle class," *Al Jazeera America*, April 11, 2015, accessed March, 2016: http://america.aljazeera.com/multimedia/2015/4/brazilian-soap-operas-slowly-cast-black-middle-class.html.

[31] Carolina Moreno, "This Latina Is Calling Out *Telenovelas* For Being 'Overtly White,'" *The Huffington Post*, March 13, 2017, accessed December, 2017: https://www.huffingtonpost.com/entry/this-latina-is-calling-out-telenovelas-for-being-overtly-white_us_58c70082e4b0428c7f1261e0.

[32] Princess Weekes, "In Lack of Representation News: Less Than 5% of TV Writers Are Black & Half of Latinx Characters Are Criminals," *The Mary Sue*, November 2, 2017, accessed December, 2017: https://www.themarysue.com/most-latinxs-black-writers/.

[33] Cristina Arreola, "13 Times White People Stole Latino Roles," *Latina Magazine*, January 29, 2016, accessed December, 2017: http://www.latina.com/entertainment/movies/roles-white-people-stole-latinos.

[34] Amen Oyiboke, "Afro-Latinos Are Missing From Pop Culture & It's Time We Right This Wrong," *Bustle*, March 6, 2016, accessed December, 2017: https://www.bustle.com/p/afro-latinos-are-missing-from-pop-culture-its-time-we-right-this-wrong-40112.

[35] For articles on these specific traditions, see David González, "A Beat Calls Puerto Ricans to Their African Roots," *The New York Times*, June 7, 2015, accessed March, 2016: https://www.nytimes.com/2015/06/08/nyregion/calling-puerto-ricans-to-their-african-roots-with-the-sound-of-his-drum.html. Also see "Bobby Sanabria: Latin Jazz's West African Roots," *NPR*, February 7, 2009 , accessed March, 2016: https://www.npr.org/templates/story/story.php?storyId=100307740 and Michael T. Luongo, "Argentina Rediscovers Its African Roots," *The New York Times*, September 12, 2014, accessed March, 2016: https://www.nytimes.com/2014/09/14/travel/argentina-rediscovers-its-african-roots.html.

[36] Associated Press, "Carlos Paez Vilaro Dies at 90; Uruguayan Mural Artist and Musician," *Los Angeles Times*, February 25, 2014, accessed December 2017: http://www.latimes.com/local/obituaries/la-me-carlos-paez-vilaro-20140226-story.html.

[37] AfroDiaspores. *Tumblr post*. May 3, 2015, accessed March, 2017: http://afrodiaspores.tumblr.com/post/118038120788/mestiza-whit-passing-or-not-is-still-mestiza-many.

[38] Eren Cervantes-Altamirano, "Understanding Mexican Nationalism and Mestizaje Through the Film 'Coco,'" *Identity Crisis*, November 27, 2017, accessed December, 2016: https://erenarruna.com/2017/11/27/understanding-mexican-nationalism-and-mestizaje-through-the-film-coco/.

[39] Julia Álvarez, "A White Woman of Color," *Hungry Mind Review*, Spring, 1998, accessed March, 2016: https://writingbb.files.wordpress.com/2010/06/alvarez_white.pdf.

[40] Chimamanda Ngozi Adichie, "The Danger of a Single Story," *TEDtalk*, 2009, accessed March, 2016: https://www.ted.com/talks/chimamanda_adichie_the_danger_of_a_single_story/transcript?language=en.

[41] Gabrielle Jackson, "Black, Undocumented And Fighting To Survive," *The Huffington Post*, June 2, 2017, accessed December, 2017: https://www.huffingtonpost.com/entry/undocumented-black_us_593178eae4b075bff0f2b281.

[42] Raquel Reichard, "10 Acts of State Violence Latinas Encounter in the U.S.," *Latina Magazine*, February 4, 2016, accessed March, 2016: http://www.latina.com/lifestyle/our-issues/state-violence-latinas.

[43] Jennifer Loubriel, "9 Simple Ways to Reduce Police Violence Against People of Color in the US," *Everyday Feminism*, September 9, 2016, accessed December, 2017:

https://everydayfeminism.com/2016/09/ways-to-reduce-police-violence/.

[44] “Stop-and-Frisk Data,” *New York Civil Liberties Union*, July 29, 2017, accessed December. 2017: https://www.nyclu.org/en/stop-and-frisk-data.

[45] Bill Chappell, “Deal Is Reached On Arizona's Hardline Immigration Law, After 6-Year Fight,” *NPR*, September 16, 2016, accessed December, 2017: https://www.npr.org/sections/thetwo-way/2016/09/16/494245921/deal-is-reached-on-arizonas-hardline-immigration-law-after-6-year-fight.

[46] “Frequently Asked Questions about the Arizona Racial Profiling Law,” *American Civil Liberties Union*, accessed March, 2016: https://www.aclu.org/other/frequently-asked-questions-about-arizona-racial-profiling-law?redirect=frequently-asked-questions-about-arizona-racial-profiling-law.

[47] Stephen Lemons, “The Enduring Sins of Joe Arpaio: Newspapermen, Michael Lacey and Jim Larkin, Speak Out in Response to Donald Trump’s Pardon of America’s Worst Sheriff,” *Phoenix New Times*, November 17, 2017, accessed December, 2017: http://www.phoenixnewtimes.com/news/lacey-larkin-speak-out-on-trump-pardon-of-arpaio-9879938.

CHAPTER 6

ANTI-BLACKNESS IN THE LATINX COMMUNITY

BY RAQUEL SOLLA

The Latinx community is extremely diverse racially. Within the Latinx community there are both whites, blacks and peoples of mixed background. Although society is slowly accepting the concept of people within the Latinx community as being something other than brown, the majority of society has yet to accept that whiteness does not solely mean Anglo-white, and blackness does not solely mean African-American. The lack of acceptance of this concept has been the result of a minimal or lack of focus in the media and elsewhere on the racial bigotry that can be seen within Latinx communities.

There's a common misconception that a racial hierarchy does not exist within the Latinx community, which is absolutely the case. White Latinos and Afro-Latinos experience two different Americas, and thus cannot be placed into this box of having the same Latino-American experience.

In the United States, this separation has manifested itself in very interesting ways. More often than not, white Latinos are able to keep their Latino identity and benefit from white privilege, while a sizable proportion of the Afro-Latinos have their Latino identity erased by our society. This may be changing, but it's changing in an agonizingly slow manner. While the cause of all this is debatable, one thing is clear, there's a distinct separation between different racial identifications within the Latino community.

Of course, with Latino whiteness, we also get the concept of white supremacy. It's been allowed to manifest itself in the following manner because Latinos are not often checked, or do not check their own privilege because they are not Anglo-Americans. In other words, white privilege, black oppression and racism is directed towards Afro-Latinos in the Latinx community and goes largely unchallenged.

In the past three years [2015], we've seen *Univision* TV Host, Rodner Figueroa, compare Michelle Obama to a simian from the "Planet of the Apes," the Miss Puerto Rico winner for Miss America get suspended over Anti-Muslim tweets [many outlets reported her suspension as being due to "poor interactions with the media"], and a slew of mostly white-Latinos attack Steve Harvey with brutally racist remarks regarding the Miss Columbia controversy at a recent Ms. Universe pageant. Most of this has gone largely under-reported in mainstream media, perhaps because many people aren't sure how to address bigotry coming from non-Anglo-Americans including African Americans and others..

There's even been speculation as to whether white Latinos have more racist tendencies than Afro-Latinos. As someone with a white mom and Latino father, you might expect that I've experienced more anti-black rhetoric from the white side of my family when in fact, the opposite is true. I'm not alone in this observation. But more often than not, it's anti-blackness that is present in the everyday lives of Latino families regardless of their defined or self-articulated racial background.

As a white Latina, I've been praised for my light skin and blue eyes, while my Afro-Latina cousins have been called "pretty for black girls." I've never really thought of ever changing my hair, while my Afro-Latina cousins constantly change their hair to look more like mine. A white-Latina cousin of mine has been criticized for dating a black man, while my other white-Latina cousin has been showered with compliments for dating her white Latino boyfriend. The bigotry present in our Latinx families can be seen when we converse outside of our families, as well.

The best evidence of this is to log onto Twitter, and check the hashtag #AllLivesMatter. A lot of these tweets are full of bigotry from Latinxs who repeat terms they've heard their own family members use to denigrate and insult black Americans. That in itself, is extremely ironic. Being a Latinx implies a cohesion of culture—native, black and European. It's painful to watch members of my Puerto Rican family and others post racist things all over Facebook when so much of Latinx culture takes from black culture. Unfortunately, the all too often denial that our own culture draws from black culture is also part of our problem.

From certain perspectives, it might seem natural that Latinx community members would stand in solidarity with movements like Black Lives Matter. In reality, we have a massive amount of silence and anti-blackness from the Latinx community. The first thing we need to do to change the anti-blackness in our community is to challenge our friends and family members who perpetuate anti-blackness. It starts in the home with our families, and it can start and also begin to end there. It may seem daunting to call out a mother, aunt, or uncle, but isn't it a bit more daunting to stay silent and let this cycle of prejudice and hate continue?

CHAPTER 7

MEXICAN AND ARGENTINIAN AMERICAN PERSPECTIVES ON WHITE LATINO PRIVILEGE

BY NICHOLLE LaMARTINA AND JULIE RAMÍREZ

Editor's Note: The two sub-chapters that follow have been written by white Latinas who have acknowledged their privileged status and have called for corrective action. Comments by white Latinos and others who have minimized or denied that there is racism and white Latino privilege in the Spanish-speaking Caribbean, its Diaspora and elsewhere are found in the Response section below [Chapter 10].

Being A White Latina: Reflections On Racial And Ethnic Identities from an Argentinian American

By Nicholle LaMartina

When speaking about my racial identity, it is impossible not to also talk about my ethnic identity because for me these two concepts have gone hand in hand. We live in a country [the U.S.] where race is a dichotomy and people are literally separated into categories of black and white, but human identities are not that simple. How one regards one's ethnicity and the cultural background with which one has grown up with, will inevitably shape the way in which one sees oneself through a racial lens, and will also affect the way one is seen from the outside. When talking about my own racial identity, I cannot just speak about the color of my skin nor the box I check off on applications, because not only would that be an injustice to myself but it would also negate the reality of the complexities and nuances that arise when we try to essentialize and simplify people's ethnological narratives.

My racial and ethnic identifications have been affected in a major way by the fact that I grew up in New York City—"the central diasporic location for [many] transnational communities historically and in our times" according to the late scholar, Juan Flores. I was born and raised in Queens to an Argentine mother and an Italian-American father, but spent my formative years with my grandmother and mother in a Spanish speaking home. While growing up in Queens, the most diverse borough of New York. Almost every single one of my friends was either an immigrant or the child of immigrant parents. Because of the wide variety of races and ethnicities that live in Queens—the question always arose—"where are you from?," "what's your nationality?," and "what are you?" These were common questions starting at a very young age. And even if your nationality is American and you were born in the States, people auto-matically connect themselves to their parent's or grandparent's countries since this is what is expected of us in this country. I have never heard anyone say "I am American" even if they technically are. When presented with these questions I used to respond with "I'm Hispanic, from Argentina" and thought it was just as easy as that. I never identified with my skin color or with the racial categorization of "white" and always found myself connecting to a greater pan-Latino community, regardless of the race of other students. My identification as a Latina from this young age was reflected in the AOL Instant Messenger username I made when I was 12 years old: "BaNgInLaTiNa17." However, after entering college and starting to travel internationally and taking ethnicity, race, and migration [ER&M] classes, I realized that my ethnic identification was complicated by both my race and my United States nationality. Since then, my ethnic and racial identity has been something I have constantly struggled with.

Although my family is from Argentina, I am from the United States, which complicates my ethnic and racial identity. During the spring semester of my sophomore year at Yale, I decided to take a semester off from school in order to live with my family in Buenos Aires. This had been one of my first experiences outside of the

States, and was the first time I realized my racial/ethnic identity changed according to context [I should note that this was before taking any ER&M classes]. I found out that within the context of Argentina itself, I was considered *estadounidense* [United States North American] and that people considered me *una gringa* [a U.S. foreign white woman]. The labels "*Latina*" and "Argentine" did not travel with me to Argentina itself. And as I continued to backpack across several other countries in South America and eventually to several countries in Europe, I realized that my own self-identifications—the ones I had grown-up with so comfortably since my elementary school days in Queens, were often-times not considered valid outside of the United States.

After returning from my semester off, I decided to take my first ER&M class at Yale. During the critical discussions of *latinidad* and how *latinidad* intersects with race, my whole outlook on my racial identification changed. Though I had become aware of my "whiteness" while in South America, I had been reluctant to identify as being white and accept that I was *una gringa.* Although I still dismiss the notion of being a *gringa*—reading scholarly material and discussing race relations with my classmates in my Latino NY seminar made it clear to me that despite being Latina, I have white privilege. Under the limited racial categories available to us in our vernacular, I am white.

During and after taking my Latino NY seminar, I began to spend much time thinking critically about my race and trying to understand how it has influenced and shaped my life. I wanted to know how my experience as a white-Latina varied from the lived experiences of other Latinos. I took note of the fact that with my European features and light skin complexion comes white privilege and the ability to merge into what is considered an "American" world which is not an option many other people of Latino descent have. For fair-skinned Latinos, the racial category of "white" is often assigned to us and available to us, which in a way seems a bit like an oxymoron. The term Latino has often been associated with marginalization and repression, while the term white is associated with control and domination. These two when combined present us with a very complicated idea or phenomenon which is difficult to come to terms with and to reflect on.

Although I certainly cannot complain about being in a

position of privilege when it comes to my skin color and Anglo features, I have realized that it has shaped the way in which I connect to my *latinidad* and to the community at large. After a few Latino studies courses, I became aware that in order to be regarded as "*Latina*," I have to assert my *latinidad* and constantly prove it – either through my use of Spanish, my ability to dance to Latin dances, or by explaining my family history, etc. This contrasts greatly with the lived experiences of many other Latinos, especially those of color. As one Dominican man who moved to Providence as a teenager said:

> "I think my children will be Dominican-Americans, my grandchildren, I don't know. But you know, we will always be Latinos. You Argentinians look like Italians, you can merge in this country, but look how we look, our skin is different, our color is different, and also our culture is different and you know how much we value very much our culture and our ways. We can never merge, we are going to be like other communities, different, powerful but different. We are always going to be Latinos."

My experiences have also been affected by the fact that I am a second-generation immigrant. I first realized this after reading Jorge Duany's book *Blurred Borders: Transnational Migration between the Hispanic Caribbean and the United States* during the summer of 2013. According to the concept of "segmented assimilation" that he discusses, it is common for second-generation immigrations of racialized groups such as Afro-Dominicans and Haitians to be stuck in a path of "downward assimilation," a phenomena in which a group of people adopts negative traits from the culture they are assimilating into rather than "mainstream values and customs" due to their inability to find support within the mainstream culture. However, most second-generation Latinos that are not racialized, such as many Cubans who experience "selective acculturation," the acquiring of certain "normative" aspects of society, and upward mobility in the United States. Through the lens of this framework, I relate more to the Cuban experience. My lived experience is very different from that of the many Latinos in NYC that have been racialized and continued to stay within what is considered a "minority" culture—thus not receiving the same opportunities that I have access to. Because of my fair skin complexion and "whiteness," I am allowed the privilege of selecting which parts of "Latino culture" I want to relate to—ergo exercising selective acculturation. After reading Duany, I realized that I could hide my Latino identity when needed in order to move upwards in our prejudiced and discriminatory society yet use my Spanish and experiences of growing up in a South American immigrant household when I so choose to do so.

My cultural identity is not static and is constantly changing depending on my geographical location, a specific situation, and who I am speaking with. Race and ethnicities are imagined concepts and they are extremely complicated to understand and define. I am Argentinian, I am white, I am not-white, I am Latina, I am *gringa*, I am European, I am South American, I am American—I am all of these things. We must not forget that race and ethnicity should not be viewed as separate, independent entities; they are concepts that are constantly at play with each other and with multiple other factors. These various forms of self-identification and of assigned identifications have had and continue to have enormous influences on people's self-perceptions, their lived experiences, and the way in which communities function. None of these issues are simple nor straightforward, and there is definitely a need to create more spaces in which people can reflect on their own racial and ethnic identities and how they have shaped their lives and the lives of their fellow humans.

A Mexican American reflects on the events that took place in Charlottesville, Virginia on August 11-12, 2017.
by Julie Ramírez

"A Charlottesville Attacker Says He "Isn't Racist Because He's Puerto Rican"

Last week I saw this headline in the news. The situation at Charlottesville was upsetting enough on its own but reading that headline took my disbelief to a new level. I have news for you: you can be racist and privileged even if you're Latinx. Colorism is a real issue within people of color, including colorism within Latinx communities. It is defined as discrimination based purely on the social values associated with skin color and it's a divisive issue that drives wedges within and between races.

As a Mexican who has fair skin, I can say that I have experienced first-hand the privilege and benefits of looking "white" both in the US and in Mexico. However, one of the biggest problems is that when we are privileged [white, straight, able-bodied, class privileged, cisgender male, or any combination of two or more of these], it can lead us to be oblivious to the experiences of others [women, POC, gay, religious, non-religious].

To be completely honest, I did not acknowledge my own privilege until I moved to the United States. When I first arrived here 6 years ago, people back home would ask me about my experience with racism in America and I remember thinking to myself "It's not that bad, I haven't had any problems." And well, here's the thing. As long as people didn't hear me talk or learn my last name, I could pass for a white American girl, which as hard as it was to admit, made me feel safe.

Yet every so often, when I meet new people, whether during an Uber [taxi] ride, or a new job, or at networking events, or at a friend's reunion, I'm asked a supposedly harmless question that becomes the gateway to casual racism: "Where are you from?"—they ask me. I know what they mean. They've heard my accent. In a subtle effort to deviate their attention from the foreignness they seek to pinpoint, I reply: "I live in Chicago." They give me a curious look and follow-up with: "No, but where are you really from?" When I say I'm from Mexico, I've gotten mixed reactions—sometimes disappointment, sometimes interest, but most of the time, it's disbelief.

"No way! You can't be! You don't look Mexican!"—they often respond as they marvel at my looks. Their tone usually implies that their reaction is meant to be a compliment, as though I should be proud not to have the common features or skin tone that come with "looking Mexican." I've never been ashamed of where I come from, but people don't understand that asking a question like this has so many implications. It is a dangerous zone because the conversation can go in a judgmental and racist direction from "I took Spanish" in High School, to "Oh, I love Mexico, I've been to Cancún/Tijuana" during my college years. I used to be most amused by their culture shock at the beginning, but the more and more I had this kind of interaction, I felt the need to explain how offensive those comments could be.

As much as it angers me when I experience this, I will admit that these kinds of stereotypical comments, among a few other occasional racial comments, are the worst experiences I've had with racism—and I have to admit that I'm privileged because of that. It does not compare with the discrimination and restriction to resources that Latinos with darker complexion or Indigenous features get. While white Latinos still experience discrimination to a certain degree from Anglo-whites, we have been able to pass as honorary whites and benefit from the inequalities formed by white supremacy. This is not new, and it has a history. The basic social and economic tenets of colonial Latin America were based on race. During the conquest and colonization of Mexico, and Latin America as a whole, the Spanish adopted a detailed and complex racial caste system which informed one's socioeconomic status in society, with the top of the hierarchy being the *criollos*, who were white [from Spain] and then the different combinations trickled down the ladder.

These racial differences and statuses are so engrained in our culture that sometimes we are guilty of offending other minorities and acting to discriminate against our own. The Charlottesville riot is not the first time Latinos have appeared in news headlines exposing our racism. The shooting of an unarmed African American teenager, Trayvon Martin, by a half-Peruvian and half-White man named George Zimmerman and the racist comments against Michelle Obama by Latinos in the media like those of Spanish language TV personality, Rodner Figueroa, are examples of this.

I am not trying to say that Latinos with fair skin or who are in a more privileged position are bad. But I do want to point out that for some of us, it is easier to have our opinions and our voices heard by the public at large. When we have access to resources, we have power and we can use that to fight oppression. We need the full spectrum of Latinos to be represented in the workforce, in TV, movies, media and most importantly in politics.

From state and local officials to Congress, most Latino politicians representing our community are light-complexioned or straight-up white-passing individuals. How can the Latino community be fairly represented when most Latinos in leadership positions have hardly experienced diversity and discrimination? Just take a look at the Latino *politicos* getting the most media attention these days—Republicans Ted Cruz and Marco Rubio. Sure they can represent us, as long as they acknowledge and most importantly share and relinquish some of their privilege. That is the key, but they seem not to—especially Ted Cruz for example.

Writing this chapter and the blog it was based-on was tougher for me than I thought because I realized that acknowledging my own privilege is not enough anymore. I need to give it up. We, minorities that have more power, need to use our privilege to fight racism. It is important to realize that just because we don't experience discrimination as other people do, it doesn't mean that it doesn't exist. We as Latinos can be our own worst enemy when it comes to racism. Just because we're within a minority doesn't give us a free pass to be offensive to others and especially not within our own community.

No matter who you are and with whom you identify, racism affects us all, and for some, it can lead to tragic consequences. Privilege can blind us. But once we open our minds and see beyond our own bubble, we are able to see when others are being mistreated. However big or small the offence may be, not everyone has the opportunity and privilege to dismiss or suppress those obstacles.

Regardless of how much privilege we have, if we have more power than someone else, then it is our job to speak-up in the face of injustice. It is our job to give voice to others when it's not our so-called place to comment on someone else's experience. It is our job to demand our workplace, school and other structured environments to ensure inclusion and equity at every level. There are other people outside our own experience. It is our job to acknowledge them. It is our job to empower them. It is our job to respect them.

CHAPTER 8

WHITE LATINO RACISM ON THE RISE: IT'S TIME FOR A SERIOUS CONVERSATION ON EURO-DIASPORIC WHITENESS

BY WILLIAM GARCÍA

A common misconception that exists today rests on the notion that there are no racial hierarchies in Latin American countries or within the Latino communities in the United States. In other words, Latino [or Hispanic] is itself a race. For many, this conversation is a pointless squabble that halts the true need for unity amongst marginalized Latinos in the United States. Unfortunately, overlooking the importance of this issue has in fact exposed the separation and a lack of interest in each other's problems.

The February 2012 shooting of unarmed African-American teenager, Trayvon Martin, by a half-Peruvian and half-white male named George Zimmerman, the rise of so-called Hispanic conservatives like Ted Cruz, Al Cardenas and Marco Rubio, and the examples of racist comments by Latinos in the media like TV personality, Rodner Figueroa, and others, have made it largely impossible to have a conversation on Latinos and race. It is becoming clear that whites from Latin America, although marginalized by Anglo-whites, have been able to pass as honorary whites and benefit from the inequalities formed by white supremacy. This is not new, and it has a history.

Many people who neglect to explore the actual history of Latin Americans in the United Sates do not know or remember people like the white Cuban, Ricky Ricardo [Desi Arnaz], who penetrated U.S. commercial TV with the comedy series *I Love Lucy* [1951] at a time when Black people were also rarely seen on TV [e.g.: the Nat King Cole show, 1956] and were not even allowed to perform next to white singers and actors. Lucy [actress and comedienne Lucille Ball] was Arnaz's real wife, and both enjoyed a long and prosperous career in the TV and film industry. In 1954, Arnaz was even able to get a role as the European Spanish Don Juan.

During this time, white Latin Americans were nevertheless seen as foreign, inferior and exotic and yet many passed and enjoyed white privilege (e.g.: film actor, Ramón Novarro, and Spanish/Cuban band leader, Xavier Cugat). Even all three of John Wayne's wives were from Latin America at a time when anti-black and anti-immigrant sentiments were powerful hateful discourses. Less mentioned is the famous Afro-Puerto Rican actor, Juano Hernández, who to date is considered one of the most successful pioneering Black actors of the African-American film industry. Despite Hernández being from Puerto Rico, he had to take Black roles precisely because he was black and experienced the same segregation as other Blacks in the United States. This was also common in Latin America, where Blacks were not allowed to be actors while whites enjoyed wearing black-face and dehumanized Black people.

According to Jill Lane (2005), "blackness" was used as a way to create a part Cuban identity independent from Spain. However, one can argue that blackness was seen as a proxy for national discourse and not for racial democracy. Anti-blackness was occurring transnationally between the United States and Latin America. A Euro-diasporic anti-black establishment was in place—a cruel phenomenon, which can be traced back to colonialism and African slavery. Arnaz was able to perform white roles and even marry an Anglo-white actress, but the same could not be remotely fathomed for Hernández.

While many invoke the idea of *mestizaje* [race mixing] and the "one-drop rule," it did not racially determine Latin American identity. The false idea that you were non-white if any of your ancestors was not white has been a common belief that undergirded racial categories and whiteness as passing in the United States. Regardless—if Arnaz was considered white or not, his whiteness allowed him to pass and have access to Hollywood. Arnaz benefited from the system of white supremacy. And while Arnaz was able to remain Cuban, Hernández was not able to be Puerto Rican because he was black.

The impossibility of Afro-descendants from Latin America being able to play Latin American [or Latino] roles would be further marked after the Civil Rights Movement. Black people from Latin America were segregated and became part of Black communities in the United Sates. Eminent figures like Arturo Alfonso Schomburg, Carlos Cooks, Chano Pozo and Mario Bauza among others formed part of the Harlem Renaissance or lived in Black neighborhoods from the 1920s to the 1960s. From the 1950s through the 1970s, there was a rise and fall of an uneasy coalition between Latinos and African-Americans. Apart from internal conflicts and the white backlash that resulted from the Civil Rights Movement, the most salient aftermath was the cementing of racial essentialisms. Blackness was seen solely as African-American and Latinos became "brown" while whiteness became Anglo-whites. These political and racial constructions remained unquestioned until recently.

The discussion of Latino whiteness was rarely brought up and instead focused minimally on Latino blackness. For example, Felipe Luciano's poem "*Jíbaro, My Pretty Nigger*" encouraged his blackness and Puertoricaness. It also appears that there was a time when you could be both Black and Latino but not white and Latino. The Nuyorican movement was occurring while the Black Arts Movements was taking place as well.

So the question remains: do Latinos "brown" themselves to create Latinos as a race because the racial discourse in the United States does not allow them to be a part of it? Another more important question is this: what occurred as a result of Latinos becoming one brown [mixed] race while blackness became exclusive to African-Americans? In this environment, Latin American markets and elites were able to carry out their anti-black agendas, which led to the rise of all-white Spanish language soap operas protected under the construction of *mestizaje* or brown-ness. Afro-Latinos and Indigenous peoples were made either invisible or reduced to adopting roles as musicians and sports athletes. This benefitted African-Americans tremendously because it allowed them to fully immerse themselves within American nationalism, which required separating their history from Latinos and Afro-Latinos while envisioning Latinos in the United States as people who were never part of the nation to begin with.

As Wilson Jeremiah Moses states in his important book, *Black Messiahs and Uncle Toms* (1982), "Black messianism is the point in our cultural mythology where nationalism and assimilationism come together most strikingly" (viii). African-American sitcoms resulted in Black essentialistic and racial hierarchies that excluded Afro-Latinos in the U.S and forced other Black migrants to assimilate to African Americanism. African-American sitcoms like "The Jeffersons," "Sanford and Son" and "Good Times" were mostly Christian, monolingual and family-based. Latino sitcoms like "¿Qué Pasa USA?," "Chico and the Man" and "A.E.S Hudson Street" were white, Christian, bilingual and also family-based.

These racially and ethnically constructed divisions not only excluded the larger diverse Black communities in the U.S., but also formed a blackness antithetical to Latino identity. While Latin American markets created all-white soap operas [which has become ever more transnational], the U.S media also created these divisions. In Christina Saenz-Alcántara's article "Who and What the Hell Is a White Hispanic?," one of the many arguments presented is that Latino whiteness is not possible because the myths of *mestizaje* in some way makes Latinos all equal:

For example, in the U.S., there is the "one-drop rule." If you have even one ancestor who is African, Asian, or Indigenous, you're automatically non-white. In Puerto Rico, the "one-drop rule" is that you are considered white if you have even one white ancestor in the previous four generations [from the Spanish colonial legal policies called *Reglas al Sacar* or *Gracias al Sacar*]. In the U.S., a Latino historically is not white since Latinos by definition are a mixture of Spanish, Indigenous, African and Asian blood.

However, we were told in a Pew Research Center report based on census records and titled, *Statistical Portrait of Hispanics in the United States, 1980-2014*, that 47.8% of U.S. based Latinos self-identified as white in the year 2000, 64.1% identified as white in 2010, and 66.2% identified as white in 2014. Incredibly, this is a steady increase in Latinos self-identifying as white at the same time that there was a very modest increase in the number self-identifying as black—in this case from 1.8% in the year 2000 to 2.0% in 2010 and 2.0% in 2014. The major change that took place during these years were the number of Latinos who self-identified as other—in this case a decline from 42.6% in the year 2000 to 28.1% in 2010 and 26.0%in 2014. Of course, these figures are not to be taken seriously because of [1] the complex reality of how Latinos have viewed and categorize skin complexion and other physical attributes over time, [2] the confusion that prevails with regard to racial categories and how these are defined and applied in both U.S. and Latin American societies, and [3] the wishful thinking of many U.S. based Latinos who have increasingly preferred to promote their alleged whiteness despite their more complex racial reality. The important "other" category in these figures, which has declined over the years, also reinforces the continuing confusion that prevails with regard to race, how it's defined in the U.S., and how it's officially recorded.

So where does this leave us?

Today, we are paying the price. The killing of Trayvon Martin by George Zimmerman in 2012 caused many to revisit the notion of Latino whiteness. The article published by *Latino Rebels*, "The White Hispanic Label: Yes People, Racism is a Latino Thing, Too," actually made some good points for the need to revisit race and Latino identity, while Cesar Vargas' "The Privilege of the White Hispanic: Leaving Out the Rest" caused, to my amazement, a stir from white Latinos (See Chapters 3 and 10 in this book). Nevertheless, we also need African-Americans to begin embracing Afro-Latinos among other Black communities who do not conform to an African American nomenclature.

Unfortunately, as I had predicted, we've seen and heard racist anti-black insults and diatribes on television [e.g.: *Univision*] and other media. This racism through media and social networks is becoming all too commonplace in the era of Trump, and it's because of this language [calling African Americans "dumb n….rs" and "monkeys"] along with other factors, that we need to have a serious conversation about Latino whiteness and Latino racism. But for this to happen, we also need to have a serious conversation about Euro-diasporic identity as well as anti-blackness. We need to have conversations about the *casta* systems [racial caste systems] that still prevail—yes, in both North and Latin America—which seems to be more powerful than ever and are the legacy of hundreds of years of African slavery and ant-black bigotry in the Americas.

White Latinos need to own up to their whiteness and its privilege in comparison to Latinos of color because we just can't afford to have the continuance or persistence of this problem any longer. We also need African-Americans to understand that Latin America has over 200 million Afro-descendants and that going to Africa should also entail going to Colombia, Brazil, Cuba and Puerto Rico, among other places. Blackness does not have to solely mean African-American and whiteness does not have to solely mean Anglo-white.

African-American academics need to stop erasing Afro-Latinos from African-American history. They also have to become more open about Latino blackness. They can't wrap their own blackness with the American flag, exclude other Black people in the U.S. [e.g.: recent African immigrants as well as Afro-Latinos] and then say they are all about black unity. History has made identity constructions that are reversible. We just have to work together and be honest about where we stand in the world.

References:

Lane, Jill. 2005. *Blackface Cuba, 1840-1895*. Philadelphia: University of Pennsylvania Press.

Latino Rebels. 2012. "The White Hispanic Label: Yes People, Racism is a Latino Thing, Too" at: http://www.latinorebels.com/2012/03/29/the-white-hispanic-label-yes-people-racism-is-a-latino-thing-too/.

Moses. Wilson Jeremiah. 2010. *Black Messiahs and Uncle Toms: Social and Literary Manipulations of a Religious Myth*. Revised Edition. University Park: Penn State University Press.

CHAPTER 9

WHAT PRIVILEGE? *MESTILEGIO*, BLACKNESS AND THE CONTOURS OF SOLIDARITY

BY RYAN HAMILTON

In April 2017, Florida state senator, Frank Artiles, in a drunken rant called his African American colleagues in the senate "n****rs." He later apologized insisting he was referring to his white colleagues and was calling them "n***as." This is not at all shocking in today's climate of Trumpian politics, but for some it was surprising that it came from the mouth of a Cuban American politician. The assumption was perhaps that a Latino should be more supportive or less inclined to use these words. For many of us Afro-descendants in Latin America, the Spanish Caribbean and AfroLatin@ communities in the United States [U.S.], this story is not surprising. The privilege of whiteness operates and exists openly and comfortably within Latin America and *latinidad.*

"Conservative" segments around the world have become emboldened with the rise of Trump to political power. The president and his battalion of millionaire administrators have made white privilege the new normal. This privilege now openly takes center stage in decision-making, public opinion, and is further implemented as state policy and exported globally. The elite and political circles in Latin America and the Spanish Caribbean have found support from their role model in the North and have further pushed their conservative agendas of division and dominance. The continued perception that class is the only stratifying force that creates unequal relations to power continues to exclude the analysis of race and gender. Now more than ever, an intersectional analysis is necessary to look beyond these privileged responses, to critique groupings of power, and be critical of constructed categories such as Latin@ and what they obscure.

Many who are vested in the struggle to build and strengthen communities of solidarity know that it cannot be done through the assumption of commonality. It takes among other things, building spaces of communication, open and equal engagement, reciprocity and patience. The assumption of Black and Brown solidarity in the U.S. seems to be based on a notion of a common experience of oppression and marginalization. Yet, this vision relies on a bounded narrative of both the Black and Latino experience and identity. These categories become solidified through a lack of discussion of the regions and geographies these identities connect to. Therefore, our assumptions of solidarity rest upon an historical disconnect which fails to analyze the similar experience of racial formations across multiple sites in the Caribbean, Latin and North America. These assumptions fail to engage or understand the experience of people of African descent, whitening and *mestizaje* in the context of Latin American national spaces.

Latin Americans and Latinos in the U.S. are from a myriad of economic, national, racial and religious backgrounds constituted within different national experiences. The hegemonic political tendency towards racial democracy may help to explain how citizens in these spaces make claims to not view each other through the lens of race while harboring racial prejudice towards each other. The notion of racial democracy, rather than expanding understandings between groups works to silence discussions of race and racism in the national contexts. Though claiming racial equality and social camaraderie, these societies have not been inclusive or responsive to Black or Indigenous needs and demands.

The idea of a racial democracy is sustained through multiple means. One of these is the category of *mestizaje*. *Mestizaje* has been theorized in multiple ways—envisioned in Latin America perhaps as a means to create a more inclusive identity born of struggle. This category was intended to denote mixture in which the different groupings are named, but easily set aside in this new configuration. For others, the category of *mestizo* rather than being inclusive erases the very same stories that it was intended to capture. *Mestizaje* has been utilized to dissuade claims from marginalized communities. *Mestizo* as a category posits a greater preference towards Europe at the expense of Indigeneity and mostly excludes Blackness from its conceptions of citizenship and nation. The process of *mestizaje* eludes to a cultural, political and social enrichment through dilution, the subduing of resistance through erasure and the maintenance of racial hierarchies.

The claim to a *mestizo* identity has become a rite of passage for many who could not access land, capital or other benefits through a proximity to whiteness. This status is achieved through improving the race "*mejorar la raza*," which requires leaving behind through further mixture that which the nation claimed could be included. By claiming mixture, many can achieve higher social status and increased possibilities in the accumulation of wealth and power. Whiteness and light skin complexion become something to strive for, and work towards over time.

As race theorist, David Theo Goldberg has noted, "race and racism can only be sustained by drawing on its support elsewhere" [1]. Notions of white supremacy are rooted in the national ideologies of many Latin American countries and also within *latinidad*. White Latino privilege has been there since the inception of the independent nations when white *criollos* liberated Latin America from Spain and even before during the Spanish colonial period. These "liberators" were not trying to transform their national societies, but rather were intent on cementing power in their own hands. By doing this, they ensured that white privilege would be a continued element in the development of the national and also in the control of the economic and the political.

Terms like Latino and Hispanic aim to lump people of Latin American and Spanish Caribbean descent together. Each Latin American nation has its own specific history of slavery, colonization, and migration that creates different experiences and treatment of their vulnerable populations. Although many Latinos and Latin Americans claim *mestizo* backgrounds, they enjoy the benefits of whiteness both in their home nations and upon arrival in the U.S. In the 2014 census, a large proportion of Latinos in the United States self-identified as white. It is not a coincidence that elite white families are the ones who have claimed political power in most Latin American nations and within the Latino Diaspora in the

U.S. Theirs are the faces that are emphasized by media outlets, cast as actors, newscasters, and other political representatives.

Latinidad in the U.S. encompasses dozens of nations, cultures, and ethno-racial groups. The Latino as both a cultural and linguistic grouping within the Empire reproduces many of the stereotypes that stem from the Empire. Within this supposedly shared category, Black and Indigenous voices are still relegated to the margins within their home nations and by extension, their new homes in the north. Mainstream *latinidad* tries to push an identity that conforms to the parameters of decency, respectability and proximity to whiteness as presented by the global north. Hence the term Latino both creates and silences, but could it not also rupture, or must it be left behind as a descriptive category? Can one take control of the category and give it further meaning through incorporating the experience of all its communities?

Though interest and research on *Afro-latinidad* has reached new heights in the last decade, there is still much to do to incorporate this information into national education frameworks. In much of my work, I highlight Black voices across multiple contexts as a way to respond to the erasure and displacement of African descendant histories and struggle in Latin America and the Spanish Caribbean. I engage in comparative work and through it, I have at times analyzed what I call "*mestilegio*" as a way to account for, critique and challenge the adhesion to a mixture that continues to privilege whiteness.

Mestilegio is a mash of words that seeks to explore white privilege in the context of Latin America and within *latinidad.* This privilege is hidden and protected by the categories of *mestizo* along with racial democracy amongst others. *Mestilegio* as an analytic term could bring us to look at the privileges of class, race, gender and sexuality that exist within the Spanish Caribbean, Latin American and Latino communities in the U.S. *Mestilegio* as a term requires us to consider power structures and the systemic ways that privilege is accorded to whiteness in regions of the south and in the north. Prevalent within Latino and Latin American contexts is the idea that whiteness assures the most benefits from power structures. These conceptions of whiteness vary from nation to nation, but still posit systems of white supremacy and white rule. *Mestilegio* can provide a rubric to continue challenging race and racism within the context of our home nations as well as to measure its impact on the Latino Diaspora, and to survey the potential for Black and Brown solidarities.

Mestilegio can simultaneously interrogate the past as it informs the present and hastens an analysis that is not only necessary, but also central to creating solidarities. Challenging *mestilegio* requires that we delve into national histories, and retell the stories of national beginnings in an effort to question the premises that continue to manifest a privileging of whiteness. The critique of *mestilegio* should begin with a dissection of three realms: the economic, the political and the personal. Through an analysis of the self, one can locate individual obstacles to achieve radical solidarities and potentialities that push us to imagine a different society. Initial targets for the analysis of *mestilegio* should be elected officials and media personalities. The lack of representation of difference replicates the models imposed by European colonizers which has led to the extension of silence towards and dispossession of communities of Indigenous and African descent. This non-representative political power replicates and institutionalizes the hierarchies that are implicit in *mestizaje*, which are reflected across the board in positions of power.

What does *mestilegio* look and feel like and what is the role that we play in perpetuating it? *Mestilegio* is that of being able to join the chorus of white supremacist thought through the performance of respectability or the improvement of an accent. It is the ability to deny others, to marginalize without flinching. It is to take up the same notions and ideas presented by broadcasters on conservative news sites. *Mestilegio* allows for the silencing of histories that challenge the white hero's within our national contexts. I have traveled extensively in Latin America and my personal experiences as an Afro-descendant have been varied depending on the communities I encounter and the spaces I navigate. Within Latin American circles I am not initially seen as part of the cultural and linguistic community spoken to in English. At home in Puerto Rico, my English sounding last name combined with my phenotype inspires a connection to other sites in the Caribbean. When encountering Mexican and Central American communities in California where I lived, I was routinely talked about in Spanish without the understanding that it was my first language. They knew not how to deal with my complexion.

Mestilegio is an attitude, it is the ability to become in-different, and therefore lose sight of the possibilities of solidarity. *Mestilegio* is what empowers white Latinos such as state senator Artiles to express themselves using racist language while claiming to do so jokingly. So many of those I called friend as a youth have assumed this position. They rationalize, justify it, and more than ever embrace their privilege and protect it from any type of questioning. Racial hierarchies and colorism are commonplace within Latino communities in the U.S. with many using various labels such as "*los prietos, morenos, cocolos*" to identify U.S. based African Americans and Afro-West Indians. When I declare to my friends that I am Black, they respond by denying that I am. You are *mulato*, you are *trigueño*, as if the category I accept impacts their vision of me. If you saw a picture of one of my childhood friends, let's call him Luis, you would not see him as Puerto Rican. You might mention places like Norway, Argentina, or Minnesota as his place of origin. For generations, his family has evaded mixture, willingly maintaining their whiteness through concerted efforts at finding white partners. Raised in a mansion by a Black nanny, he frolicked on the family owned yacht and was handed a company to run once he graduated from college. He belongs to the elite in Puerto Rico, but this description could be from any Latin American or European nation.

Luis exudes privilege, making it known wherever he goes, sharing it on social media and chats with friends. Instead of receiving a critique, he is met with laughter, sometimes even applauded by the many who believe in meritocracy and accept the hierarchies and elitism that prevail on the island and among most Puerto Ricans in the Diaspora. Because of our childhood friendship, Luis presumes he can share his thoughts freely with me during our chats. These have included comments such as "the problem is the poor people, they don't want to work, they are accustomed to getting everything given to them," "education should be privatized, public schools aren't good for anything," "women should stay home and take care of the kids," "Blacks are in that position because they see themselves as inferior," "the labor unions should be destroyed, they don't want to work." We no longer share conversations, but what is frightening is that there are so many others who share the perspectives articulated by Luis.

People are on the move, but they move with ideas and stereotypes. Many arriving from Latin America arrive with a cultural baggage of prejudice that does not get unpacked within the context of U.S. society, but is reinforced. Beginning the work of building solidarity between Black and Brown requires that we get beyond the assumptions of each and observe the contours of connections between the two. We should not presume to bring together that which does not see its reflection in the other. These connections can be situated through a deeper exploration and critical analysis of the plight of people of African descent across the Americas rather than privileging the site of the U.S. as the sole space for the production of Blackness. Solidarity requires a more equal exchange between African Diasporas in the global north and south. A necessary step to create any terms of solidarity is a confrontation with many Latinos and Latin Americans who are white and exude and continually benefit from the privilege of whiteness. Through this necessary engagement we can perhaps develop a shared consciousness around whiteness and power and develop a response.

Many claim that racism does not exist in Latin America but that it persists in the U.S. Yet, those arriving from Latin America, along with Latinos in the U.S. already have the baggage, stereotypes, prejudices and sometimes, racist tendencies. In the U.S., legal frameworks have existed for the creation or maintenance of segregation in U.S. society especially in the south. This has created the impression that better conditions and less racial animosity prevailed in the U.S. north as opposed to the south. In Latin America, the treatment of Black bodies has not been different from the treatment of Black bodies in the north. In Latin America, most nations failed to establish legal frameworks that encouraged or prevented segregation, racism, and racial discrimination. As a result, these nations in their own way have normalized prevailing racism and other stereotypes allowing for their preservation. Much like in the U.S., anything gained for Black folks has only happened when rights have been demanded. Although people of African descent have lived and have been a part of the formation of each Latin American nation for hundreds of years, they largely remain invisible to many Latin Americans. Too many people of African descent from Latin America are asked where they are from. Within the context of their home countries, they are seen as foreign, precisely because of the erasure of their presence and contributions. That erasure of their presence in the homeland countries is also part of the experience of their arrival in the U.S.

In the last twenty years, different national groups and movements organized by Afro-descendants around Blackness have risen across Latin American spaces. Their initial claims were for visibility and their demands shifted to calls for equal treatment before the law and national recognition through their addition into census categories and the creation of government entities that directly deal with the plight of people of African descent. These actions of recognition have taken much longer in the south than in the north partly because of conceptions of racial democracy that shut down any conversation of difference within these national contexts. The silencing of conversations and honest discussions across national spheres has deeply contributed to the vision of Blackness as foreign to Latin America, other than Brazil. The ability and language to talk about race and racism is necessary to build a shared vocabulary to criticize it in order to act against it.

There is an unintentional complicity of many Latino and Black academics and activists who have not properly addressed their own stereotypes, prejudices or racism. This is certainly true within many Latino academic circles and a salient obstacle in building solidarity between two groups that may not see their experiences as similar. Narratives of either solidarity or conflict through the exclusivity of the categories of Latino and Black are conveniently pushed in many arenas including education. A necessary step to tackle these disconnects is to approach academic faculty across disciplines and teachers at all levels of schooling and provide updated narratives to counter and push beyond their geographic and linguistic limitations.

Challenging *mestilegio* will only occur when people of African descent and Indigenous. communities demand it. The condemnation and illegality of racism and racist language around Blackness has begun to take-on greater importance in many Latin American countries in recent years. African American narratives of

Blackness and anti-racism have been a starting point for some of these movements but are not the only methods of resistance to follow. The work being done in these national contexts should have a global support system and more specificall, a support system from the Diaspora. "Anti-racism can only exist anywhere by being supported elsewhere."

It is through this lens of *mestilegio* that we could perhaps understand the words of Frank Artiles. The words used on his colleagues makes a clear distinction between him and them. His vision of *latinidad* and mixture placed Blackness not as absent but as inferior. The challenge to *mestilegio* has to happen at all levels and requires confrontation with the vision of racial democracy that is falsely exposed across the hemisphere. It requires that we construct national histories that don't attempt to exclude Black and Indigenous voices. It requires a more direct intervention into specific arenas of power to destabilize structures and categories that have existed for many years and were never intended to be inclusive. Through this work we can push the boundaries of media outlets to share different perceptions and images of the populations that inhabit, make and claim the space of *latinidad*.

[1] David Theo Goldberg speaking at the Institute for Black Europe in Amsterdam, June 2017.

CHAPTER 10

INTERNET RESPONSES TO THE ORIGINAL POSTINGS OF THEIR CHAPTERS

BY WILLIAM GARCÍA AND CESAR VARGAS.

***Editor's Note**: Comments in this section have been edited, names have been changed, the writing has been cleaned-up where necessary, and clarified in some instances. I also eliminated some of the truly ridiculous and absurd comments and many of the efforts to divert attention from the subject. Readers will note that there was support for García and Vargas in many if not all the statements made in response to their original postings, but there was also considerable resistance from many of the respondents to the reality of white Latino privilege in major areas of our society and culture. Quite a number of the respondents promoted the ideals of mestizaje at the same time that they were reluctant or refused to discuss the issue of white Latino privilege and the actual reality of racialist mestizaje as a hierarchical construct and its impact. Even some of those respondents who recognized the problem of white Latino privilege called for people to simply move-on without the need for further discussion. Of course, there were also those white Latino respondents [claimed as such] who denied that there was a problem in the first place, or claimed that they were not accountable for their privilege—and there were also more basic problems. For example, there was much confusion from persons who did not understand the difference between the fact that science does not recognize the existence of races and the reality of the social and political construction of race. Many assumed that race was real* *from a scientific perspective and some even articulated their unquestioning adherence, commitment and promotion of the social construction of race and its impact in their daily lives. There was also much presumptuousness and at times, gratuitous personal insults directed at García and Vargas from persons who arrogantly claimed to be familiar with the facts or the specifics of the issues when in fact they were not. The editor has at times interjected some comments to clarify these problems where necessary.*

Comments in Response to William García's original posting on "White Privilege and the Effacement of Blackness..."

From MrMestizaje ----- Puerto Rico has definitely always had a huge problem with identity. It has been a constant struggle since the first "*criollos*" stopped considering themselves Spanish and called themselves *Puertorriqueños*. There have been many attempts throughout history to clearly identify what it is to be Puerto Rican: Luis Pales Matos writing *Tun Tun de Pasa y Grifería* in the 1930s coining the term "*Afroantillano*" to include Black Caribbeans as part of the Puerto Rican diaspora; the adoption of Cuban writer Luis Carbonell's saying "*Y tu abuela donde esta*" ["and your grandmother, where is she?"] to counter the dominating white class dissociation with the Black race; even the Puerto Rican Parade held in New York every year allowing mainland Puerto Ricans to celebrate their heritage. Therefore, we can definitely conclude that Puerto Ricans have been eager and yearning to establish what it means to be Puerto Rican. Yet doing so has proven to be a very complicated feat as our history, like most of the Western Hemisphere's history, has been so complex.

Being Puerto Rican entails being Taino [Indigenous], European, African, American, and even Chinese. And along with each, being Puerto Rican also entails embracing the full history, not just the history that happened within the island. There have been so many peoples that have contributed to our rich history and our culture, that denying or obviating any aspect of each history would be to deny the true fabric of our existence.

To be able to start the process of identification, we need to have some radicals who dare speak-out their reality, their story, their truth. It will not be the same for every person, and Amen Hallelujah to that! So, even though I am not completely in favor of what the author of this article has to say, I commend him for starting a dialogue for identifying what being a Puerto Rican is. But I must argue against the biased viewpoint of the author in criminalizing and distancing "white" Puerto Ricans from defining the Puerto Rican race. "*Y tu abuela donde esta*" goes both ways!

What really defines a Puerto Rican is how diverse we are. I have family in Dominican Republic, the U.S., the Middle East, China, Europe and South America. I have family who physically resemble other races: Black, white, Asian, Indigenous. Some are straight, others queer, even transgender. Some live in ghettos, others in Guaynabo, and others like me prefer to go beyond Puerto Rican and U.S. soil. And you know what. We're all Puerto Rican.

Instead of trying to point out our differences and fight over who is more Puerto Rican, I would actually invite all of us to start viewing our similarities. Don't forget our history, as it does define us, but learn to forgive the atrocities committed equally by invaders and locals in the past and accept that these things did change us, and for better or worse, they are part of who we are now-a-days. I've had enough of our pointing fingers at others and making ourselves victims. Let's not allow our identity to be defined by what others do, rather let's take control of who we are and embrace it. Let's look at the diversity and richness that makes us truly beautiful, and let's aim to represent that 100%. That's all I have to say…

From BalancedView ----- To MrMestizaje: Thank you so much for those words. This is exactly how I feel. It's always good to read someone who has a balanced point of view.

From Jincha/Grifa ----- And if I consider myself a member of the human race. Am I a minority? This article completely invisibilizes the problem of my race because even if you do not believe it, I share my habitat with millions of micro-organisms and we are more than what you think. There isn't even a box that includes my race when I fill it out on official documents. I'm tired of this abuse. In Puerto Rico, I am this— a member of the human race. In the U.S.A. I am this—typically very *jincha* [pale] for Black people, very *grifa* for white people [a person who can pass for white except for an "African" hair texture].

From MentallySaneRican ----- It seems to me that the author has a serious mental complex. If he would seek counseling instead of talking so much s..t, his life would be better!

From William García ----- There is no racism in Puerto Rico? See the following: http://youtu.be/bs4trwwtwtA.

From MrMestizaje ----- Sure, there is racism in Puerto Rico. There is racism against Blacks, against whites, against *mestizos*, against Dominicans, against the *gringos*, against everyone, as in the rest of the world.

From UnderstandingRican ----- This essay does raise valid issues. I would enjoy talking about it more than writing about it. I migrated before Guaynabo city was a "thing" so the term is new to me. In my opinion, it is true that there is a significant segment of Puerto Ricans that discriminate against Blacks, other Hispanics, women and LGBT—all for ignorant and incorrect reasons. I don't think that race is the main causation of this. Race is not a biological definition, it's a cultural one. If you look at a large part of *reggaeton* and *salsa* and the artists who perform this music—most are considered white in Puerto Rican society. If you look at all societies regardless of color, discrimination exists based on ignorant beliefs.

Most of the time, this discrimination aligns more with income level. The problem of capitalism is that it's not designed to create equality. Yankee hats and Nike's are also no more Puerto Rican than surfer or hipster clothes when it comes to fashion. They are capitalist status symbols that have become Puerto Rican. I remember as a kid, it was uncool not to have Jordans.

I'm curious about the statistics that back the demographics of the Puerto Ricans migrating to the U.S through the years. Also, when do you consider someone Black. Looking at some of my forefathers, they were considered Black as seen in the census. And I count my Afro hair as part of my African heritage. The latest consensus in science is that modern humanity came from Africa, which says that every society is based on African culture. I would like more data backing some of the anecdotes. Other books that agree only with your statements don't give you an objective idea of the findings. As someone who lived during the growth of gated communities, I don't see them motivated by race. The times I was mugged—the mugger was usually what would be considered a white person in Puerto Rico. Keep in mind that this is an anecdote with a small sample size.

From DarkPRican ----- It's always dangerous to indulge in over-simplifications when it comes to the very complex socio-cultural ramifications of the Puertorrican condition. As a student at the UPR Mayaguez campus in the late 70's, I can tell you that there was a well-defined structure, but not of racially biased attitudes. There was in the least an issue of privileged status. It always baffled me to hear expressions like: "*Ustedes, los de la Isla*" [Those of you from the island] mainly coming from those "*blanquitos*" referenced in the article. To say that there is no prejudice in Puerto Rico means that either you never lived there or you prefer to stick your neck in the ground. As a dark skinned Puertorrican, I lived through this even with my own family after they migrated to the U.S. in the 1980s—and I'm still experiencing it. Racial bias is the condition of a weak spirit and I don't think it will ever be eradicated as long as there are humans living on this planet.

From Anti-Nuyorican ----- The author of this posting is an Afro-Nuyorican by way of Staten Island. Enough said! Do go back and study Puerto Rican history. And, do feel free to research your subject matter before putting pen to paper, you would benefit from searching sources predating the 1990's.

From UnderstandingRican ----- I don't agree with some of what the author said but it takes courage to publish one's words and be judged by the world. If you disagree with something you should say what it is.

From William García ----- To UnderstandingRican. Yes, thank you for your comment. And to Anti-Nuyorican—as a historian I have knowledge of the Puerto Rican canon. I have read many books that are important to my topic such as *Narciso Descubre su Trasero*, *El País de Cuatro Pisos*, books from Guillermo Baralt and so forth. The reason I didn't put these works in the biblioraphy was in order to let people know about the more recent works that are out there. Also, in my bibliography you will find some important books that predate the 1990s.

From ActivistPRican ----- Many Boricuas are "wounded and bleeding!" Read! Actively participate in the politics, culture, history and social justice for our Island or outside it—all those movements that promote a logical and creative conversation / dialogue for all of us on our Planet Earth. Thank you very much William Garcia for having the knowledge and bravery that distinguishes all the warriors of our country, Puerto Rico, and to bring to light a subject so guarded under the mattress. You become a voice that claims our "decorated blackness"—so ignored at a level of humanism and understanding. The fact that so many people have reacted is very positive. It has brought the theme of social privilege, "cultural romance" and the beauty of our Boricua *negrura* ["negroidness"]in the light of a new song. This is good medicine. What a cure, and if it burns—you blow!

From William Garcia ----- Narcissus Discovers his black Boricua queer by Zenon Cruz rescued me the first time I read it. Also, as a graduate of the UPR, it enabled me to slap the Boricua canon exemplified by the racist Antonio Pedreira and Thomas White. It gives me *pena* ["sadness"] that later, the famous book of the four floors and various other writings were still using the same discourse to deny, or to justify it. The arguments are: [1] To the light—do not lay your eyes here—you don't know what you're saying [2] United States racism is different [therefore worse] compared to the Puerto Rican and [3] we are all mixed, therefore, there is no racism and don't talk about it here. Cheap and sad rationalizations. Thanks for the support.

From Fascinated ----- It is fascinating that this article creates so much anger. Yes, we are a racist country. But it is a racism different from that of the United States. It is complicated because it is intermixed with a classism and is not institutional racism as it was in the United States. The Nuyoricans are surprised to see "humble" Puerto Ricans treat with such deference the Puerto Ricans of the upper middle or upper class, who are mostly white. They think it is due to racism. There is a racist element but there is also a legacy of paternalism and privilege that results in some "educated" or "good family" people treated differently from others, not with disdain but with indifference. I think it is this attitude to which the article refers.

From William Garcia ----- Somehow, I agree with what you say. Sure there is class and race. Thanks for your comment.

From BornInUSA ----- Born in the USA. white, entered Navy, Caucasian, WTH am I????

From Presumptuous Alex ----- To William García. You know you are not Puerto Rican, right?

From William Garcia ----- Why am I not Puerto Rican?

From presumptuous Clara ----- Because you were apparently in your teens when you came to PR, late 20s when you first met a *guaynabito* and lack basic knowledge about PR while pushing 40. I can call myself the world's biggest Pokemon fan, but if the only critter I can mention is Pikachu, then I may certainly like Pokemon, but I'm certainly not "the biggest fan." What's more, I'll probably give more credibility about Puerto-Ricanness to the whitest *gringo* that ever gringoed if he put in the time actually living in PR and can name two beers beyond *Medalla* and he'd still be more Rican than you.

William Garcia ----- "Puertorican beers like Heineken?" Shoo! Go away white Puerto Rican racist lady!

From presumptuous Clara ----- Bye, black *gringo*.

From William Garcia ----- Too bad for you I was born in Puerto Rico. It's all good though. I know you don't know what you're talking about.

From IslandCentric ----- Born in Puerto Rico but not raised there. You are the product of being raised in Staten Island and you are culturally different from Puerto Ricans, just accept that. No different than Italian Americans are different from Italians in Italy, and Irish Americans are different from the Irish in Ireland.

From William Garcia ----- Did you even read the article? We're five million strong in the Diaspora, and we'll let you islanders know who is Puerto Rican from now on—in heh, heh. Peace. "You really are very smart." Even if I had not been born in Puerto Rico, I had lived in Puerto Rico for almost ten years [especially with the va-y-ven: that is], studying in elementary schools in Candelaria in Toa Baja, eating *frozing*, playing roosters and spins, etc. Children of Puerto Rican parents and having been educated in the UPR, would have remained Puerto Rican. You of the island are a minority and I do not know if you have noticed, we are not asking your permission for you to legitimize us as Puerto Ricans. A Boricua from the Bronx is probably more Boricua than you and probably has flagged more than you.

From Island B-Boy ----- When I entered the IUPI [UPR - Rio Piedras] it was in 1998 with a Yankees cap, a Che Guevara shirt and Adidas tennis shoes. We were a band of rappers with Afros, and although we were not all Blacks of color, we represented our African heritage and listened to the hip-hop of our New York brothers. There I made friends with the rappers Luis Días "Intifada." DJ Nature, E.A. Flow, who were students there and for them I became friends with SieteNueve who is the best rapper who talks about being Black in Puerto Rico in his songs [The hell with Tego Calderón!]. All Nuyorican students became our friends because we accepted them and understood their tastes. I'm a b-boy and sometimes we were going to dance and dance circles in front of the amphitheaters with boombox radios that we brought. We put a name, "The Rapkaholiks." and from there came the hip-hop collective *Vanguardia Subterranea*. I left the "dread-locks" on for a year despite having straight hair. I had a Nuyorican teacher who gave the class "Sociology in Protests Movements," and I took many courses on Puerto Rican migration.

My experience in the IUPI was different from that of the author since in the UPR, I learned more about my African side. Of course, I entered in 1998, the author is class of 2009 and rap was not so annoying. William, I am completely in agreement with everything that you wrote, I read it completely. And if these *guaynabitos* from crap leave you a bunch of hate in the comments, you know that you did well.

¡PA'LANTE! ONE LOVE!!!

From AfricaRican ----- Man, listen! In the U.S.A, everyone doubts the fact that I'm Puerto Rican. My mother was raised there, and I was born there. That's enough for me. If the children of white people fleeing Cuba can say "I'm more Puerto Rican" than me, the child of a Surinamese man and a woman born in Guadeloupe but raised in Rio Piedras, they can say that too.

I never understood until I was grown why my mother insisted that my English and French be top-shelf, but my Spanish be *puro Jibaro* ["pure peasant"]. people have said to me, half in jest, "every time I listen to you speak Spanish, I want to go cut sugar cane." Yeah, my accent is that thick and I'm totally unapologetic about it.

Having my *latinidad* constantly put under the spotlight and doubted is a major reason why I now live in Africa. nobody doubts it here. "I'm from a Spanish-speaking island in the Caribbean." "Cool!" I often don't elaborate because if I say Puerto Rico, then people who know the island know that Puerto Ricans are U.S. citizens, and I try to keep that low-key.

From ChicagoRican ----- Only a few words to those who think in terms of black or white. I am a Puertorican raised in Chicago. While growing up, I found that most races have both types of persons. Whites that hate blacks and blacks that hate whites. I lived in Chicago for more than 20 years and never lived among Puerto Ricans. Most of the time I lived with Italians and Irish. There was always someone that did not accept me for my race but there was more that did. I have been in Puerto Rico the last 40 years and find the same to be true here. The difference is that here I feel that I am with my people. I can talk to anyone I want to—black or white, and I am treated as a *Puerto-Riqueño* not as white. It's true that we are all different colors but it is also true that the most beautiful pictures are in color. If you only see the people of Puerto Rico in black and white then you have a defective vision problem. Look at us in color and you'll see the beauty of our race. The rest is only prejudice learned from bad experiences or lack of love for your race. No matter what color we are, we are all beautiful.

From MoveForward ----- Still beating dead horses instead of moving forward. How sad.

From WhiteBoricua ----- There is racism everywhere, we Puerto Ricans just have less of it, but there is racism none the less. As a white *Boricua*, I celebrate my blackness proudly. As a culture, we sing songs about our blackness and even call each other *negro* as a term of endearment.

From Appreciative ----- Enjoyed every bit of your article. Really looking forward to read more. Cool.

Editor's Note*: Readers who have looked at these comments should know that William García's position on white Latino privilege and racism at the University of Puerto Rico, Rio Piedras, is supported by research completed* by "*collegefactual.com,*" *a program that advises potential undergraduate and graduate students on various issues of importance that may influence their choice of a particular college or university. It turns out that the University of Puerto Rico, and other UPR campuses, such as those in Utuado and Carolina [which is in the midst or near San Juan's largely Afro-Puerto Rican neighborhoods in Carolina, Loiza and Piñones] have terrible records when it comes to their ethnic and racial diversity. It is actually worse on these campuses than it is in mainland U.S. colleges and universities. The same is also true of the Interamericana and the Pontifical Catholic University in Ponce which have also been highlighted by CF.C. Collegefactual.com was not able to actually obtain statistics on this problem which is usually obtained from mainland institutions. We can assume that this was the result of the usual obfuscation and/or denial that claims that there is no race problem on the island and that all Puerto Ricans regardless of their background are part of "La gran familia puertorriqueña." However, a complication may arise as a result of how race is defined by collegefactual.com as opposed to how it's defined in Puerto Rico. We can assume [in contrast to the application of the "one drop rule" on the U.S.mainald] that the racism that prevails in island institutions as reported by William García and others is directed primarily at the medium to dark brown complected "African looking" Puerto Ricans [with "pelo malo"] as opposed to the lighter complected "fino" and "off white trigueños" and even certain "jabaos." However, it's important to note that collegefactual.com also visited these institutions and observed what follows: [1] that these institutions "are not ethnically diverse, or have "very low ethnic diversity," [2] that the "University of Puerto Rico - Rio Piedras is ranked 2,561* *[out of 2,718] in ethnic diversity nationwide with a student body composition that is far below the national average" when it comes to diversity [also true of the rankings for the other institutions], [3] that the faculty in all of these institutions "are not ethnically diverse," [4] that "It may be difficult for college students to meet and learn from student peers from different ethnic and racial backgrounds at" these schools.... We can also note that this would be a problem with faculty at these institutions as well.*

These comments are found in the following:

https://www.collegefactual.com/colleges/university-of-puerto-rico-rio-piedras/student-life/diversity/

https://www.collegefactual.com/colleges/university-of-puerto-rico-utuado/student-life/diversity/

https://www.collegefactual.com/colleges/university-of-puerto-rico-carolina/student-life/diversity/?_ga=2.157785274.1236023961.1509027738-334805201.1509027737#EthnicDiversity&show_messages=1

https://www.collegefactual.com/colleges/inter-american-university-of-puerto-rico-fajardo/student-life/diversity/
https://www.collegefactual.com/colleges/inter-american-university-of-puerto-rico-barranquitas/student-life/diversity/

https://www.collegefactual.com/colleges/pontifical-Catholic-university-of-puerto-rico-ponce/student-life/diversity/

Comments in Response to the original postings of "The Privilege of the White Hispanic: Leaving Out the Rest with Facts, Stats, and Cognitive Dissonance" by Cesar Vargas [These comments are no longer online]

From UnderstandingWhiteLatiino ----- The intersection of race and privilege is an ominous crossroads. It pops up whenever a white person says something like, "People have made jokes about my Irish ancestry, and I never get offended. So, what's with all these Latinos getting upset about wetback jokes?" If you've said something like this and fail to see the problem, I'm not sure I can help you. But let me just point out that the inability—indeed, the outright refusal—to see the world through anyone else's eyes is a hallmark of privilege. In America, the concept of privilege is closely related to race. White privilege is even its own catch-phrase and subset of cultural angst. Recently, my friend Hector Luis Alamo wrote a piece for *Latino Rebels* in which he stated that "resentment towards whites runs deep in Latino communities." He went on to list the reasons for this resentment, including the fact that "Latinos in America aren't granted nearly as many tools and opportunities as whites." This is all true, of course, but it doesn't stop there. Over at *Huffington Post*, César Vargas stated that white privilege seeps into the Latino community itself. He implied that Latinos who are lighter in skin [like me] receive benefits that darker-skinned Hispanics do not. Vargas wrote that the "Latino representation in the States seems to be a microcosm of the racial and social disparity in Latin America" and that "white Hispanics [are] ill-equipped to speak for the rest of us." At about this time, we all start getting a bit uncomfortable with these ideas. After all, we're not talking about some Klan member shouting that whites are the master race. We're referring to good, sincere white people—and even light-skinned Latinos—who enjoy an easier life by virtue of their skin tone, and who are repulsed at the very idea of bigotry. But white privilege is a powerful and quite real thing. It sneaks up on its recipients in ways that they may not even recognize. For example, many studies have shown that people are more likely to help individuals who resemble them—ergo—whites in positions of power are more likely to mentor and guide their fellow whites, regardless of their actual talents or abilities. And of course, if you're a white cop who shoots an unarmed black kid under the most suspicious of circumstances, literally hundreds of thousands of people will rush to your defense. And they will most likely be white. What does all this mean? Well, at the very least, it should mean that if you've benefitted from white privilege, give thanks for your lucky genes and strive to make America a place where such randomness doesn't prop up our entire social structure. And if someone makes a joke about you being Irish, don't think it lets you off the hook.

From WhiteAntiVargasLatino ----- I found this article written by some Latino from New York by the name of Cesar Vargas. I know he's not Chicano or Mexican because he doesn't even know the definition of a Chicano for starters. Anyway, his article is the most ridiculous thing I've ever read. Now, they want to divide white looking Latinos from the rest of the majority non-white looking Latinos. His tactics are more divide and conquer. It gets me mad because he thinks we get everything handed to us without working for it. I would like to know from white looking Latinos who live in America if they have had everything handed out to them for simply looking white? What about it—light skin Latinos?—have any of you had everything handed out to you by whites just because you had a lighter skin color?

From WhiteEhecatl ----- No, not at all since I have black hair and they usually think Middle Eastern or something similar to that. Seriously though, I don't know what to say. Am I supposed to get stuff handed to me?

From WhitePRScientistSympathizer ----- As for my experience as a white Puerto Rican living in the States, I can say my experience is nothing like those self-identified Hispanics/Latinos who are *Indio*, *mestizo*, Black or *mulato*; aka someone of color. No question about it, I've never once experienced prejudice or racism first hand because I go invisible as a Hispanic. But I see how they are treated and how the white majority interacts with them and it is ugly. How can I, a white Hispanic, speak for them and their experience? They simply face more difficult struggles and prejudice. So, I kind of sympathize with what he is saying. He isn't saying we have it easy, it's just that they face a far more difficult path than whites do. As for if there's an imbalance of representation, whether that's in pop culture, politics or business—I'm not sure. I haven't thought about it honestly, maybe because I don't have to.

From WhiteEhecatl ----- Yeah, you could say the darker Latinos face racism more than we white Latinos would, but he is saying we get hired more easily due to our looks, not because of our job background. He also suggests that the majority representing Latinos are white Latinos. Since when is Cesar Chavez, Dolores Huerta, Sonia Sotomayor, originations like the Young Lords from NY, or the Brown Berets from California white? I think he is passing people like Eva Longoria and other similar Hispanics for white because in American movies and TV, a majority of the Hispanics look white. I still don't understand quite what he is talking about. Whether or not he likes it, a majority of the white looking Latinos didn't make a choice to be born the way they did. The only group that I do see not being very well represented in the media here in America are Black Hispanics. I think they have had a lot of struggle even being accepted as Hispanics—especially when you have African Americans trying to claim them, and Anglos thinking they can't be Hispanic because they look Black. I also think they have it harder just like African Americans since they are no different from them.

From LA-Latino ----- I think white Hispanics are mixed people, but still have white privilege [to the extent that it even exists]. The major exception is the white *barrio* Chicano. For them, whiteness can't quite balance the negative associations of being from hood.

From LatinoObserver ----- White Hispanics are privileged in the sense that they will not be racially profiled, assumed to be illegal immigrants, or discriminated against for being nonwhite. White Hispanics are more likely to experience xenophobia, but this often will depend on whether they have an accent or not. I have a co-worker who is Mexican and looks white, he is often assumed to be Greek until people find out he is Mexican, and then they say "really? I wouldn't have guessed it!" [This, despite his Spanish surname!] and go back to forgetting that he is Hispanic until it comes up again in conversation. But either way, white Latinos won't usually face institutionalized racism, and at best will be asked "Wait, you're Hispanic, I thought you were white?" and having to justify their identity. This is very different than the experience of someone who is visibly admixed with African and Amerindian. White privilege doesn't go away just because someone speaks Spanish. And if it does, and white Hispanics get lumped in with nonwhites—the Spanish should have thought of that when they colonized areas heavily populated by Amerindians and also brought many African slaves to their colonies.

From LatinoObserver ----- what I would like to know is what is a white Hispanic to some of you, and what is a white looking Latino to some of you. I have a feeling that some of the white Hispanics that some people have in mind [very Mediterranean looking] wouldn't be taken for white in America. For example, this white woman from Portugal [in picture] would never be taken for white in my area, but for a Mexican—yes. She would also face the same discrimination that other Mexicans face. Yes, racist whites will call her a wetback, beaner, and they will tell her to go back to Mexico, blah, blah, blah. But wait, she's white but not white enough for America. I think people need to keep that in mind. Now it's different if those white Hispanics looked something similar to Vargas. We can say this Hispanic wouldn't face any discrimination and pass more easily, but these types of white Hispanics are a tiny minority in America.

From DNALatino ----- To hell with white Hispanics! Brown power! Let's breed them into extinction! Who's with me?! I may look [off] white, but I'm: Mediterranean 29.00%, North European 27.23%, North Amerindian + Arctic 15.74%, West African 9.37%, Southwest Asian 9.77%, Caucasian 7.10%, and Siberian 1.79%

From LatinoObserver ----- White Hispanic to me means they can pass for a European ethnicity of some sort. Whether they look authentically Iberian or whether they look pseudo East Mediterranean like a Sicilian or Greek. For instance, Gloria Estefan for me is a white Hispanic. My issue is they get the privilege for being white and the benefits of being a minority. It should be one or the other. ...And since they are always going to have white privilege, being "Hispanic" should not be enough to be a minority for diversity purposes in the US. It should require that you be nonwhite [*mestizo*, *genizaro*, *mulato*, etc.].

From UnderstandingWhiteLatiino ----- LOL. I think you'd be a white Hispanic to them. I'm going to try to message Cesar Vargas and invite the man to this forum so he can tell us if you make it as a white Hispanic.

From MexTlaloc ----- Thank you for this! I feel that this is often seen in organizing social justice spaces. The white Latino is always privileged over others, and no one realizes why. It would also be great to examine how white supremacy [as a system] lives in all of us.

From PleaseSympathize ----- Cesar, do not underestimate somebody else's plight. As a light-skinned Latina myself, I am aware of the conflict of equality and social justice that surrounds skin color. However; to say one group is advantaged over another is not understanding the complexity of human behavior. Because of my so called "advantages," it has been pointed out by my own sister that I am privileged which has also resulted in my success since she is the one who looks Indigenous and has been less successful. I have worked since I was 16 and have taught for 10 years in elementary education and can tell you that I have never had a school year in which I had felt safe from the chopping block because I treat all students equal and have high expectations for all [I tend to forget the list of who are the ones who don't have to follow the rules]. It seems that the teachers who are loved by the parents the most are those who identify with Caucasian looks, hair dye and culture even if they are Afro or Indigenous looking. Those teachers usually look the other way and fear high expectations of themselves and others. Not to mention that when you are an Aztec dancer for years, and you do not look Indigenous, it is difficult to receive teachings from certain "teachers" because they do not consider it to be your birthright. Reverse discrimination exists. Regardless of the situation, it is wrong, it should be stopped and not propagated among our children who are literally our future as a society.

From William García ----- A good example here of white Latino racism and denial.

From LatinoHillbilly ----- The comment above from Please Sympathize suggests that one of the things that complicate the idea of white Latino privilege is that most of us come from families where dark, medium, and light complected are members. So, when a white Latino sees him/herself, they see their family, which may be darker. Thus, their identity is not clearly "white." This does not mean there is no white Latino privilege, but it does suggest that this privilege is different from and more complicated than the privilege of white Americans.

From William García ----- Great research. Fantastic journalism. Right on the money.

Response to William García's original posting on the need "for a Serious Conversation on Euro-Diasporic Whiteness."

From OneHumanRacePR ----- There is no scientific recognition of race in the human Species. We are all one race, homo sapiens-sapiens. The amount of melanin in your skin is an environmental variation not a racial distinction. Race just like borders are an artificial human construct.

From AfroAmPR ----- Unfortunately, that doesn't stop the white Latinos he speaks of from being racist/anti-black.

From Free to Be Racist ----- It doesn't stop the Blacks and Latinos of any color that he speaks of from being racist either. Personally, if you believe in freedom, anyone should be able to be racist unapologetically.

From OneHumanRacePR ----- To Mr. Free to Be Racist ----- And they can, but we are also free to call then on their ignorance.

From AfroPR ----- To Mr. Free to Be Racist ----- The difference is that white Latinos are in a position of power and privilege in this country [regardless of class] and precisely because of their phenotype. It puts an additional responsibility on them to use this privilege for a good purpose.

From AfroAmPR ----- To OneHumanRacePR ----- Thank you.

From AfroAmPR ----- To Mr. Free to Be Racist ----- White racism is way more potent than so called Black racism. I take it your interpretation of racism is simplistic.

From Flowers ----- The amount of melanin in your skin determines a huge number of your lifetime experiences [due to the ways in which others perceive you] and a huge number of human interactions, as well as opportunities that will or won't come your way.

From OneHumanRacePR ----- To Flowers ----- I did not say racism does not exist. I am simply pointing out that it's based on ignorance. Most people do not know that science does not recognize race as a scientific reality. Most people are under the false impression that there are genetic differences among the races when the reality is that all humans are close cousins and we can all be traced back to the same origin. If more people understood that the person you are discriminating against is basically your cousin things might get better.

AfroDominicanCuban ----- To OneHumanRacePR ----- keep on believing that mainstream scientific nonsense.

From OneHumanRacePR ----- To AfroDominicanCuban ----- What is hard to understand is this nonsensical comment you just posted.

From OneHumanRacePR ----- To AfroDominicanCuban ----- Science is not about belief. The data are clear. This isn't belief—this is fact whether you believe it or not. The facts remain indisputable. Genetics shows that there is no significant variation in our genetic codes which would qualify as racial differences. Humans are one species—homo sapiens-sapiens. There is no other species of humans.

From OneHumanRacePR ----- To AfroDominicanCuban ----- In my experience, white racists tend to have superiority complexes and Black racists are resentful. Black racists do not walk around thinking they are superior. They tend to hate and distrust whites because they feel whites act superior. Latino racism is similar, but actually more diverse. Latinos don't like whites because they think they are superior. They don't like Blacks because they feel superior to Blacks. At the end of the day, it's all ignorant stupidity.

From OneHumanRacePR ----- To AfroDominicanCuban ----- brilliant comment. Are you ten years old? The thoughts of my twelve year old are more complete than that.

Editor's Note*: Afrocentric extremists and the members of the Nation of Islam can be and are racists. See especially, the literature of Afrocentric extremists from Frances Cress Welsing, Clyde (Ahmad) Winters, and David Imhotep among others.*

From Blogger ----- To Free to Be Racist ----- Personally, I can't handle the fact that white people benefit more in this society because they've historically trampled on people of color. So I have to make everybody racist in my mind because then it's not so bad when I'm also a victim!

From RaceBelieverMD ----- To OneHumanRacePR ----- I enjoy your passion but you are incorrect in what you are saying. You are misrepresenting the science. You are correct in saying that there is only one species, but race and species are different. Race is a classification below the level of subspecies. The differences in the human races we see on earth are not simply melanin in the skin. The differences in races are adaptations to a particular area where one population of a species was isolated from other populations of a species. It is a little deeper than just skin color. This is why certain medications work better in one race than they do in another, or certain substances are tolerated in one race better than others. There are very real physiological differences. I know it is popular to say that the only race is the human race but that is because people don't seem to understand what a race is. You seem to confuse race with species. That's like confusing species with family as it pertains to organization.

***Editor's Note**: These comments are nonsense coming from "Race-BelieverMD"—a physician no less! Race and subspecies in humans and any connection between the two are no longer considered scientifically valid in part because of the simple reason that scientists cannot agree on how to divide the human species into races or any other conceptualized subgroup. There is too much biological and genetic overlapping between seemingly distinct populations along with other complications. Human differences are considered minor from a scientific standpoint and no longer sufficient to justify the categorization of certain groups as races or as a subspecies. What we have is the social and political construction of race which is not scientific. Overlapping between socially and politically constructed races can be seen in the greater resistance to sickle-cell anemia that prevails among "white" Italians and "black" sub-Saharan Africans in contrast to [e.g.] "white Germans and Scandinavians because of a shared history* *of malaria in both "white" Italy and "black" sub-Saharan Africa. South Asians in Great Britain are also defined as black, but in the United States they are said to be Asians. At one point, "Race-BelieverMD" states that "people don't seem to understand what a race is," but scientifically—neither does he. Even his reading of claims by those scientists and science writers who are currently trying to resurrect a new version of the old "social Darwinistic" science of race is flawed. See comments further down.*

From OneHumanRacePR ----- To RaceBelieverMD ----- Quote: "More recently, molecular techniques have developed to examine genetic differences between individuals and populations, including karyotypes providing chromosomal number and patterns, deoxyribonucleic acid [DNA] hybridization, protein sequences, and nuclear and mitochondrial base sequences from ancient and modern DNA. From all this evidence, it is clear that populational, but not racial differences, do exist within the human species. Race should not be equated with ethnicity, "

From OneHumanRacePR ----- To RaceBelieverMD ----- It is you who has the science wrong. See:

http://www.newsweek.com/there-no-such-thing-race-283123

http://www.pbs.org/wgbh/nova/evolution/does-race-exist.html

From OneHumanRacePR ----- To RaceBelieverMD ----- The concept of race stems from ignorance and is antiquated. DNA has already debunked the concept that race would be a form of speciation or sub-speciation. The genetic difference between two white individuals is greater than between a black man and a white man. The hereditary differences you describe have nothing to do with the artificial concept of race.

From RaceBelieverMD ----- To OneHumanRacePR ----- Yes you are correct, race is NOT ethnicity. It is also not species, nor is it sub-species. It does not matter what the genetic difference between two individuals within a race is. DNA sequences of humans are 99.5% the same with other humans, but DNA sequences between homo-sapiens and Neanderthal is 99.84 percent identical. What does that tell you? According to your theory, not only would homo-sapiens be the same species as Neanderthal but the same subspecies and same race. We both know that is not true.

Now the link you put up defined race as "The biological definition of race is a geographically isolated breeding population that shares certain characteristics in higher frequencies than other populations of that species, but has not become reproductively isolated from other populations of the same species." This I agree with. And this is exactly why your final statement—The "hereditary differences you describe have nothing to do with the artificial concept of race"—is wrong. According to that definition from the link you posted the hereditary differences have everything to do with race because that's all that race is. There are currently race specific drugs [e.g.: Bidil] There are currently a great number of diseases that are predominantly found in one race over another because these diseases may have evolved as a way to help the affected person and their descendants. There has been research showing the lack or prevalence of muscle fiber types between different races. There are so many things pointing to there being different human races and we choose to ignore it. I tell you what, if God forbid, make sure to pay attention to the doctor's documentation of the race of a patient because that will affect the drugs they give them... Yes, the thing that you say that do not exist will affect the way drugs work in their bodies—I guess by magic since race does not exist. I know this is uncomfortable but race is real. Maybe what is faulty is the way you define race.

***Editor's Note**: The physician seems to contradict himself in parts of his posting. His follow-up comments on Neanderthals are also most problematic. The classic Neanderthal "type" in Europe and the "Middle East" became extinct about 35,000 years ago according to a now obsolescent or obsolete hypothesis. Recent research has demonstrated that the Neandertals had so much in common with so-called "physically modern" humans that scientists have begun to equate the two groups as part of a single species. Recent excavation work has demonstrated that there was interbreeding between Neandertals and "physically modern" humans and as a result, they are now no longer seen as significantly different. Individuals who have recently had their genetic background tested by Ancestry.com or National Geographic [etc.]*

are now being told that there are traces of Neandertal or "Denisovan" DNA [another group previously seen as "transitional"]in their genome. My second and most recent genetic test revealed that I am one percent "Denisovan." The good doctor seems to be unaware of the recent research on Neanderthals and its conclusions. The physician also makes a big deal about drugs that are targeted at certain socially constructed races but fails to mention targeted ethnic groups that are not defined as races—and like all medications, targeted drugs can also work on non-targeted populations and also don't necessarily work on all individuals in targeted populations.

From OneHumanRacePR ----- To RaceBelieverMD ----- I'm not reading your opinions sorry. But if you don't have a PhD and are not published why should I bother with your opinions? Fact—science does not recognize race amongst the human species. This is a fact not my opinion.

From RaceBelieverMD ----- To OneHumanRacePR ----- Actually I do have an M.D. degree and I have published work on pharmacological efficacy of specific drugs in specific races. So I guess I am exactly who you should listen to. However, I see you like links and I do not have much time today, so I will post some that will help you understand. Oh btw, just saying "fact" does not make what you are writing after that a real fact. Science very rarely has a universal view on anything and this is how I know you are not a scientist. Here are some links that challenge you.

From RaceBelieverMD ----- To OneHumanRacePR ----- http://time.com/.../what-science-says-about-race-and.../ [*Time Magazine*] Pay close attention to the part that says "Analysis of genomes from around the world establishes that there is a biological basis for race, despite the official statements to the contrary of leading social science organizations."

From RaceBelieverMD ----- To OneHumanRacePR ----- https://www.wsj.com/articles/nicholas-wade-race-has-a-biological-basis-racism-does-not-1403476865 [*Wall Street Journal*].

From RaceBelieverMD ----- To OneHumanRacePR ----- http://blogs.discovermagazine.com/crux/2012/05/02/human-races-may-have-biological-meaning-but-races-mean-nothing-about-humanity/#.WhQh73lOkqM [*Discover Magazine*].

From OneHumanRacePR ----- To RaceBelieverMD ----- These links do not challenge me They question the accepted science. They do not refute it. Again, science does not recognize race. These journalistic articles of opinion have not changed this. Let's repeat—science does not recognize race. This is fact. The rest is opinion. There have always been those, and there will always be those who reject accepted science. This does not change the facts. I could show you papers that deny evolution. I can show you papers that deny climate change. Does that mean evolution and climate change are not accepted science? That is hardly the case. Dr. Ben Carson is an MD, but it doesn't stop him from believing ridiculous s..t and having false opinions. You posted two links from the opinion sections of newspapers and magazines—one from the blog section. My links are from the science sections, not the opinion sections. Learn the difference.

***Editor's Note**: The sources cited by "RaceBelieverMD" above are indeed poor. There are some published peer reviewed scientific studies that make controversial claims about "race," but "Race-BelieverMD" does not cite them. Instead, he cites someone like Nicholas Wade, a former New York Times science writer whose book "A Troublesome Inheritance: Genes, Race and Human History" has been trashed by biologists, geneticists and anthro-pologists in scientific journals. See two reviews of Wade's book in "Science" and the "American Scientist" at:*

http://www.sciencemag.org/news/2014/08/geneticists-decry-book-race-and-evolution

https://www.americanscientist.org/article/a-troubling-tome

From RaceBelieverMD ----- To OneHumanRacePR ----- Now I know you are losing it. You are confusing the "accepted science" with facts. If I can offer evidence to the contrary, it is not a scientific fact, although it may be the accepted concept at the time. If people can write a biologically sound paper highlighting differences between races, if pharma can come up with medications that work in one race and not another, then I would hardly say that race does not exist because there are too many examples that show that it does in a biological capacity. If your goal is to point out that it's a fact that mainstream publications and mainstream scientists say race does not exist, you are correct. However, it is not a fact that they are correct. An MD is a scientist like a car mechanic is a scientist. This has to be the worst comment I have ever heard. You must be an undergrad because your arguments have a great deal of ignorance in them. Do you even understand the training of an MD? Do you understand that MD's and PhD's work hand in hand in labs and within clinical trials? You compare them to Mechanics? I have not words for that. You honestly think that something listed in the science section of a newspaper is not someone's opinion? These are not peer reviewed journals. They are all people's opinion.

From RaceBelieverMD ----- To OneHumanRacePR ----- I will have to take a page out of your book and say if you do not have a doctorate degree or any scientific publications, you really do not belong at the table arguing with me on this topic. I will leave you to believe whatever you want to believe. But as a Hispanic I think it is important that you understand how your race will play a part in your future healthcare.

Editor's Note: *The physician really loses it here! Hispanics are not a race!*

From OneHumanRacePR ----- To Race BelieveMD ----- LMAO. I have been clear that these are not my opinions. I am stating facts. I know science is not fact. That is not my claim. The fact I stated is that "science does not recognize Race amongst the human species." This is a fact.

From RaceBelieverMD ----- To OneHumanRacePR ----- No, it's not that science does not recognize race. A large number of scientists base their research on racial differences. Your Healthcare is based on racial differences. Your drugs are based on racial differences. To say science does not recognize it is to ignore the obvious. Mainstream publications only print the words of scientists that do not recognize it. There are a great many social reasons for this. The fact is that the scientific community is split on this. You will see this if you ever visit an evolutionary biology conference. Heated debates happen within science on this topic. So if scientists cannot agree on this topic, I am not sure how you can say "Science does not recognize race amongst the human species. This is a fact." The only fact is that there is no agreement among scientists and for most, it's not worth the negative attention to present the hard science so they just back away from the conversation.

Editor's Note*: It is an utterly gross exaggeration that our health-care and drugs are based on "racial differences." In addition, there is the physician's bogus claim that "a large number of scientists base their research on racial differences." These scientists are in fact a small group who are very much on the defensive. They are mostly concentrated in the United States—trying to resurrect revised versions of the old social Darwinist ideas with regard to race. They tend to be in the medical profession or they're involved in biological research connected to the medical profession. They focus on socially constructed races and tend to, or conveniently ignore, the overlaps and contradictions that render the idea of race invalid from a scientific perspective. They are also in the business [for profit] of completing research that may result in the creation of targeted remedies and treatments that may be applied to socially constructed races and ethnic groups—for example, targeted treatments for Ashkenazi Jews, a defined "racially white" ethnic group [not a race] within the broader population of socially constructed "Caucasians." These researchers are a small minority in the global scientific community and it's clear that "RaceBelieverMD" is one of them.*

The good doctor also claims that he has "published work on [the] pharmacological efficacy of specific drugs in specific races," but so far, he cites none here.

From RaceBelieverMD ----- To OneHumanRace PR ----- I believe this conversation has run its course. Have a very merry Christmas, all the best to you and yours.

From OneHumanRacePR ----- To Race BelieverMD ----- I'll take the last word since I am right. This conversation ran its course when you refused to accept the facts. You're still stating opinion pretending to be the bigger man in this conversation while trying to argue that race is a real thing and not an artificial construct. Are there genetic difference amongst populations?—Yes. Can those differences be exploited for medical reasons?—Yes. Is this the same as Race?—not even close. You posted opinion after opinion. There was not one valid scientific link to support your claim and you want to pretend this argument is on an equal footing. Sorry, but that's dishonest. Humans are one race—homo sapiens-sapiens. It's called the human race. That BS that scientists are debating this issue is a typical rejectionist cop-out. Heated debates do not mean s..t in science. If anyone would have any data to support the idea of race, it would be published. Your BS would go over better with someone more ignorant of the scientific process. You are taking pages out of the bogus creationist handbook to make your argument.

From CentroMex ----- To Free to Be Racist ----- Are they free to spread their hate and offend others based on their freedom? Then I guess freedom causes harm, and conceptualized to not make people happy.

From RaceBelieverMD ----- To OneHumanRacePR ----- I stopped because it is clear you have no idea what you are talking about. It is obvious you do not have a science background. You woke up one morning read one book and three newspapers and you think you know. You do understand that you have given me nothing but opinions. *New York Times*, *PBS*, *Newsday* are no different than if it was publish in *Fox News*. They will publish what they feel is right and not the whole story. Everything you posted was opinion until you posted a peer review journal. Why do I even bother? This is like a basketball player arguing with a baker. Finally, look again at what you wrote—"Are there genetic difference amongst populations?—Yes. Can those differences be exploited for medical reasons?—Yes. Is this the same as race?—not even close." This is exactly what race is, "genetic difference amongst a population." For some reason, you just don't want to call it race. From a science standpoint, there is chromosomal race, physiological race, and geographical race look up the definitions of these and ask yourself if they apply.

Perhaps what you are saying is that there is no biological basis for the way you define race, or you are saying that the social definition or race has no scientific basis. I am not sure what race means to you. Race means a different thing in the USA from what it means in Brazil. However, look up the strict biological [not social] definition of race and you will see that I am right.

***Editor's Note**: Again, genetic differences between populations are not sufficient to categorize populations into different "races." There are the genetic similarities and overlaps between populations that "RaceBelieverMD" ignores. He also states falsely that from "a scientific standpoint, there is "chromosomal race, physiological race, and geographical race." These are scientifically bogus constructs. They have no basis in science. He also demonstrates his actual confusion on the race issue when he states that "race means a different thing in the USA than it does in Brazil, and of course, this is true because there are different non-scientific social and political constructions of race in these countries. ...And what is the strict biological definition of race? "RaceBelieverMD" cites none. He doesn't cite any link that would justify the idea of race from a scientific standpoint. You can "Google" the biological definition of race on the internet, but you would more or less get the following at the end of any statement of its definition: "Genetic diversity has resulted from the extensive hybridization that has occurred in the last two hundred thousand years, hiding any clear evidence for typological classification of race. Moreover, when selection pressures [temperature, altitude] are coupled with phenotypic variation, phenotypic expression defies taxonomic assignment of race. The genetic diversity within any historically defined race swamps the small amount of difference between such groups, making the boundaries of these categories entirely arbitrary. Therefore, race in humans does not have a biological meaning." Quoted from "Biology Reference Forum" at:*

http://www.biologyreference.com/Ar-Bi/Biology-of-Race.html

From RaceBelieverMD ----- To OneHumanRacePR ----- Ok I said it before, but now I am really done..lol. If you would like I would suggest you enroll in a biological concepts of race course. Universities normally have one. Then you will see how incomplete your view on race is... Ok I am done now, I promise..lol.

***Editor's Note**: To my knowledge, there are no reputable universities that would have courses that would teach the biological concept of race the way "RaceBelieverMD" would like it to be taught.*

From OneHumanRacePR ----- To RaceBelieverMD ----- As soon as I saw your reply I knew it would be some kind of ego driven personal attack. You are very predictable.

From CraniofacialRacialist ----- There is most definitely a scientific [anthropological] recognition of race among the human species and it's determined by craniofacial anthropometry and morphology not skin color. Quote: "For the time being at least, the people in 'race denial' are in 'reality denial' as well. Their motivation [a positive one] is that they have come to believe that the race concept is socially dangerous. In other words, they have convinced themselves that race promotes racism. Therefore, they have pushed the politically correct agenda that human races are not biologically real, no matter what the evidence." See:

http://www.geocities.ws/racial_reality/race.html

***Editor's Note**: Craniofacial anthropometry was discredited many decades ago and often seen as racist in the way it was applied, but there are still attempts to resurrect this flawed approach with problematic and/or bogus results (e.g.: see the controversy that arose with the discovery of "Kennewick Man" in 1996—a "paleoIndian" first thought to be European:*

<https://www.npr.org/sections/codeswitch/2016/05/05/476631934/a-long-complicated-battle-over-9-000-year-old-bones-is-finally-over>.

The link posted above by "CraniofacialRacialist" is an internet posting that highlights the conclusions and opinions of George W.

Gill, a professor of anthropology, who along with geneticist, Neil Risch, and a few others, is trying to resurrect the idea that humans can be subdivided scientifically into racial categories. However, as already noted, Gill's position [and those of the others with similar views] are not supported by the overwhelming majority of scientists based on the evidence and for the reasons already noted.

From ProudWhiteLatinoRacialist ----- To OneHumanRacePR ----- Tell that politically-over-corrected fairy-tale to Obama who insists he's "black" despite his very white mother...you can't have it both ways...either race exists or it doesn't, and in today's world, it does!

From ProudWhiteLatinoRacialist ----- To OneHumanRacePR ----- Be sure you share it with Obama...you know, that Uncle Tom in the White House who calls himself "black" with the inconveniently white mother. Then we can talk about "constructs."

From AfroAmRacialist ----- To CraniofacialRacialist ----- I agree 1000%—understanding that there are distinctions or that diversity is threatening or uncomfortable for some people. That color blind rhetoric only serves to sweep conversations under the carpet.

From Australian Racialist ----- Late to the party here, but genetic distance is a very real thing and only an idiot believes melanin levels is what separates us. Human biodiversity and ability is a very real thing, it's just a sliding scale so the distinctions are man-made. Race is a very useful taxonomic classification system for human populations. Quit living in fantasy land.

From AfroAmOaklander ----- I have a Hispanic ancestor and I don't even really talk about it if not asked because it doesn't matter in the scope of things. I was always a bit confused about Mexicans in the San Fran Bay area. On the one hand, they called themselves *La Raza*, but they would have "white" on their driver's license and birth certificates. Clearly, they were brown and Hispanic, but they were pushing that white envelope anyway. And what do they have against Black folks? I always hear "Oh, Mexican and Blacks don't get along." Well, I don't get that at all. We fight the same battle. We have the same enemies.

From Concerned AfroAm ----- I don't think we have the same exact battle. I think Hispanics are on the way to replace Blacks in the work force and have been given "white privilege" to a certain degree which is evident in how the illegal immigration movement was turned into a civil rights issue.

From AfroAmOaklander ----- To Concerned AfroAm ----- I don't agree. Latinos aren't replacing Black people in the workplace as far as I can see. They are still pretty much working in kitchens and garages and doing menial labor. A very few work in office jobs and higher up. This is what I've seen. Most are farm laborers too. Black people have a different rung on that ladder since we are not immigrants, and we don't have the bilingual issue. That said we both fight the battle of racism, bigotry and other "isms."

From FloridaLatino ----- To Concerned AfroAm ----- If undocumented Latinos [who tend to be brown and not white] had white privilege, they would have gotten their papers on arrival like white immigrants did. I do think that the struggles have some differences, but it's certainly a civil rights issue.

From Concerned AfroAm ----- To AfroAmOaklander ----- I'm just curious to know what state you live in? I live in Los Angeles, California, and I can tell you that Latinos aren't or weren't just working in kitchens and garages and doing the jobs Americans don't want to do. In L.A., I met a guy who had no papers working for Boeing. I have a friend who is Mexican working in construction with illegal status making decent money, so the stereotype that they are all doing menial jobs is ridiculous within itself. In Los Angeles county, Black people are largely absent from the work force and I believe that although white racism does affect Latinos, there is a preference for them over Blacks. Yes—they are still considered minorities and many of them don't know their rights, but they are still preferred over Black workers because of their whole docile, hardworking and non-confrontational stereotype. In many places, Black unemployment in this country is higher than Latino unemployment, and while racism does affect us all, there is a racial hierarchy that rewards lighter skin people in this country [Asians, Latinos, etc.].

From Concerned AfroAm ----- To FloridaLatino ----- Stopping people who look illegal or just because they are so called Hispanic/Latino is a civil rights issue. However, millions of people crossing the border illegally is not a civil rights issue and I'm willing to bet if the official faces of illegal immigration were Nigerian or Haitian or from any other predominately Black nation, we wouldn't be having this discussion because the United States of America is very selective in her application of justice, liberty and democracy.

From OneHumanRacePR ----- To Concerned AfroAm ----- Question. Are there no Hispanic dark skin people in the world? There are Hispanics with white privilege because some Hispanics are white. It is as simple as that. The people you call illegal immigrants would be called refugees if they had lighter skin.

From OneHumanRacePR ----- To Concerned AfroAm ----- If you think your problems have anything to do with Latino people or immigrants, you are falling for the right-wing propaganda on this issue. meanwhile the 1% who have 90 % of the wealth laugh while we fight each other for scraps.

From OneHumanRacePR ----- Question. Every Latino you see just has to be undocumented? LOL. Do you know that much of the land we walk on used to be Mexico and those "Latino" people are actually Indigenous to that land. Just because they speak Spanish does not mean they are not Native American. I am always baffled when people call Mexicans illegal immigrants on their ancestral lands.

From Arizona Latino ----- To Concerned AfroAm ----- The notion of ranking oppressions is ... so 1970s... There is an entire federal police force charged with hunting down brown Latino people, not just along the border, but across the entire country. I would hardly call that privilege, and get ready for the current administration as ICE, according to the *Washington Post*, is set to hunt down 100,000 Central Americans. What is this—Trump lite? Again, no need to rank oppression. We all fight together or else. You can fill in that part.

From FriscoLatina ----- I do not agree. As a Hispanic women living and working in San Francisco, your viewpoint just does not flow right. Yes, many work in kitchens, but there are also teachers, administrators, city employees, business owners, housekeepers, etc. Jobs that provide food, clothing and rent with dignity. People trying to make it in this world. I would ask that you further research some of your comments and hope you realize that the struggles of Hispanics, Blacks and Asians are very real. It should not be about one versus another. We need to have a conversation that every human being regardless of skin color deserves to live with human dignity. From native San Franciscan and human being.

From ProudWhiteLatinoRacialist ----- To FloridaLatino ----- When I was in graduate school, a Scottish PhD student I was friends with for five years returned to Scotland after his course work and research were done. He had to return because his "white privilege" [in fact he was pink] had no influence on ICE. Yours is the typical hate-whitey clap-trap that we read on the internet everyday...it is very boring! However, I will agree that the majority of illegals are brown and from Latin America—primarily Mexico.

From RicanAntiSemite ----- All "Latinos" come from Black people just like whites, Asians, "Middle Easterners," and Native Americans. It was these Russian cave dwellers—aka the Khazars —aka the supposed Jews who invented racism, colorism and the seven white identities from the *Talmud.* The Khazars control *Univision,* the Spanish language TV network. That's why the media is anti-Black. FYI. Even TV personality, Don Francisco, is a Talmudic, Zionist, cabalist Khazar from Chile.

From FloridaRican ----- please stop getting your information from memes.

From CollegeAntiSemiteLatino ----- To RicanAntiSemite ----- Truth there sister. Nothing but love to FloridaRican, but you're just a sheep. Ignorance is bliss, so pick up a book and look into history. This article is talking about people like you who are brainwashed. Get educated and quit being an internet idiot.

From Rican AntiSemite ----- To FloridaRican ----- What memes? What are you talking about *ovejo*?! [sheep].

From RicanAntiSemite ----- To FloridaRican ----- Colonized, brainwashed, sheep-like. You make me laugh. So yes, I'm laughing at your ignorant ass. Get the hell outta here!

From ProudWhiteLatinoRacialist ----- To RicanAntiSemite ----- Oh please!!! Next, you'll be singing Kum-Bay-Yah with extra-terrestrials. The fact is that race is a social, cultural, ethnic and historical reality in all of the Americas and the world. Go to sub-Saharan African nations where they butcher each other with machetes for having the wrong-colored kinte cloth turban on their heads...get real!

From RicanAntiSemite ----- To ProudWhiteLatinoRacialist ----- Good bye troll. Good bye! Don't get butt-hurt by the truth. At least I'm not whitewashed like you. I'm decolonizing myself. I will be awake and conscious next year unlike you. I'm going to practice *palo monte* in Louisiana— voodoo, hoodoo, Kemetism, Native American shamanism, and the 21 *divisiones*. I've given up my Catholic roots, so I've been getting real. What the hell are you talking about? I would love to offer you a seat, tie you up, then go 300 on you so you can be the hell quiet—OK?

From ProKhazarAntiBlack ----- I'm sorry but the "Khazars" aren't the ones responsible for "anti-Blackness." It's Black people's behavior. You can dance around the subject all you want, but in the end, any negativity surrounding Black people is their own doing by the way they act.

From Carolinian ----- To FlordiaRican ----- Actually the only part she did not get wrong is that all races come from Africa including the "Khazars."

From ProudWhiteLatinoRacialist ----- To RicanAntiSemite ----- Ghetto classy I see.

From FloridaRican ----- To RicanAntiSemite ----- What I'm saying is that memes tend to be the main conductors of these sorts of conspiracy theories. I think we need materially verifiable claims. A lot of what you've said was created by the Nazis to excuse the crisis of capitalism and scapegoat Jews. Of course, I'm not saying you're a Nazi. Getting to the point: the real enemy is the ruling class—those who exploit us on a daily basis.

From RicanAntiSemite ----- To Carolinian ----- White people are the African albinos who couldn't tolerate the African sun and heat so they moved into the caves in the Caucasus mountains.

From Australian Racialist ----- This is just embarrassing Afrocentric garbage.

From RicanAntiSemite ----- To Australian Racialist ----- ??? Here's to your white fragility. There's nothing "garbage" about the truth. So please shut the hell up!

From ProKhazarAntiBlack ----- To RicanAntiSemite ----- LOL. Boyz in the Hood? That's your big point? Sorry, I don't baby Black people. I hold Black people accountable for their actions.

Editor's note: *The Khazars became an important part of the European anti-Semitic conspiracy theories of the nineteenth century based on distortions of their history. The Khazars came from the steppes of Central and Eastern Asia—migrating westward like their predecessors and successors [e.g.: Huns, Bulgars, Turks and Mongols] and came to rule what is now the Ukraine along with some neighboring regions to the north and west of the Black Sea, and towards the east, including the Caucasus region. They ruled these regions from [CE] the 7th to the 11th century. They were never cave dwellers and they certainly were not the creators of western European racism. This is a totally bogus claim [See Chapter 1 in this book].*

The Khazar leadership and the Khazars themselves were apparently quite tolerant when it came to religion. Fleeing Christians, Jews, Zoroastrians, and others were given refuge in their domains. They were also courted as allies by their important neighbors to the south who tried religious conversion as part of their efforts to recruit them as allies. The Eastern Roman Byzantines tried to convert them to Eastern Orthodox Christianity. The Sassanid Persians [Iranians] tried to convert them into the

Zoroastrianism up until the CE 640s. The Muslims also tried conversion to Islam, but the rulers [Khagans], aristocrats and many others converted to Judaism [still a controversial claim] sometime between CE 740 and CE 920. It's also clear that their rulers also adopted Jewish names in the 9th and 10th centuries—including Zachariah, Manasseh, Benjamin, Aaron, Joseph, and David.

It is unfortunate but predictable that this 19th century anti-Semitic conspiracy theory [later adopted by the Nazis and others] is still very much alive and has also been adopted by groups here in the United States including Louis Farrakhan's Nation of Islam, the Afrocentric extremists, and the folks who have posted these claims in the current debate.

From William García ----- All I'm saying is that before we talk about the *mescolanzas* [mixing] of races that people often mention, It's important for white Latinos—white Puerto Ricans for example, to embrace their European heritage [as many do] in ways that is not racist and obviously not clinging to *mestizaje*. Before we all dance *bomba* and *plena*, it's important to come to terms with whiteness instead of avoiding it in order to avoid white guilt or because it's associated with that of being colonizers. You have to look at yourself in the mirror and understand that you bear the mark of colonialism. I know it's hard but it's even harder to bare the mark of those that were African slaves and freed Blacks. People like me don't have the luxury of ignoring this reality. I understand that those that have the privilege of not having to do that can ignore it, but they should not ignore it for the sake of everyone. As a white Latinx, you should write your own honest reflections on how your whiteness has treated you [especially if you have white counterparts]. You should know very well the racial differences and similarities between whiteness and white supremacy in Latin America and the United States. There are similarities but white does NOT have to solely mean Anglo-white and Black does not have to mean solely African American. Afro-Latinos have stepped up to the plate. Now it's the turn of white-Latinos to step up and talk about how they occupy space in the world.

From AfroAmPR ----- To William Garcia ----- Damn Will, you blew me away with that one. I just can't imagine embracing my Euro heritage at all. I guess since I physically look black in quotes. What is there worthy of embracing when considering that Euro-heritage came from colonialism?

From Whitehead ----- To AfroAmPR ----- That's a ridiculous statement. As ridiculous as saying you can't accept your Indigenous roots because they practiced human sacrifice and slavery.

From William García ----- To AfroAmPR ----- European culture is very important in ways that have different dimensions than that of global colonizers, enslavers and racism. In Puerto Rico, for instance *aguinaldos* [a folk genre of Spanish origin Christmas music] have a baroque history which I find fascinating. The famous Caribbean carnivals have a European background as well. There are countless examples that are intriguing and worthy of human admiration and integrity.

From PuertoRicanArtist ----- To William García ----- I would think that part of the issue is that we are required to learn about European culture in such a glorified way that you would believe that all other cultures are inferior. This is reinforced by the teachings [in schools and through media] that before slavery, people of color were [and still are] savages. From Africa to the Middle East to New York. These teachings breed ideas of inferiority and are untrue. If you were taught that the founders of civilization were in Africa and all humans began there, maybe you'd think differently. If the balance of history was taught equally, and we were taught how great all cultures were, you may even see each other as kin. But the truth is that a Spaniard does not see a Puerto Rican as a Spaniard, which is why we are called Hispanics. You may find it easier as a white Latino to assimilate because of the color of your skin, but I'm sure a confederate flag toting Southerner may most likely lump you into the category of Mexican [not the *Telemundo* or *Univision* variety]. And what categorizes an individual to embrace their white Hispanic skin color? I'm sure, you being Puerto Rican, know the saying for those who think they are better…"show me your grandmother."

In Puerto Rico, you can be light enough to pass for white, but your grandmother is as dark as Wesley Snipes. So, the idea of Hispanic race mixing with Blacks is ridiculous. You're already Black. In fact the irony of the Hispanic could be the fact they are walking proof that we are all the same. I personally know Hispanic born dark people that can be considered Black, but with age grow to be white looking, and vice versa. …And no, I'm not talking about Sammy Sosa.

From Carolinian ----- To William Garcia ----- From what I've seen in genetics, most Puerto Ricans are tri-racials. Why not embrace all of yourself?

From ProudWhiteLatinoRacialist ----- To Carolinian ----- From what you have seen? Perhaps looking at verifiable immigration records from Europe would be more informative than watching Afrocentric nonsense YouTube videos of fake Taínos and Blackface Negroes doing Apache war dances, in Hopi war paint while screaming Navajo war cries.

From AfroAmAntiPurity ----- You are not of pure blood if you are from Latin America. Your people have been laying on their backs giving birth to the white man's baby for centuries and proud to do it. These are white people who look down on you, yet you are so willing to be their lap dogs. I really can't feel bad for the things that happen to you.

From AfroAmPR ----- PuertoRicanArtist said it all. Until racial equality exists globally, which I doubt, and people are taught about the greatness of all groups, it's going to be real difficult to celebrate non-racist European heritage. Today's political climate makes it all the more discouraging.

From Concerned AfroAm ----- While that bit of science sounds great and seems very informative, at the end of the day, it's irrelevant because in the real world, the amount of melanin in your skin determines your social, economic status, class, and societal distinction. Racism and bigotry based on skin color and ethnicity, like borders, are very real, debilitating and a demobilizing human construct.

From OneHumanRacePR ----- To Concerned AfroAm ----- I disagree that it's irrelevant. Racism and bigotry based on skin color and ethnicity exists because most people are ignorant of the fact that race is an artificial construct. The solution is not to just ignore the facts and accept the current norms. The solution is to embrace the truth and educate the ignorant.

From CaliLatina ----- What about people who identify as *mestizo*, Indigenous and Spanish?

From William García ----- *Mestizo* [mixed] is a broad and undefined term. It can simply mean a mix of European and Indigenous but it also has other meanings. There are many *mestizos* who pass for white while many also pass for dark brown Indigenous. While many *mestizos* who can pass for white can enjoy white privilege and claim indigeneity, dark brown Indigenous *mestizos* cannot benefit from privilege. These hierarchies need to be further discussed. If TV personality, Ricky Ricardo, would've been *mestizo*, it wouldn't have really mattered because it wouldn't have changed anything. Mentioning *mestizos* would've only strengthen my argument.

From WoodworkMex ------ To William Garcia ----- There are many *mestizos* who pass for white. I presume you're referring to *castizos*? Many also pass for dark brown Indigenous—probably "*cholos*. "Hispanic" is basically a cultural construct, more than anything else.

From CaliLatina ----- To William Garcia ----- I'm *mestizo* and I look Asian. What about *mestizo's* who look Asian?

From AntiChicanoMovement ----- Latin America is a patch work of races. There are Indigenous people, Blacks who are the descendants of African slaves, and European migrants. That's why you see people like George López who looks Indigenous, the late Celia Cruz who was Black and the descendant of African slaves brought to Cuba against their will, and people like Ted Cruz and Marco Rubio who are the descendant of Spaniards. In my opinion, the confusion over race in Latin America was created by elitist intellectuals in the Chicano movement who in order to piggy back on the Black civil rights movement, started insisting that all Hispanic nationalities be erased and that we all start being called "Latino" instead of by our individual Hispanic country of origin. Then they started insisting that we all be called "brown." White Hispanic racism isn't on the rise, it has always existed. Racism is always going to exist as long as there are differences in humans. In fact, bigotry exists even among white people. You think that all Europeans think of themselves as equals? There's a hierarchy in Europe with some Europeans thinking of themselves as superior to others. The British think of themselves as superior to the Irish, the Germans think of themselves as superior to the Mediterraneans, the Russians think of themselves as superior to the other Slavs, etc.

From ArizonaLatino ---- To AntiChicanoMovement ----- Don't know where you get your info, but at best you are half right. What you described was the antithesis of the Chicano Movement. Hispanic refers to the European. Chicanos were fed up with hundreds of years of European imposed culture and identities among Mexican Americans. Just remember that most Mexicans, Central Americans and peoples from the Andes in the U.S. constitute probably 80% of all so-called "Hispanics/Latinos," which is a government invented category... and this population is heavily Indigenous or de-Indigenized Indigenous people. There are white Latinos, especially in other countries, and on that part, I do agree. Yes, they get lots of privilege and many of them want nothing to do with brown or Black peoples.

From AntiChicanoMovement ----- To ArizonaLatino ----- Read Cristina Mora's book, *Making Hispanics: How Activists, Bureaucrats, and Media Constructed a New American*. She explains it all there.

***Editor's Note**: Yes, it's explained in Mora's book, but it wasn't just Mexican Americans [and it wasn't promoted by the Chicano movement]. The process of creating the "Hispanic" category involved other Latinos, most notably Cubans and Puerto Ricans. All of this is discussed in Mora's book.*

From ArizonaLatino ---- To AntiChicanoMovement -----_ I will read her book, but I don't have to read it to tell you that it's fiction to say that the Chicano Movement produced the label and category called "Hispanic." That is the antithesis of everything the Chicano Movement stood for. Think about it. If 75% of all "Hispanics" are Mexican and Central American, then this "Hispanic" concept at best dilutes and invisibilizes the Mexicans, Central American, and the Latino Indigenous.

From WoodworkMex ----- To Arizona Latino ----- I was under the impression that the Chicano Movement basically believed that they were a hybrid people, where Spanish/Hispanic elements fused with the Native Indigenous to create something new and distinct.

From HighYellowDominican ----- To William García ----- Thank you for this article. It is well researched and very badly needed. As a Dominican American who grew up in Washington Heights, I never thought of myself as white, white Hispanic or otherwise. I saw my struggle closely aligned with the African American kids I grew up with but also did not identify as Afro-Latina. I am what would be called in Black circles—high yellow—light skinned—*mulato.* What Dominicans refer to as *rubia* [although I am nowhere close to blond or red haired]. I have the privilege of seeing someone that kinda looks like me on *Telemundo* but I also have been "excluded" because my mannerism are seen as a bit too "urban." I am saying all this to say that identity is complex and layered and although I'm 100% there with you as far as our people's internalized racism is concerned, I am hesitant to use the restricting Black/White racial terms in relation to Latinos/Hispanics. I think we—Latinos/Hispanics—offer an opportunity to have a deeper, non-binary conversation about race and identity. Thank you again for opening up this conversation. *Pa'lante!*

From AfroAmPR ----- To HighYellowDominican ----- I'm glad you mentioned this. Recently, I was heartbroken because a very pale skinned Dominican student of mine, who also grew up in the Heights says that [1], he renounces his Dominican-ness and opts for American, [2] He wants to forget his Dominican background and go for straight-up white and believe it or not, that doesn't even bother me that much. What bothered me—what really, really, really stung was [3], that he won't research his genetic background because he's afraid he's going to encounter African DNA and that will mess up his whole view of himself, and lastly [4], he sometimes tells people he's Irish or even Italian and even refuses to speak Spanish, but he clearly understands it well. [3] and [4] stung the most, mainly because this student is really, really, really bright and really determined to excel in life. He reminds me of this article, how light skin Latinos want to assimilate so badly that they join the oppressive status quo and yearn to embody it, to engulf in it, to lose themselves in it. The Dominican people can actually use someone with his creativity and talent, but instead, he can care less. I don't know why I'm telling you this. I just needed to vent after reading your post.

From HighYellowDominican ----- To AfroAmPR ----- The self-hatred is real. Perhaps this young man has not seen enough people who look like him, or from his world, that have "achieved." This is why I think it's so important for us who have "made it" to keep pulling our people up, but also to keep it real and remember where we came from. And there might be hope for him yet. His fear of looking at his DNA is a realization that he knows there's more to his story.

From ProudWhiteLatinoRacialist ----- Good thing you are so dedicated to your job with the race police.

From PintoLatino ----- Timely. Excellent. A badly needed national conversation.

From ProudWhiteLatinoRacialist ----- From white men and from behind their white faces...*dio' mio chico, coje verguenza ya y no te jorobes tanto...* Nowhere in the world will you be mistaken for Mandingo, Mayan or Mandarin. You walk in the world as a white man and so did your parents. So, drop the PC. "Race just doesn't exist?" nonsense! I think Asia and Africa are jammed with people who would disagree with that crap!

From WhiteMontaña ----- This article is poorly written and edited. Many of the points made by the author are not fully developed. Race and ethnicity are not the same thing. This article is all over the place.

From AfroDominicanCuban ----- Wow[!]—the conversation with the original savage beast of this planet. We're dealing with a worldwide system that was designed to keep "whites" in power, although they've done nothing of substance to be powerful. All that the so called "whites" have done is pillage, brainwash and destroy the original peoples together with the environment of our planet for vanity and thirst for blood. No conversation is going to bring these unconscious deficient-minded creatures from coming into awareness, especially when their power is at stake! The great majority of this specie represents the imbalance of the economic system and the peace of our planet. -----Me, as an Afro-Diasporan of immediate Cuban and Dominican lineage, has come to the conclusion that the "Euro-Latinos" are more implicitly racist in contrast to those other "white" pests that inhabit our Earth. At least the English speaking "Euros" give the Afro-Diasporans hand-outs in their efforts to appear inclusive. For decades, *Univision* and *Telemundo* has had no Afro-programming" that caters to those that gave culture to Latin America—us Black people! And please, don't count the whitewashed Celia Cruz programming crap on *Telemundo*.

From William García ----- See Raymond Arrieta: "Stop Doing Brown or BlackFace" and please share this at:

https://petitions.moveon.org/sign/raymond-arrieta-stop.fb51?source=c.fb&r_by=14871722

From Victorinus ----- I think the author discredits himself and his whole argument by using "so-called Hispanic" to describe GOP politicians who are Hispanic. Just because you disagree with someone's politics doesn't give you the right to disavow their heritage. Marco Rubio appears white so he's not Latino to you? Also, to Felipe Luciano, the "comedian" in the clip above, *Güagäncó* is as much Afro as he is Cuban. That's the beauty of our culture in our mixture. It's when we take sides that we all lose.

From MexicoLion ----- It really baffles me how everything boils down to skin color. That in itself explains absolutely nothing about human nature. Racism/prejudice is a stupid concept, but unfortunately part of human nature. There is racism among and within

Hispanics. For example, in Mexico, a lighter skin Mexican of European descent will never marry a Mexican of Indian [native tribes] descent. Just look at Mexican soap operas. The maids are usually Indian-looking women whereas the protagonists are usually white of European descent. At the same time, within America's Black/African-American community, racism and classism is also alive and well. Lighter skin Blacks are discriminated against as not being "Black-enough" at the same time many lighter skinned Blacks either try to find someone as light as they are, or marry outside their race. The bottom line is that racism/prejudice will never disappear. In every civilization that has existed, there has always been a group that has considered itself to be superior to another group either because of physical, intellectual or other attributes. Racism is stupid. It's a waste of time and solves nothing.

From AfroAmJef ----- Light skinned Blacks are notorious for their anti-blackness? Really? What the hell are you talking about?

From HongKongAfroAm ----- This author suggests that African Americans have erased "Afro-Latinos" from the discussion of "blackness" in America. The issue is that Afro-Latinos choose a role in an ongoing narrative in America of mixed feelings on the issue of race. The ambivalence doesn't exist within African American culture. The problem with identification and identity resides with so called "Latinos." The Harlem Renaissance didn't depend on Afro-Latinos who choose to join the collection of artist and musicians who spearheaded the movement. The question of who is Black, shouldn't be an issue. The discussion should be "who is African?" I'm from *Nueva York* and too many of my Afro-Latino brothers and sisters waiver on this issue. One minute, they're Taino, the next "Latino" and then, when it is convenient or when there is African American scholarship money, they are Black. Puerto Ricans, like Felipe Luciano were definitely integral to the development of rap music in America. But, he joined a group of poets, and a movement that already existed. African Americans were rhyming over drum beats before "The Last Poets." This takes nothing away from Afro-Latinos who have been integral members of several "pro Black" movements. However, in many instances, whether it was rap music, the Black Panthers, or even the recent Black Lives Matter movement, they were not the progenitors within the culture. Had Puerto Ricans been on the forefront of rap, they would have been rapping in Spanish since their arrival in the 1950s or 70s in the Bronx. This article tries to incriminate African Americans as excluding Afro-Latinos from their important role in America. I don't see how this was the case when during Black history month, individuals like Roberto Clemente and Arturo Alfonso Schomburg have always been given acknowledgement. The question about Blackness is irrelevant. We need to have a discussion about who is African. And too many light skinned Latinos who have Caucasian features can refute this claim. Of course, this is, and has always been done when it's convenient.

From William García ----- Afro-latinos can't choose when to be black, we can't be one thing one day and something else the next day. Not the first time I've heard this faulty logic from African Americans. Furthermore, it's interesting how Afro-Latinos, Puerto Ricans and other silenced contributors to movements are seen as people who come late to the party. The person who was actually the catalyst for the Harlem riots of 1935 was Puerto Rican. So I guess that means that the Harlem riots was a Puerto Rican event? This chicken-or-the-egg argument should instead focus on cultural, political and ideological hybridities and begin to envision the African-diaspora as something centrifugal, fluid and inter-connected. This whole "we were here first" is a way to minimize or erase Afro-Latinos.

From HongKongAfroAm ----- To William Garcia ----- African American's never silenced your role in the American struggle for equality. You may not deny your African identity, but many and the majority of your brethren do. Puerto Rico is a country; which includes Europeans, Africans and those who carry the Taino blood line. Are the Europeans classified as "Black?" You're suggesting that African Americans minimized your identity in America. This isn't true. This isn't a "chicken-or-the-egg" argument because Puerto Ricans joined the narrative willingly, while African Americans were forming their own identity in the wake of slavery. A

Puerto Rican may have participated in the inception of the 1935 Harlem Riots, but as your article erroneously noted, Puerto Ricans were not the progenitors of the cultural renaissance that took place in Harlem. I'll share. I'm a social dancer from NYC. As I learned the roots of Salsa in NYC, according to a documentary by Henry Chalafant on Puerto Ricans [Titled I believe *From Mambo to Hip-Hop*] and their influence on Hip Hop and their creation of the New York City Mambo scene, I learned that African Americans were the first musicians to play for a Latino audience. So, does this mean that African Americans started Mambo? Nah man! We were there, but as I'm so constantly reminded, "It's our Latin thing." They joined a narrative that was already set in motion by Latinos. One of the worst things that happened to African Americans post slavery is that they didn't have their own separate state or land like many in the Caribbean. Anything that the African American creates is co-opted by other ethnic groups. African Americans have never marginalized Afro-Latinos because we've never had that kind of power. Again, this isn't about chickens and eggs, it's about why we're fighting over a color [re: the invention of the White Race] and not who identifies with Africa. Anyone can be Black. Rachel Dolezal proved that. The question is: is she African?

***Editor's Note**: "HongKongAfroAm" makes a number of exaggerated and problematic assertions. The claim that "African Americans were the first musicians to play for a Latino audience" is absurd and no evidence is provided. Arturo Alfonso Schomburg's Puerto Rican heritage has only been acknowledged in recent years. It was not that long ago that he was simply called Arthur Schomburg—period! ...And does "HongKongAfroAm" know anything about Carlos Cooks among others? There has also been the erasure of the Puerto Rican/Latino presence and community in Central Harlem from 1900 to the early 1950s [research findings forthcoming]. Rap's origins and development are also in dispute.*

From ThreeTimesMixed ----- The irony behind the racial reality of Cuban Americans here in the U.S. is that even the whitest Cuban on the Island has an African admixture which blows the whole one drop rule in the U.S. right out of the universe !!!!! Yes, if DNA tests were administered to Ted Cruz, and Marco Rubio, both of them would be legally black in the U.S. if "the one drop rule" was applied.

From ProudWhiteLatinoRacialist ----- "legally black???" That's as stupid as saying "legally white" I think you stand a better chance of being designated "legally stupid" with a comment like that based on the fallacious, fictitious and totally fraudulent "1-drop-rule" that was created by illiterate, toothless, syphilitic white slave owners who created this non-scientific "rule" so they could exclude all the mulatto children from inheriting a slave owner's estate in competition with his white offspring. …And FYI, between 1898 and 1940 over one million Europeans migrated to Cuba. That was yesterday, historically speaking. My grandparents in Puerto Rico came from Corsica and other European countries. Did they step-off the boats and start race mixing right then and there??? C'mon!!! Did they become Aztecs? Apaches? Mandingos? Eskimos? Go read a book, you idiot!

From ProudWhiteLatinoRacialist ----- To ThreeTimesMixed ----- You're a bit late to the party. This "discussion" needed to have happened five centuries ago...and today, with the dishonest, duplicitous and deceitful identity politics of the fake "Latino" mythology obstructing constructive discourse of race in the U.S. [they still worship at the altar of the ignorant "1-drop-rule"] I wouldn't hold out much hope of any exchange embracing intelligence, insight or integrity.

***Editor's Note**: The claim by "ProudWhiteLatinoRacialist" that Europeans who came to Puerto Rico in the 1800s or whenever did not "step-off the boats and start race mixing right then and there is not true. Most did in fact intermarry (etc.) with individuals who were mixed in various ways including (frequently unbeknownst to them) many Puerto Ricans defined as "white" with a "white" look who were actually mixed as demonstrated by the results of their genetic tests.*

It wasn't that long ago when versions of the "one drop rule" were still legally applied in a number of southern states along with anti-miscegenation laws. The U.S. Supreme Court judged both of these laws to be legally unconstitutional in "Loving versus Virginia" [miscegenation] and the "Virginia Racial Integrity Act [the one drop rule] in 1967. However, the unofficial cultural articulation and application of "the one drop rule" persists up to the present. See for example:

https://news.harvard.edu/gazette/story/2010/12/one-drop-rule-persists/.

As seen on this thread, "ProudWhiteLatinoRacialist" also emphasizes his white ancestry but never acknowledges or discusses the main issue to be discussed on this thread—Latino white privilege. The same can be said of other white Latinos on this thread. That, or they otherwise minimize or deny the existence of Latino white privilege.

From CaliLatina ----- Don't forget about the *mestizo's* who look Asian or Arabic. People always tell me that they thought I was Asian until I said something in Spanish. I'm like, um-OK with that.

From AfroAmFem #1 ----- This article is so dumb. Facts are messed up. "We don't include Afro Latinos?" LOL. They don't want to be associated with Blacks in America. Let's be real. This article just adds to the divide between Latinos.

From AfroAmFem #2 ----- Preach! As an African-American, I've never tried to deny the Blackness of Afro-Latinos! They go out of their way to deny it themselves—even when it's obvious that they are Black! From my point of view, if you're of predominantly sub-Saharan African descent and look like you are— then you're Black regardless of your nationality! When I was growing up, an African-American friend told me that Roberto Clemente was a Black man. We're Pittsburghers, and she's proud of the fact that he played for the Pittsburgh Pirates.

From HoustonLatina ----- My Dad is Latino and my Mom is white. What does that make me? White Hispanic? It's a label. It does not mean I'm a racist. I have noticed that if you can pass as white and you tell a Hispanic person you're a mix, you get made fun of and told you come from the old country. They have a hard time accepting white Hispanics.

From CraniofacialRacialist ----- To HoustonLatina ----- You appear to be a fully Caucasian individual [of the Alpine variety]. So, I'm assuming that your "Latino" dad is white too. As a kid growing up in Miami, Florida [Where the majority of Latin Americans are White Cubans], I did not hear the terms "Hispanic" or "Latino" until I was in my late teens [let alone someone being thought of as non-white simply because they were of Latin American descent], and I clearly distinguished individuals who were Amerindian or Black and people significantly admixed with those races [such as George López or the typical Dominican] from the obviously Caucasian ones [such as Andy García or yourself].
From ProudWhiteLatinoRacialist ----- To HoustonLatina ----- First of all, you say one of your parents is "Hispanic." That is not a race. All people from Hispanic-cultural backgrounds have some racial background—white, Black, Indigenous, Asian and even Middle Eastern, or any mixture of the above—just like in the U.S.A.! Think of it this way—if you're in Texas, most Hispanic-cultured people are of Mexican origin, and of those, most are of Indigenous [Indian] background, or they're mixed Indian and white, but most Mexicans in Texas are so ashamed of their Mexican background that they reach immediately for the "Hispanic" label, which they think minimizes the discrimination they endure.

From CraniofacialRacialist ----- Prior to the terms Hispanic and Latino, no average American would've thought of someone as "inferior" simply because they were of Latin American extraction. Also the "one drop rule" only applied to Black ancestry and aside from white supremacists and Afrocentrists, regular people do not subscribe to such an ideology. Another more important question is this: what occurred as a result of "Latinos" becoming one brown [mixed] race and Blackness exclusive to African-Americans? Latin American markets and elites were able to carry out their anti-Black agendas, which led to the rise of all-white soap operas protected under the construction of *mestizaje* or brownness. Anyone who thinks that such people are "brown" either has a severely impaired eyesight or suffers from profound mental retardation. With that being said, all I can say is this—the "Hispanic/Latino" nonsense needs to be canned because as a blogger so rightly put it, the whole "Hispanic" identity as it exists in the United States, is a political racket—it's rigged to include as many people as possible in an effort to create a separateness from mainstream America. People of Latin American descent should be considered individually for what they are [e.g.: a white Cuban-American, a mulatto Puerto Rican, etc.] and not collectively under this bogus pan-ethnicity.

***Editor's Note**: "CraniofacialRacialist" is wrong when he arrogantly claims without evidence that "no average American would've thought of someone as "inferior" simply because they were of Latin American extraction." Taking into consideration the use of the word "average," it's clear that Latin Americans have indeed been seen as inferior. "CraniofacialRacialis" needs to read the history [e.g.: "Manifest Destiny," etc.], and he also needs to focus on recent articulations of this idea in the works of [for example] Samuel Huntington in his book "Who Are We?: The Challenges to America's National Identity" (2004). See also the articulation of this prejudice by President Trump, former President Woodrow Wilson and former secretary of state, Henry Kissinger, and others at:*

https://www.dissentmagazine.org/blog/trump-wall-latin-america-us-foreign-policy-hostility.

From ProudWhiteLatinoRacialist ----- To CraniofacialRacialist ----- As a Puerto Rico-born person of Corsican, Irish, Basque, Mallorcan, Canary Islander, German, Dutch and French background, I can only say that yours is the most intelligent comment on this thread. It always shocks people when they learn that I am born in Puerto Rico because I speak fluent English, Spanish, French, Mandarin and Arabic. Why? Because in different socio-linguistic contexts, I am obviously a white person and I don't embrace a ghetto-Spanglish mentality or a fake brown identity, like you find among white "Latinos" on most campuses.

From CraniofacialRacialist ----- To ProudWhiteLatinoRacialist ----- Thank you Sir and my sentiments are more than mutual. All I can say is that we could sure use 1 million more like me and you!

From ProudWhiteLatinoRacialist ----- To CraniofacialRacialist ----- That "million" is actually much bigger, but most people who share our racial, cultural and ethnic coordinates within the artificial Hispanic/Latino rubric don't engage this self-defeating bigotry because it is a lot easier to go with the flow, even when the flow is over the cliff. Regards to you!!!

From NewMexSpanish ----- Interesting points—my Dad's family is from New Mexico and from the Spanish – don't ever call them Mexican. A lot of the old families from Texas and New Mexico are Spanish and Sephardic Jews. The Hispanic construct is crap at best. I think it is a cop-out as much as Irish Americans are Anglos. My mom is a white Mexican [DNA proof] but if you look at me, I did my DNA and I'm a lot of things but I'm not Latino or Hispanic! Spanish, Native American, Jewish, and French. Go figure

Editor's Note: *The "Spanish" from New Mexico and Texas ["Spanish Americans"]—also the "Californios" [in California], trace their ancestry to the original Spanish conquistadors and settlers of the pre-1821 Spanish colonial period—before these regions became part of the independent Mexican nation state. There is currently, considerable tension between these "Spanish Americans" and Mexican Americans [defined by national origin] and especially with the Indigenous. The Mom might also be a "white Mexican," but is most probably of mixed background. See:*

http://www.uexpress.com/georgie-anne-geyer/1998/7/30/the-war-of-the-statues

From PrivilegedPhilippis ----- Why does whiteness or white people have to get dragged into everything? Damn!! It's so irritating. Sorry, my sensitive white privilege is getting the better of me. Instead of venting, I should stick to oppressing. Carry on.

From AngoAmerican #1 ----- Because they don't want to conform to your PC nonsense and privileged tribalistic ideology They're the problem? what a joke.

FromChapelHill-U Latina ----- white Latinos are no more racist or anti Black than any other white. If anything, as the article very clearly says, white Latinos are not really fully accepted as white by other whites and thus have a tendency to be more compassionate towards Blacks, because they themselves have experienced stupid racism, ignorance, hatred.....

From ProudWhiteLatinoRacialist ----- To ChapelHill-U Latina ----- And what you say would be of more consequence if anyone with a brain would give a s..t about what ignorant, provincial, stupid Americans think about them. I don't shape my identity around the ignorance of others. The Irish and Italians were once considered "non-white" by the American WASP establishment. Do you think the Kennedys and the Mondales give a s..t today in their mansions, yachts and penthouses?

Editor's Note: True in this case on the history of the Irish and Italians in the U.S. On the Irish, See for example:

https://www.amazon.com/Irish-Became-White-Routledge-Classics/dp/0415963095

From AfroAmFem #1 ----- To ProudWhiteLatinoRacialist ----- You are really lost. You are a people who cannot accept responsibility for the racism you throw our way. Then you blame us for your reactions to your negative feelings for dark skin. You are brainwashed and too ill-educated to know it. Hello Trump! He wants your light brown ass gone! So that should tell you how whites feel about you. You are here to pick their damn fruit, wash their dishes and be their whores. Any rights you enjoy as a people are due to Blacks putting their lives on the line and dying for those right. Yet you think you earned those rights. Hispanics do not fight for any one's rights. At least I have never seen you do it.

***Editor's Note**: OK on the critique of "ProudWhiteLatinoRacialist" in my opinion, but totally wrong when the claims are made that Hispanics were not activists in civil rights along with African Americans during the 1960s and 1970s and also at present. This story tends to be minimized or ignored. See for example, the 1954 U.S. Supreme Court "Hernández versus Texas" decision and the multipart documentary [total—four hours] on the Mexican American and Chicano civil rights movement.*

http://www.nytimes.com/2004/05/15/opinion/a-quiet-victory-for-civil-rights.html?mcubz=3&_r=0 and

https://www.youtube.com/results?search_query=chicano+civil+rights+movement%2C+full+documentary+

There was also César Cháves and his movement on behalf of the mostly Mexican farmworkers and also the mostly Puerto Rican eastern seaboard "Young Lords" and "Macheteros" [etc.], who were inspired by the Black Panthers and the Mexican American Brown Berets.

From Carlos ----- This is an excellent article. And I really do hope more Hispanics read articles like this. Racism and white superiority need to be talked about in the Hispanic community.

From Joseph ----- Racism in the Latino community is very strong but colorism is even worse. Darker skinned Latinos get the shaft while the lighter skinned Latinos are loved and get benefits.

From AfroAmJef ----- Bravo!

From Australian ----- White Latinos are very real. It's quite clear John Wayne's wives were white Latinos [one was a European Spaniard for goodness sake!]. Even with cultural differences, they are going to assimilate into white Anglo culture much more readily than Negroes who have been there centuries.

UPR Rican ----- This white Latino Racism has an explanation. White Anglos or non-Hispanic whites created it. Wherever in the country white Anglos are a clear majority, they discriminate against all Latinos. Once their majority dwindles—suddenly white Latinos are their new buddies; the explanation being that they do not like feeling that they're in the minority. They also fear that minorities will do to them just as they have done to minorities. There are examples of this in Florida where Latinos are already in the majority in some counties and cities. White Anglos suddenly started showing statistics for white Latinos as a separate demographic based on the census and then adding them to the total number of whites making them part of a white majority—and Hispanic whites are falling for it.

From MexicoLion ----- I find it funny that Americans are now realizing that Latino racism is something that even exists. In Latin America, racism is alive and well and in many instances, it's supported even by the government. Let's look for example at Mexico. Although Mexico has a significant Black population, there isn't one individual in the Mexican government that is Black or even close to the Indigenous of the country. In addition, it is interesting to look at the Mexican soap operas and you can clearly see that racism in the country is alive and well. The vast majority of actors in Mexican television are usually those of European descent or those who look white. Normally those that look very native or Indigenous are relegated to the menial roles such as maids or poor people. Having said this, it is important to also note that many Hispanics/Latinos do not have any Indigenous admixture. A good example of this is Argentina. There are lots of Argentinians who are direct descendants of Germans and Italians who have not mixed with Indigenous people. In Cuba as well, although there are many Cubans that are mixed with Black/Africans, there are also Cubans that can only trace their heritage back one or two generations, and from there, they can trace their family or even have a family tree that goes back to Spain. The issue of Hispanic racism is nothing new, it has always existed and will continue to exist—just like it exists in the US.

From ProudWhiteLatinoRacialist ----- Don't confuse these knuckle-draggers with facts, political fictions and fantasies are more to their liking...

***Editor's note**: There are current and historical exceptions to the claim that "there isn't one individual in the Mexican government that is Black or even close to the Indigenous of the country." This is certainly not true of the lower levels of government; however visibly African descended individuals seem to be rare. At the top, there are the historical examples of presidents Vicente Gerrero ["Afro-mestizo"—1829, one year], Benito Juarez ["Zapotec" Indian—1858-1872 with interruptions], president and dictator Porfirio Díaz [mestizo—1876-1880, 1884-1911], and Gustavo Díaz Ordáz [clearly mestizo but not acknowledged as such—1964-1970].*

From LatinaArab ----- The U.S. census by removing "Latino" or "Hispanic" has encouraged the divide. There are many, many of us who don't choose to identify as white or Black, and we shouldn't have to. Which side of your family do you choose?

From ProudWhiteLatinoRacialist ----- To LatinaArab ----- Are you aware that "Latino" and "Hispanic" are bogus bean-counter labels? Neither has ever been a "race" since the beginning of time on the planet earth. That is why they were removed—White, Black, Asian, Native American are racial groups. Time to stop belly-dancing and read a book...*dio' mio chica.*

Editor's Note: *-----Where do these individuals get this from—with regard to the U.S. census? There is currently a proposal to change the Hispanic category from a multi-ethnic group to a "race" in the 2020 census and it appears that the change will be implemented.*

From LatinaArab ----- To ProudWhiteLatinoRacialist ----- Learn how to debate and/or discuss an issue irrespective of your opinion. The question remains. For those who don't consider themselves all of one race, how should, and why should they seek to identify as one or the other? As for the belly dancing, baby, I can dance while reading.

From ProudWhiteLatinoRacialist ----- To LatinaArab ----- There is no "debating" fictions, fallacies and identity con-job frauds. Keep dancing. Your talents apparently require shimmying and shaking not engaging in intelligent, factual and historically verified facts.

From AngoAmerican #2 ----- Maybe it's just me, but I have always viewed Latinos, Spaniards, and Hispanics as non-whites or minorities. As a white American, this was just my way of thinking. Don't consider it right or wrong just my views.

From ProudWhiteLatinoRacialist ----- To AngoAmerican #2 ----- You are not the only one who thinks this. Stupidity about Spanish-speaking people is very wide-spread among American idiots who get their information about us from the Taco Bell drive-up window menu, dancing Chihuahuas and looking at the brown illegals they see on TV running across the US border. For the rest of the people of the planet who are educated, are informed, and are not provincial American idiots, they know "Hispanic" has never been a racial category in the history of man since the caveman started walking upright.

Editor's Note: *-----Dare I say so in several ways with regard to "stupidity" (etc.)? Including from these guys above—"Proud-White-LatinoRacialist," "CraniofacialRacialist" and others in this debate.*

LIST OF CONTRIBUTORS

Dorothy Bell Ferrer is a writer at *La Tinta es Negra* and for other internet programs. She has studied at the University of Puerto Rico, Rio Piedras campus, and manages *La Tinta es Negra*, see: https://www.facebook.com/latintaesnegra/?pnref=lhc.

William García is currently a Ph.D. candidate in American Studies at the University of Kansas in Lawrence, Kansas. A recipient of an MA degree in history at the University of Puerto Rico, Rio Piedras, and another MA degree in curriculum and teaching from the Columbia University Teachers College, Mr. García has also been a research assistant at Columbia and an adjunct professor in the Latin American and Latino Studies Program at the City College of the City University of New York.

Ryan Hamilton recently earned his Ph.D. degree in anthropology at the Graduate School of the City University of New York. It is expected that his path breaking dissertation on the mostly Afro-descended communities of the Samaná peninsula in the Dominican Republic will be published as a book in the near future. He is also currently teaching at the LaGuardia Community College of the City University of New York.

Gabriel Haslip-Viera is a retired emeritus professor, Department of Sociology, the City College of the City University of New York. He is most recently the author or co-editor *of Latinos in New York: Communities in Transition* (2017), *Thieves of Civilization: Afrocentric Attempts to Appropriate the Cultural Heritage of Native Americas and Latino Indo-Mestizos in America* (2014), and *Race, Identity and Indigenous Politics: Puerto Rican Neo-Taínos in the Diaspora and the Island* (2014).

Jennifer Loubriel earned her B.A. degree from Oberlin College majoring in religion and English. She identifies as an amateur Latinx ethicist and speculative fiction enthusiast. She also has worked as a community organizer and educator where she has taught and has "[un] learned" with some deeply fabulous young women. Ms. Loubriel is a co-founder and moderator of the Tumblr *Women of Color, in Solidarity* program—a safe space for and by women of color. Jennifer is also an aspiring radical librarian who thinks a lot about policing in community spaces. See: https://everydayfeminism.com/author/jenniferl/?utm_content=buffer04da0&utm_medium=social&utm_source=facebook.com&utm_campaign=buffer.

Nicholle LaMartina: is a writer from New York City who currently lives in New Haven Connecticut. Her chapter in this book is an updated version of an article that was originally posted on the website "Thought Catalogue" in February 2014.. See: https://thoughtcatalog.com/nicholle-lamartina/2014/02/being-a-white-latina-a-reflection-on-racial-and-ethnic-identities/.

Julie Ramírez: is in charge of the digital marketing program at Catharsis Productions. She holds a BA degree in entertainment and media management with a concentration in live performances from Columbia College in Chicago, Illinois, and writes for various online journals.

Raquel Solla: was attending Emory University as a student when the original posting for this chapter was posted on the internet program ODESSEY in July 2016. See: https://www.theodysseyonline.com/anti-blackness-in-the-latinx-community.

Cesar Vargas: César Vargas was born and raised in the Dominican Republic and came to the U.S. when he was thirteen years old. He received a B.A. in Film Studies from Queens College, CUNY and has worked in the fashion and film industry. He is the founder of UPLIFTT [United People for Latinos in Film, TV and Theater], and a producer, writer, and director. He is also a published columnist [*Fox News, Huffington Post, and NBC*, among others]. As a poet and social media autodidact, he writes about pop culture, human behavior, and other social issues. See: http://www.upliftt.com/author/cesar-vargas/.

Made in the USA
San Bernardino, CA
03 December 2019

60756932R00124